Misquoting Jesus

MISQUOTING JESUS

The Story Behind Who Changed the Bible and Why

BART D. EHRMAN

HarperSanFrancisco
A Division of HarperCollins*Publishers*

Photography and Illustration Credits

Introduction—The Pierpont Morgan Library, New York; M. 777, f.3v, f. 24v, f. 37v, and f. 58 v

Chapter 1—Biblioteca Laurenziana, Florence, Italy; Photo: Scala/Art Resource, NY

Chapter 2—Courtesy of Bart Ehrman

Chapter 3—Victoria & Albert Museum, London; Photo: Victoria & Albert Museum, London/Art Resource, NY

Chapter 4—British Library, London; Photo: HIP/Art Resource, NY

Chapter 5—From the Winchester Psalter, British Library, London; Photo: HIP/ Art Resource, NY

Chapter 6—Golden Gospels of Henry VIII, Germany, Abbey of St. Maximin, Trier. The Pierpont Morgan Library, New York; Photo: The Pierpont Morgan Library/ Art Resource, NY

Chapter 7—The Pierpont Morgan Library; Photo: The Pierpont Morgan Library/ Art Resource, NY

Chapter 8—British Library; Cott. Nero.D.I.V. Folio No:211; Photo: HIP/Art Resource, NY

HarperCollins books may be purchased for educational, business, or sales promotional use. For information please write: Special Markets Department, HarperCollins Publishers, 10 East 53rd Street, New York, NY 10022.

HarperCollins Web site: http://www.harpercollins.com

HarperCollins®, 📕 ®, and HarperSanFrancisco™ are trademarks of HarperCollins Publishers

FIRST EDITION

Library of Congress Cataloging-in-Publication Data is available.

ISBN-13: 978-0-06073817-4
ISBN-10: 0-06-073817-0

06 07 08 09 RRD(H) 20 19 18 17 16 15 14 13 12

To Bruce M. Metzger

Contents

Acknowledgments

I owe a debt of gratitude to four keen and careful scholars who have read my manuscript and suggested (occasionally urged and pleaded for) changes: Kim Haines-Eitzen of Cornell University; Michael W. Holmes of Bethel College in Minnesota; Jeffrey Siker of Loyola Marymount University; and my wife, Sarah Beckwith, a medieval scholar at Duke University. The scholarly world would be a happier place if all authors had readers such as these.

Thanks are also due to the editors at Harper San Francisco: John Loudon, for encouraging the project and signing it up; Mickey Maudlin, for bringing it home to completion; and above all Roger Freet, for a careful reading of the text and helpful comments.

Translations of biblical texts, unless otherwise indicated, are my own.

I have dedicated this book to my mentor and "Doctor-Father," Bruce M. Metzger, who taught me the field and continues to inspire me in my work.

The Four Gospel Writers, with their traditional animal symbols, each highlighting an aspect of their portrayal of Jesus: Matthew as a man (humanity), Mark as a lion (royalty), Luke as an ox (servility), and John as an eagle (divinity).

INTRODUCTION

More than almost anything I've ever written about, the subject of this book has been on my mind for the past thirty years, since I was in my late teens and just beginning my study of the New Testament. Because it has been a part of me for so long, I thought I should begin by giving a personal account of why this material has been, and still is, very important to me.

The book is about ancient manuscripts of the New Testament and the differences found in them, about scribes who copied scripture and sometimes changed it. This may not seem to be very promising as a key to one's own autobiography, but there it is. One has little control over such things.

Before explaining how and why the manuscripts of the New Testament have made a real difference to me emotionally and intellectually, to my understanding of myself, the world I live in, my views of God, and the Bible, I should give some personal background.

I was born and raised in a conservative place and time—the nation's heartland, beginning in the mid 1950s. My upbringing was nothing out of the ordinary. We were a fairly typical family of five, churchgoing but not particularly religious. Starting the year I was in fifth grade, we were involved with the Episcopal church in Lawrence,

Kansas, a church with a kind and wise rector, who happened also to be a neighbor and whose son was one of my friends (with whom I got into mischief later on in junior high school—something involving cigars). As with many Episcopal churches, this one was socially respectable and socially responsible. It took the church liturgy seriously, and scripture was part of that liturgy. But the Bible was not overly emphasized: it was there as one of the guides to faith and practice, along with the church's tradition and common sense. We didn't actually talk about the Bible much, or read it much, even in Sunday school classes, which focused more on practical and social issues, and on how to live in the world.

The Bible did have a revered place in our home, especially for my mom, who would occasionally read from the Bible and make sure that we understood its stories and ethical teachings (less so its "doctrines"). Up until my high school years, I suppose I saw the Bible as a mysterious book of some importance for religion; but it certainly was not something to be learned and mastered. It had a feel of antiquity to it and was inextricably bound up somehow with God and church and worship. Still, I saw no reason to read it on my own or study it.

Things changed drastically for me when I was a sophomore in high school. It was then that I had a "born-again" experience, in a setting quite different from that of my home church. I was a typical "fringe" kid—a good student, interested and active in school sports but not great at any of them, interested and active in social life but not in the upper echelon of the school's popular elite. I recall feeling a kind of emptiness inside that nothing seemed to fill—not running around with my friends (we were already into some serious social drinking at parties), dating (beginning to enter the *mysterium tremendum* of the world of sex), school (I worked hard and did well but was no superstar), work (I was a door-to-door salesman for a company that sold products for the blind), church (I was an acolyte and pretty devout—one had to be on Sunday mornings, given everything that happened on Saturday nights). There was a kind of loneliness associated with being a young teenager; but, of course, I didn't realize that it was part of being a teenager—I thought there must be something missing.

That's when I started attending meetings of a Campus Life Youth for Christ club; they took place at kids' houses—the first I went to was a yard party at the home of a kid who was pretty popular, and that made me think the group must be okay. The leader of the group was a twenty-something-year-old named Bruce who did this sort of thing for a living—organized Youth for Christ clubs locally, tried to convert high school kids to be "born again" and then get them involved in serious Bible studies, prayer meetings, and the like. Bruce was a completely winsome personality—younger than our parents but older and more experienced than we—with a powerful message, that the void we felt inside (We were *teenagers!* All of us felt a void!) was from not having Christ in our hearts. If we would only ask Christ in, he would enter and fill us with the joy and happiness that only the "saved" could know.

Bruce could quote the Bible at will, and did so to an amazing degree. Given my reverence for, but ignorance of, the Bible, it all sounded completely convincing. And it was so unlike what I got at church, which involved old established ritual that seemed more geared toward old established adults than toward kids wanting fun and adventure, but who felt empty inside.

To make a short story shorter, I eventually got to know Bruce, came to accept his message of salvation, asked Jesus into my heart, and had a bona fide born-again experience. I had been born for real only fifteen years earlier, but this was a new and exciting experience for me, and it got me started on a lifelong journey of faith that has taken enormous twists and turns, ending up in a dead end that proved to be, in fact, a new path that I have since taken, now well over thirty years later.

Those of us who had these born-again experiences considered ourselves to be "real" Christians—as opposed to those who simply went to church as a matter of course, who did not really have Christ in their hearts and were therefore simply going through the motions with none of the reality. One of the ways we differentiated ourselves from these others was in our commitment to Bible study and prayer. Especially Bible study. Bruce himself was a Bible man; he had gone to Moody Bible Institute in Chicago and could quote an answer from the Bible to every question we could think of (and many we would never think of). I soon became envious of this ability to quote scripture and got involved with Bible studies myself, learning some texts, understanding their relevance, and even memorizing the key verses.

Bruce convinced me that I should consider becoming a "serious" Christian and devote myself completely to the Christian faith. This meant studying scripture full time at Moody Bible Institute, which, among other things, would involve a drastic change of lifestyle. At Moody there was an ethical "code" that students had to sign off on: no drinking, no smoking, no dancing, no card playing, no movies. And lots of Bible. As we used to say, "Moody Bible Institute, where *Bible* is our middle name." I guess I looked on it as a kind of Christian boot camp. In any event, I decided not to go half-measures with my faith; I applied to Moody, got in, and went there in the fall of 1973.

The Moody experience was intense. I decided to major in Bible theology, which meant taking a lot of biblical study and systematic theology courses. Only one perspective was taught in these courses, subscribed to by all the professors (they had to sign a statement) and by all the students (we did as well): the Bible is the inerrant word of God. It contains no mistakes. It is inspired completely and in its very words— "verbal, plenary inspiration." All the courses I took presupposed and taught this perspective; any other was taken to be misguided or even heretical. Some, I suppose, would call this brainwashing. For me, it was an enormous "step up" from the milquetoast view of the Bible I had had as a socializing Episcopalian in my younger youth. This was hard-core Christianity, for the fully committed.

There was an obvious problem, however, with the claim that the Bible was verbally inspired—down to its very words. As we learned at Moody in one of the first courses in the curriculum, we don't actually have the original writings of the New Testament. What we have are copies of these writings, made years later—in most cases, many years later. Moreover, none of these copies is completely accurate, since the scribes who produced them inadvertently and/or intentionally changed them in places. All scribes did this. So rather than actually having the inspired words of the autographs (i.e., the originals) of the Bible, what we have are the error-ridden copies of the autographs. One of the most pressing of all tasks, therefore, was to ascertain what the *originals* of the Bible said, given the circumstances that (1) they were inspired and (2) we don't have them.

I must say that many of my friends at Moody did not consider this task to be all that significant or interesting. They were happy to rest on the claim that the autographs had been inspired, and to shrug off, more or less, the problem that the autographs do not survive. For me, though, this was a compelling problem. It was the words of scripture themselves that God had inspired. Surely we have to know what those words were if we want to know how he had communicated to us, since the very words were his words, and having some other words (those inadvertently or intentionally created by scribes) didn't help us much if we wanted to know *His* words.

This is what got me interested in the manuscripts of the New Testament, already as an eighteen-year-old. At Moody, I learned the basics of the field known as textual criticism—a technical term for the science of restoring the "original" words of a text from manuscripts that have altered them. But I wasn't yet equipped to engage in this study: first I had to learn Greek, the original language of the New Testament, and possibly other ancient languages such as Hebrew (the language of the Christian Old Testament) and Latin, not to mention modern European languages like German and French, in order to see what other scholars had said about such things. It was a long path ahead.

At the end of my three years at Moody (it was a three-year diploma), I had done well in my courses and was more serious than ever about becoming a Christian scholar. My idea at the time was that there were plenty of highly educated scholars among the evangelical Christians, but not many evangelicals among the (secular) highly educated scholars, so I wanted to become an evangelical "voice" in secular circles, by getting degrees that would allow me to teach in secular settings while retaining my evangelical commitments. First, though, I needed to complete my bachelor's degree, and to do that I decided to go to a top-rank evangelical college. I chose Wheaton College, in a suburb of Chicago.

At Moody I was warned that I might have trouble finding real Christians at Wheaton—which shows how fundamentalist Moody was: Wheaton is only for evangelical Christians and is the alma mater of Billy Graham, for example. And at first I did find it to be a bit liberal for my tastes. Students talked about literature, history, and philosophy rather than the verbal inspiration of scripture. They did this from a Christian perspective, but even so: didn't they realize what *really* mattered?

I decided to major in English literature at Wheaton, since reading had long been one of my passions and since I knew that to make inroads into the circles of scholarship, I would need to become well versed in an area of scholarship other than the Bible. I decided also to commit myself to learning Greek. It was during my first semester at Wheaton, then, that I met Dr. Gerald Hawthorne, my Greek teacher and a person who became quite influential in my life as a scholar, teacher, and, eventually, friend. Hawthorne, like most of my professors at Wheaton, was a committed evangelical Christian. But he was not afraid of asking questions of his faith. At the time, I took this as a sign of weakness (in fact, I thought I had nearly all the answers to the questions he asked); eventually I saw it as a real commitment to truth and as being willing to open oneself up to the possibility that one's views need to be revised in light of further knowledge and life experience.

Learning Greek was a thrilling experience for me. As it turned out, I was pretty good at the basics of the language and was always eager for more. On a deeper level, however, the experience of learning Greek became a bit troubling for me and my view of scripture. I came to see early on that the full meaning and nuance of the Greek text of the New Testament could be grasped only when it is read and studied in the original language (the same thing applies to the Old Testament, as I later learned when I acquired Hebrew). All the more reason, I thought, for learning the language thoroughly. At the same time, this started making me question my understanding of scripture as the verbally inspired word of God. If the full meaning of the words of scripture can be grasped only by studying them in Greek (and Hebrew), doesn't this mean that most Christians, who don't read ancient languages, will never have complete access to what God wants them to know? And doesn't this make the doctrine of inspiration a doctrine only for the scholarly elite, who have the intellectual skills and leisure to learn the languages and study the texts by reading them in the original? What good does it do to say that the words are inspired by God if most people have absolutely no access to these words, but only to more or less clumsy renderings of these words into a language, such as English, that has nothing to do with the original words?[1]

My questions were complicated even more as I began to think increasingly about the manuscripts that conveyed the words. The more I studied Greek, the more I became interested in the manuscripts that preserve the New Testament for us, and in the science of textual criticism, which can supposedly help us reconstruct what the original words of the New Testament were. I kept reverting to my basic question: how does it help us to say that the Bible is the inerrant word of God if in fact we don't have the words that God inerrantly inspired, but only the words copied by the scribes—sometimes correctly but sometimes (many times!) incorrectly? What good is it to say that the autographs (i.e., the originals) were inspired? We don't *have* the originals! We have only error-ridden copies, and the vast majority of these are centuries removed from the originals and different from them, evidently, in thousands of ways.

These doubts both plagued me and drove me to dig deeper and deeper, to understand what the Bible really was. I completed my degree at Wheaton in two years and decided, under the guidance of Professor Hawthorne, to commit myself to the textual criticism of the New Testament by going to study with the world's leading expert in the field, a scholar named Bruce M. Metzger who taught at Princeton Theological Seminary.

Once again I was warned by my evangelical friends against going to Princeton Seminary, since, as they told me, I would have trouble finding any "real" Christians there. It was, after all, a Presbyterian seminary, not exactly a breeding ground for born-again Christians. But my study of English literature, philosophy, and history—not to mention Greek—had widened my horizons significantly, and my passion was now for knowledge, knowledge of all kinds, sacred and secular. If learning the "truth" meant no longer being able to identify with the born-again Christians I knew in high school, so be it. I was intent on pursuing my quest for truth wherever it might take me, trusting that any truth I learned was no less true for being unexpected or difficult to fit into the pigeonholes provided by my evangelical background.

Upon arriving at Princeton Theological Seminary, I immediately signed up for first-year Hebrew and Greek exegesis (interpretation) classes, and loaded my schedule as much as I could with such courses. I found these classes to be a challenge, both academically and personally. The academic challenge was completely welcome, but the personal challenges that I faced were emotionally rather trying. As I've indicated, already at Wheaton I had begun to question some of the foundational aspects of my commitment to the Bible as the inerrant word of God. That commitment came under serious assault in my detailed studies at Princeton. I resisted any temptation to change my views, and found a number of friends who, like me, came from conservative evangelical schools and were trying to "keep the faith" (a funny way of putting it—looking back—since we were, after all, in a Christian divinity program). But my studies started catching up with me.

A turning point came in my second semester, in a course I was taking with a much revered and pious professor named Cullen Story. The course was on the exegesis of the Gospel of Mark, at the time (and still) my favorite Gospel. For this course we needed to be able to read the Gospel of Mark completely in Greek (I memorized the entire Greek vocabulary of the Gospel the week before the semester began); we were to keep an exegetical notebook on our reflections on the interpretation of key passages; we discussed problems in the interpretation of the text; and we had to write a final term paper on an interpretive crux of our own choosing. I chose a passage in Mark 2, where Jesus is confronted by the Pharisees because his disciples had been walking through a grain field, eating the grain on the Sabbath. Jesus wants to show the Pharisees that "Sabbath was made for humans, not humans for the Sabbath" and so reminds them of what the great King David had done when he and his men were hungry, how they went into the Temple "when Abiathar was the high priest" and ate the show bread, which was only for the priests to eat. One of the well-known problems of the passage is that when one looks at the Old Testament passage that Jesus is citing (1 Sam. 21:1–6), it turns out that David did this not when Abiathar was the high priest, but, in fact, when Abiathar's father Ahimelech was. In other words, this is one of those passages that have been pointed to in order to show that the Bible is not inerrant at all but contains mistakes.

In my paper for Professor Story, I developed a long and complicated argument to the effect that even though Mark indicates this happened "when Abiathar was the high priest," it doesn't really mean that Abiathar was the high priest, but that the event took place in the part of the scriptural text that has Abiathar as one of the main characters. My argument was based on the meaning of the Greek words involved and was a bit convoluted. I was pretty sure Professor Story would appreciate the argument, since I knew him as a good Christian scholar who obviously (like me) would never think there could be anything like a genuine error in the Bible. But at the end of my paper he made a simple one-line comment that for some reason went straight through me. He wrote: "Maybe Mark just made a mistake." I started thinking about it, considering all the work I had put into the paper, realizing that I had had to do some pretty fancy exegetical footwork to get around the problem, and that my solution was in fact a bit of a stretch. I finally concluded, "Hmm . . . maybe Mark *did* make a mistake."

Once I made that admission, the floodgates opened. For if there could be one little, picayune mistake in Mark 2, maybe there could be mistakes in other places as well. Maybe, when Jesus says later in Mark 4 that the mustard seed is "the smallest of all seeds on the earth," maybe I don't need to come up with a fancy explanation for how the mustard seed is the smallest of all seeds when I know full well it isn't. And maybe these "mistakes" apply to bigger issues. Maybe when Mark says that Jesus was crucified the day *after* the Passover meal was eaten (Mark 14:12; 15:25) and John says he died the day *before* it was eaten (John 19:14)—maybe that is a genuine difference. Or when Luke indicates in his account of Jesus's birth that Joseph and Mary returned to Nazareth just over a month after they had come to Bethlehem (and performed the rites of purification; Luke 2:39), whereas Matthew indicates they instead fled to Egypt (Matt. 2:19–22)—maybe that is a difference. Or when Paul says that after he converted on the way to Damascus he did *not* go to Jerusalem to see those who were apostles before him (Gal. 1:16–17), whereas the book of Acts says that that was the first thing he did after leaving Damascus (Acts 9:26)—maybe that is a difference.

This kind of realization coincided with the problems I was encountering the more closely I studied the surviving Greek manuscripts of the New Testament. It is one thing to say that the originals were inspired, but the reality is that we don't have the originals—so saying they were inspired doesn't help me much, unless I can reconstruct the originals. Moreover, the vast majority of Christians for the entire history of the church have not had access to the originals, making their inspiration something of a moot point. Not only do we not have the originals, we don't have the first copies of the originals. We don't even have copies of the copies of the originals, or copies of the copies of the copies of the originals. What we have are copies made later—much later. In most instances, they are copies made many *centuries* later. And these copies all differ from one another, in many thousands of places. As we will see later in this book, these copies differ from one another in so many places that we don't even know how many differences there are. Possibly it is easiest to put it in comparative terms: there are more differences among our manuscripts than there are words in the New Testament.

Most of these differences are completely immaterial and insignificant. A good portion of them simply show us that scribes in antiquity could spell no better than most people can today (and they didn't even have dictionaries, let alone spell check). Even so, what is one to make of all these differences? If one wants to insist that God inspired the very words of scripture, what would be the point if we don't *have* the very words of scripture? In some places, as we will see, we simply cannot be sure that we have reconstructed the original text accurately. It's a bit hard to know what the words of the Bible mean if we don't even know what the words are!

This became a problem for my view of inspiration, for I came to realize that it would have been no more difficult for God to preserve the words of scripture than it would have been for him to inspire them in the first place. If he wanted his people to have his words, surely he would have given them to them (and possibly even given them the words in a language they could understand, rather than Greek and Hebrew). The fact that we don't have the words surely must show, I reasoned, that he did not preserve them for us. And if he didn't perform that miracle, there seemed to be no reason to think that he performed the earlier miracle of inspiring those words.

In short, my study of the Greek New Testament, and my investigations into the manuscripts that contain it, led to a radical rethinking of my understanding of what the Bible is. This was a seismic change for me. Before this—starting with my born-again experience in high school, through my fundamentalist days at Moody, and on through my evangelical days at Wheaton—my faith had been based completely on a certain view of the Bible as the fully inspired, inerrant word of God. Now I no longer saw the Bible that way. The Bible began to appear to me as a very human book. Just as human scribes had copied, and changed, the texts of scripture, so too had human authors originally *written* the texts of scripture. This was a human book from beginning to end. It was written by different human authors at different times and in different places to address different needs. Many of these authors no doubt felt they were inspired by God to say what they did, but they had their own perspectives, their own beliefs, their own views, their own needs, their own desires, their own understandings, their own theologies; and these perspectives, beliefs, views, needs, desires, understandings, and theologies informed everything they said. In all these ways they differed from one another. Among other things, this meant that Mark did not say the same thing that Luke said because he didn't mean the same thing as Luke. John is different from Matthew—not the same. Paul is different from Acts. And James is different from Paul. Each author is a human author and needs to be read for what *he* (assuming they were all men) has to say, not assuming that what he says is the same, or conformable to, or consistent with what every other author has to say. The Bible, at the end of the day, is a very human book.

This was a new perspective for me, and obviously not the view I had when I was an evangelical Christian—nor is it the view of most evangelicals today. Let me give an example of the difference my changed perspective could have for understanding the Bible. When I was at Moody Bible Institute, one of the most popular books on campus was Hal Lindsay's apocalyptic blueprint for our future, *The Late Great Planet Earth*. Lindsay's book was popular not only at Moody; it was, in fact, *the* best-selling work of nonfiction (apart from the Bible; and using the term *nonfiction* somewhat loosely) in the English language in the 1970s. Lindsay, like those of us at Moody, believed that the Bible was absolutely inerrant in its very words, to the extent that you could read the New Testament and know not only how God wanted you to live and what he wanted you to believe, but also what God himself was planning to do in the future and how he was going to do it. The world was heading for an apocalyptic crisis of catastrophic proportions, and the inerrant words of scripture could be read to show what, how, and when it would all happen.

I was particularly struck by the "when." Lindsay pointed to Jesus's parable of the fig tree as an indication of when we could expect the future Armageddon. Jesus's disciples want to know when the "end" will come, and Jesus replies:

> *From the fig tree learn this parable. When its branch becomes tender and it puts forth its leaves, you know that summer is near. So also you, when you see all these things you know that he [the Son of Man] is*

What does this parable mean? Lindsay, thinking that it is an inerrant word from God himself, unpacks its message by pointing out that in the Bible the "fig tree" is often used as an image of the nation of Israel. What would it mean for it to put forth its leaves? It would mean that the nation, after lying dormant for a season (the winter), would come back to life. And when did Israel come back to life? In 1948, when Israel once again became a sovereign nation. Jesus indicates that the end will come within the very generation that this was to occur. And how long is a generation in the Bible? Forty years. Hence the divinely inspired teaching, straight from the lips of Jesus: the end of the world will come sometime before 1988, forty years after the re-emergence of Israel.

This message proved completely compelling to us. It may seem odd now—given the circumstance that 1988 has come and gone, with no Armageddon—but, on the other hand, there are millions of Christians who *still* believe that the Bible can be read literally as completely inspired in its predictions of what is soon to happen to bring history as we know it to a close. Witness the current craze for the Timothy LaHaye and Jerry Jenkins series *Left Behind,* another apocalyptic vision of our future based on a literalistic reading of the Bible, a series that has sold more than *sixty million* copies in our own day.

It is a radical shift from reading the Bible as an inerrant blueprint for our faith, life, and future to seeing it as a very human book, with very human points of view, many of which differ from one another and none of which provides the inerrant guide to how we should live. This is the shift in my own thinking that I ended up making, and to which I am now fully committed. Many Christians, of course, have never held this literalistic view of the Bible in the first place, and for them such a view might seem completely one-sided and unnuanced (not to mention bizarre and unrelated to matters of faith). There are, however, plenty of people around who still see the Bible this way. Occasionally I see a bumper sticker that reads: "God said it, I believe it, and that settles it." My response is always, What if God *didn't* say it? What if the book you take as giving you God's words instead contains and that settles it." My response is always, What if God *didn't* say it? What if the book you take as giving you God's words instead contains human words? What if the Bible doesn't give a foolproof answer to the questions of the modern age—abortion, women's rights, gay rights, religious supremacy, Western-style democracy, and the like? What if we have to figure out how to live and what to believe on our own, without setting up the Bible as a false idol—or an oracle that gives us a direct line of communication with the Almighty? There are clear reasons for thinking that, in fact, the Bible is not this kind of inerrant guide to our lives: among other things, as I've been pointing out, in many places we (as scholars, or just regular readers) don't even know what the original words of the Bible actually were.

My personal theology changed radically with this realization, taking me down roads quite different from the ones I had traversed in my late teens and early twenties. I continue to appreciate the Bible and the many and varied messages that it contains—much as I have come to appreciate the other writings of early Christians from about the same time and soon thereafter, the writings of lesser-known figures such as Ignatius of Antioch, Clement of Rome, and Barnabas of Alexandria, and much as I have come to appreciate the writings of persons of other faiths at roughly the time, the writings of Josephus, and Lucian of Samosata, and Plutarch. All of these authors are trying to understand the world and their place in it, and all of them have valuable things to teach us. It is important to know what the words of these authors were, so that we can see what they had to say and judge, then, for ourselves what to think and how to live in light of those words.

This brings me back to my interest in the manuscripts of the New Testament and the study of those manuscripts in the field known as textual criticism. It is my conviction that textual criticism is a compelling and intriguing field of study of real importance not just to scholars but to everyone with an interest in the Bible (whether a literalist, a recovering literalist, a never-in-your-life-would-I-ever-be-a-literalist, or even just anyone with a remote interest in the Bible as a historical and cultural phenomenon). What is striking, however, is that most readers—even those interested in Christianity, in the Bible, in biblical studies, both those who believe the Bible is inerrant and those who do not—know almost nothing about textual criticism. And it's not difficult to see why. Despite the fact that this has been a topic of sustained scholarship now for more than three hundred years, there is scarcely a single book written about it for a lay audience—that is, for those who know nothing about it, who don't have the Greek and other languages necessary for the in-depth study of it, who do not realize there is even a "problem" with the text, but who would be intrigued to learn both what the problems are and how scholars have set about dealing with them.[2]

That is the kind of book this is—to my knowledge, the first of its kind. It is written for people who know nothing about textual criticism but who might like to learn something about how scribes were changing scripture and about how we can recognize where they did so. It is written based on my thirty years of thinking about the subject, and from the perspective that I now have, having gone through such radical transformations of my own views of the Bible. It is written for anyone who might be interested in seeing how we got our New Testament, seeing how in some instances we don't even know what the words of the original writers were, seeing in what interesting ways these words occasionally got changed, and seeing how we might, through the application of some rather rigorous methods of analysis, reconstruct what those original words actually were. In many ways, then, this is a very personal book for me, the end result of a long journey. Maybe, for others, it can be part of a journey of their own.

An image from the famous Rabula Gospels, an elegant
biblical manuscript from sixth-century Syria.

I

THE BEGINNINGS OF
CHRISTIAN SCRIPTURE

To discuss the copies of the New Testament that we have, we need to start at the very beginning with one of the unusual features of Christianity in the Greco-Roman world: its bookish character. In fact, to make sense of this feature of Christianity, we need to start before the beginnings of Christianity with the religion from which Christianity sprang, Judaism. For the bookishness of Christianity was in some sense anticipated and foreshadowed by Judaism, which was the first "religion of the book" in Western civilization.

JUDAISM AS A RELIGION OF THE BOOK

The Judaism from which Christianity sprang was an unusual religion in the Roman world, although by no means unique. Like adherents of any of the other (hundreds of) religions in the Mediterranean area, Jews acknowledged the existence of a divine realm populated by superhuman beings (angels, archangels, principalities, powers); they subscribed to the worship of a deity through sacrifices of animals and other food products; they maintained that there was a special holy place where this divine being dwelt here on earth (the Temple in Jerusalem), and it was there that these sacrifices were to be made. They prayed to this God for communal and personal needs. They told stories about how this God had interacted with human beings in the past, and they anticipated his help for human beings in the present. In all these ways, Judaism was "familiar" to the worshipers of other gods in the empire.

In some ways, though, Judaism was distinctive. All other religions in the empire were polytheistic—acknowledging and worshiping many gods of all sorts and functions: great gods of the state, lesser gods of various locales, gods who oversaw different aspects of human birth, life, and death. Judaism, on the other hand, was monotheistic; Jews insisted on worshiping only the one God of their ancestors, the God who, they maintained, had created this world, controlled this world, and alone provided what was needed for his people. According to Jewish tradition, this one all-powerful God had called Israel to be his special people and had promised to protect and defend them in exchange for their absolute devotion to him and him alone. The Jewish people, it was believed, had a "covenant" with this God, an agreement that they would be uniquely his as he was uniquely theirs. Only this one God was to be worshiped and obeyed; so, too, there was only one Temple, unlike in the polytheistic religions of the day in which, for example, there could be any number of temples to a god like Zeus. To be sure, Jews could worship God anywhere they lived, but they could perform their religious obligations of sacrifice to God only at the Temple in Jerusalem. In other places, though, they could gather together in "synagogues" for prayer and to discuss the ancestral traditions at the heart of their religion.

These traditions involved both stories about God's interaction with the ancestors of the people of Israel—the patriarchs and matriarchs of the faith, as it were: Abraham, Sarah, Isaac, Rachel, Jacob, Rebecca, Joseph, Moses, David, and so on—and detailed instructions concerning how this people was to worship and live. One of the things that made Judaism unique among the religions of the Roman Empire was that these instructions, along with the other ancestral traditions, were written down in sacred books.

For modern people intimately familiar with any of the major contemporary Western religions (Judaism, Christianity, Islam), it may be hard to imagine, but books played virtually no role in the polytheistic religions of the ancient Western world. These religions were almost exclusively concerned with honoring the gods through ritual acts of sacrifice. There were no doctrines to be learned, as explained in books, and almost no ethical principles to be followed, as laid out in books. This is not to say that adherents of the various polytheistic religions had no beliefs about their gods or that they had no ethics, but beliefs and ethics—strange as this sounds to modern ears—played almost no role in religion per se. These were instead matters of personal philosophy, and philosophies, of course, *could* be bookish. Since ancient religions themselves did not require any particular sets of "right doctrines" or, for the most part, "ethical codes," books played almost no role in them.

Judaism was unique in that it stressed its ancestral traditions, customs, and laws, and maintained that these had been recorded in sacred books, which had the status, therefore, of "scripture" for the Jewish people. During the period of our concern—the first century of the common era,[1] when the books of the New Testament were being written—Jews scattered throughout the Roman Empire understood in particular that God had given direction to his people in the writings of Moses, referred to collectively as the Torah, which literally means something like "law" or "guidance." The Torah consists of five books, sometimes called the Pentateuch (the "five scrolls"), the beginning of the Jewish Bible (the Christian Old Testament): Genesis, Exodus, Leviticus, Numbers, and Deuteronomy. Here one finds accounts of the creation of the world, the calling of Israel to be God's people, the stories of Israel's patriarchs and matriarchs and God's involvement with them, and most important (and most extensive), the laws that God gave Moses indicating how his people were to worship him and behave toward one another in community together. These were sacred laws, to be learned, discussed, and followed—and they were written in a set of books.

Jews had other books that were important for their religious lives together as well, for example, books of prophets (such as Isaiah, Jeremiah, and Amos), and poems (Psalms), and history (such as Joshua and Samuel). Eventually, some time after Christianity began, a group of these Hebrew books—twenty-two of them altogether—came to be regarded as a sacred canon of scripture, the Jewish Bible of today, accepted by Christians as the first part of the Christian canon, the "Old Testament."[2]

These brief facts about Jews and their written texts are important because they set the backdrop for Christianity, which was also, from the very beginning, a "bookish" religion. Christianity began, of course, with Jesus, who was himself a Jewish rabbi (teacher) who accepted the authority of the Torah, and possibly other sacred Jewish books, and taught his interpretation of those books to his disciples.[3] Like other rabbis of his day, Jesus maintained that God's will could be found in the sacred texts, especially the Law of Moses. He read these scriptures, studied these scriptures, interpreted these scriptures, adhered to these scriptures, and taught these scriptures. His followers were, from the beginning, Jews who placed a high premium on the books of their tradition. And so, already, at the start of Christianity, adherents of this new religion, the followers of Jesus, were unusual in the Roman Empire: like the Jews before them, but unlike nearly everyone else, they located sacred authority in sacred books. Christianity at its beginning was a religion of the book.

CHRISTIANITY AS A RELIGION OF THE BOOK

As we will see momentarily, the importance of books for early Christianity does not mean that all Christians could read books; quite the contrary, most early Christians, like most other people throughout the empire (including Jews!), were illiterate. But that did not mean that books played a secondary role in the religion. In fact, books were centrally important, in fundamental ways, to the lives of Christians in their communities.

Early Christian Letters

The first thing to notice is that many different kinds of writing were significant for the burgeoning Christian communities of the first century after Jesus's death. The earliest evidence we have for Christian communities comes from letters that Christian leaders wrote. The apostle Paul is our earliest and best example. Paul established churches throughout the eastern Mediterranean, principally in urban centers, evidently by convincing pagans (i.e., adherents of any of the empire's polytheistic religions) that the Jewish God was the only one to be worshiped, and that Jesus was his Son, who had died for the sins of the world and was returning soon for judgment on the earth (see 1 Thess. 1:9–10). It is not clear how much Paul used scripture (i.e., the writings of the Jewish Bible) in trying to persuade his potential converts of the truth of his message; but in one of his key summaries of his preaching he indicates that what he preached was that "Christ died, in accordance with the scriptures . . . and that he was raised, in accordance with the scriptures" (1 Cor. 15:3–4). Evidently Paul correlated the events of Christ's death and resurrection with his interpretation of key passages of the Jewish Bible, which he, as a highly educated Jew, obviously could read for himself, and which he interpreted for his hearers in an often successful attempt to convert them.

After Paul had converted a number of people in a given locale, he would move to another and try, usually with some success, to convert people there as well. But he would sometimes (often?) hear news from one of the other communities of believers he had earlier established, and sometimes (often?) the news would not be good: members of the community had started to behave badly, problems of immorality had arisen, "false teachers" had arrived teaching notions contrary to his own, some of the community members had started to hold to false doctrines, and so on. Upon hearing the news, Paul would write a letter back to the community, dealing with the problems. These letters were very important to the lives of the community, and a number of them eventually came to be regarded as scripture. Some thirteen letters written in Paul's name are included in the New Testament.

We can get a sense of how important these letters were at the earliest stages of the Christian movement from the very first Christian writing we have, Paul's first letter to the Thessalonians, usually dated to about 49 C.E.,[4] some twenty years after Jesus's death and some twenty years before any of the Gospel accounts of his life. Paul ends the letter by saying, "Greet all the brothers and sisters with a holy kiss; I strongly adjure you in the name of the Lord that you have this letter read to all the brothers and sisters" (1 Thess. 5:26–27). This was not a casual letter to be read simply by anyone who was mildly interested; the apostle *insists* that it be read, and that it be accepted as an authoritative statement by him, the founder of the community.

Letters thus circulated throughout the Christian communities from the earliest of times. These letters bound together communities that lived in different places; they unified the faith and the practices of the Christians; they indicated what the Christians were supposed to believe and how they were supposed to behave. They were to be read aloud to the community at community gatherings—since, as I pointed out, most Christians, like most others, would not have been able to read the letters themselves.

A number of these letters came to be included in the New Testament. In fact, the New Testament is largely made up of letters written by Paul and other Christian leaders to Christian communities (e.g., the Corinthians, the Galatians) and individuals (e.g., Philemon). Moreover, the letters that survive—there are twenty-one in the New Testament—are only a fraction of those written. Just with respect to Paul, we can assume that he wrote many more letters than the ones attributed to him in the New Testament. On occasion, he mentions other letters that no longer survive; in 1 Cor. 5:9, for example, he mentions a letter that he had earlier written the Corinthians (sometime before *First* Corinthians). And he mentions another letter that some of the Corinthians had sent *him* (1 Cor. 7:1). Elsewhere he refers to letters that his opponents had (2 Cor. 3:1). None of these letters survives.

Scholars have long suspected that some of the letters found in the New Testament under Paul's name were in fact written by his later followers, pseudonymously.[5] If this suspicion is correct, it would provide even more evidence of the importance of letters in the early Christian movement: in order to get one's views heard, one would write a letter in the apostle's name, on the assumption that this would carry a good deal of authority. One of these allegedly pseudonymous letters is Colossians, which itself emphasizes the importance of letters and mentions yet another one that no longer survives: "And when you have read this epistle, be sure that it is read in the church of the Laodiceans, and that you read the letter written to Laodicea" (Col. 4:16). Evidently Paul—either himself, or someone writing in his name—wrote a letter to the nearby town of Laodicea. This letter too has been lost.[6]

My point is that letters were important to the lives of the early Christian communities. These were written documents that were to guide them in their faith and practice. They bound these churches together. They helped make Christianity quite different from the other religions scattered throughout the empire, in that the various Christian communities, unified by this common literature that was being shared back and forth (cf. Col. 4:16), were adhering to instructions found in written documents or "books."

And it was not only letters that were important to these communities. There was, in fact, an extraordinarily wide range of literature being produced, disseminated, read, and followed by the early Christians, quite unlike anything else the Roman pagan world had ever seen. Rather than describe all this literature at great length, here I can simply mention some examples of the kinds of books that were being written and distributed.

Early Gospels

Christians, of course, were concerned to know more about the life, teachings, death, and resurrection of their Lord; and so numerous Gospels were written, which recorded the traditions associated with the life of Jesus. Four such Gospels became most widely used—those of Matthew, Mark, Luke, and John in the New Testament—but many others were written. We still have some of the others: for example, Gospels allegedly by Jesus's disciple Philip, his brother Judas Thomas, and his female companion Mary Magdalene. Other Gospels, including some of the very earliest, have been lost. We know this, for example, from the Gospel of Luke, whose author indicates that in writing his account he consulted "many" predecessors (Luke 1:1), which obviously no longer survive. One of these earlier accounts may have been the source that scholars have designated Q, which was probably a written account, principally of Jesus's sayings, used by both Luke and Matthew for many of their distinctive teachings of Jesus (e.g., the Lord's Prayer and the Beatitudes).[7]

Jesus's life, as we have seen, was interpreted by Paul and others in light of the Jewish scriptures. These books too—both the Pentateuch and other Jewish writings, such as the Prophets and Psalms—were in wide use among Christians, who explored them to see what they could reveal about God's will, especially as it had been fulfilled in Christ. Copies of the Jewish Bible, usually in Greek translation (the so-called Septuagint), were widely available, then, in early Christian communities as sources for study and reflection.

Early Acts of the Apostles

Not just the life of Jesus, but also the lives of his earliest followers were of interest to the growing Christian communities of the first and second centuries. It is no surprise, then, to see that accounts of the apostles—their adventures and missionary exploits, especially after the death and resurrection of Jesus—came to occupy an important place for Christians interested in knowing more about their religion.

One such account, the Acts of the Apostles, eventually made it into the New Testament. But many other accounts were written, mainly about individual apostles, such as those found in the *Acts of Paul,* the *Acts of Peter,* and the *Acts of Thomas.* Other Acts have survived only in fragments, or have been lost altogether.

Christian Apocalypses

As I have indicated, Paul (along with other apostles) taught that Jesus was soon to return from heaven in judgment on the earth. The coming end of all things was a source of continuous fascination for early Christians, who by and large expected that God would soon intervene in the affairs of the world to overthrow the forces of evil and establish his good kingdom, with Jesus at its head, here on earth. Some Christian authors produced prophetic accounts of what would happen at this cataclysmic end of the world as we know it. There were Jewish precedents for this kind of "apocalyptic" literature, for example, in the book of Daniel in the Jewish Bible, or the book of 1 Enoch in the Jewish Apocrypha. Of the Christian apocalypses, one eventually came to be included in the New Testament: the Apocalypse of John. Others, including the *Apocalypse of Peter* and *The Shepherd* of Hermas, were also popular reading in a number of Christian communities in the early centuries of the church.

Church Orders

The early Christian communities multiplied and grew, starting in Paul's day and continuing in the generations after him. Originally the Christian churches, at least those established by Paul himself, were what we might call charismatic communities. They believed that each member of the community had been given a "gift" (Greek: *charisma*) of the Spirit to assist the community in its ongoing life: for example, there were gifts of teaching, administration, almsgiving, healing, and prophecy. Eventually, however, as the expectation of an imminent end of the world began to fade, it became clear that there needed to be a more rigid church structure, especially if the church was to be around for the long haul (cf. 1 Corinthians 11; Matthew 16, 18). Churches around the Mediterranean, including those founded by Paul, started appointing leaders who would be in charge and make decisions (rather than having every member as "equally" endowed with the Spirit); rules began to be formulated concerning how the community was to live together, practice its sacred rites (e.g., baptism and eucharist), train new members, and so on. Soon documents started being produced that indicated how the churches were to be ordered and structured. These so-called church orders became increasingly important in the second and third Christian centuries, but already by about 100 C.E. the first (to our knowledge) had been written and widely disseminated, a book called *The Didache* [Teaching] *of the Twelve Apostles*. Soon it had numerous successors.

Christian Apologies

As the Christian communities became established, they sometimes faced opposition from Jews and pagans who saw this new faith as a threat and suspected its adherents of engaging in immoral and socially destructive practices (just as new religious movements today are often regarded with suspicion). This opposition sometimes led to local persecutions of Christians; eventually the persecutions became "official," as Roman administrators intervened to arrest Christians and try to force them to return to the old ways of paganism. As Christianity grew, it eventually converted intellectuals to the faith, who were well equipped to discuss and dismiss the charges typically raised against the Christians. The writings of these intellectuals are sometimes called apologies, from the Greek word for "defense" (*apologia*). The apologists wrote intellectual defenses of the new faith, trying to show that far from being a threat to the social structure of the empire, it was a religion that preached moral behavior; and far from being a dangerous superstition, it represented the ultimate truth in its worship of the one true God. These apologies were important for early Christian readers, as they provided them with the arguments they needed when themselves faced with persecution. Already this kind of defense was found in the New Testament period, for example, in the book of 1 Peter (3:15: "always be prepared to make a defense to anyone who asks you to give an account of the hope that is in you") and in the book of Acts, where Paul and other apostles defend themselves against charges leveled at them. By the second half of the second century, apologies had become a popular form of Christian writing.

Christian Martyrologies

At about the same time that apologies began to be written, Christians started producing accounts of their persecutions and the martyrdoms that happened as a result of them. There is some portrayal of both matters already in the New Testament book of Acts, where opposition to the Christian movement, the arrest of Christian leaders, and the execution of at least one of them (Stephen) form a significant part of the narrative (see Acts 7). Later, in the second century, martyrologies (accounts of the martyrs) began to appear. The first of them is the *Martyrdom of Polycarp,* who was an important Christian leader who served as bishop of the church of Smyrna, in Asia Minor, for almost the entire first half of the second century. The account of Polycarp's death is found in a letter produced by members of his church, written to another community. Soon afterward, accounts of other martyrs began to appear. These too were popular among Christians, as they provided encouragement to those who were also persecuted for the faith, and guidance about how to face the ultimate threats of arrest, torture, and death.

Antiheretical Tractates

The problems Christians faced were not confined to external threats of persecution. From the earliest times, Christians were aware that a variety of interpretations of the "truth" of the religion existed within their own ranks. Already the apostle Paul rails against "false teachers"— for example, in his letter to the Galatians. Reading the surviving accounts, we can see clearly that these opponents were not outsiders. They were Christians who understood the religion in fundamentally different ways. To deal with this problem, Christian leaders began to write tractates that opposed "heretics" (those who chose the wrong way to understand the faith); in a sense, some of Paul's letters are the earliest representations of this kind of tractate. Eventually, though, Christians of all persuasions became involved in trying to establish the "true teaching" (the literal meaning of "orthodoxy") and to oppose those who advocated false teaching. These antiheretical tractates became an important feature of the landscape of early Christian literature. What is interesting is that even groups of "false teachers" wrote tractates against "false teachers," so that the group that established once and for all what Christians were to believe (those responsible, for example, for the creeds that have come down to us today) are sometimes polemicized against by Christians who take the positions eventually decreed as false. This we have learned by relatively recent discoveries of "heretical" literature, in which the so-called heretics maintain that their views are correct and those of the "orthodox" church leaders are false.[8]

Early Christian Commentaries

A good deal of the debate over right belief and false belief involved the interpretation of Christian texts, including the "Old Testament," which Christians claimed as part of their own Bible. This shows yet again how central texts were to the life of the early Christian communities. Eventually, Christian authors began to write interpretations of these texts, not necessarily with the direct purpose of refuting false interpretations (although that was often in view as well), but sometimes simply to unpack the meaning of these texts and to show their relevance to Christian life and practice. It is interesting that the first Christian commentary on any text of scripture that we know about came from a so-called heretic, a second-century Gnostic named Heracleon, who wrote a commentary on the Gospel of John.[9] Eventually commentaries, interpretive glosses, practical expositions, and homi-lies on texts became common among the Christian communities of the third and fourth centuries.

I have been summarizing the different kinds of writings that were important to the lives of the early Christian churches. As I hope can be seen, the phenomenon of writing was of uppermost importance to these churches and the Christians within them. Books were at the very heart of the Christian religion—unlike other religions of the em-pire—from the very beginning. Books recounted the stories of Jesus and his apostles that Christians told and retold; books provided Christians with instruction in what to believe and how to live their lives; books bound together geographically separated communities into one universal church; books supported Christians in their times of persecution and gave them models of faithfulness to emulate in the face of torture and death; books provided not just good advice but correct doctrine, warning against the false teachings of others and urging the acceptance of orthodox beliefs; books allowed Christians to know the true meaning of other writings, giving guidance in what to think, how to worship, how to behave. Books were completely cen-tral to the life of the early Christians.

THE FORMATION OF THE CHRISTIAN CANON

Eventually, some of these Christian books came to be seen not only as worthy of reading but as absolutely authoritative for the beliefs and practices of Christians. They became Scripture.

The Beginnings of a Christian Canon

The formation of the Christian canon of scripture was a long, in-volved process, and I do not need to go into all the details here.[10] As I have already indicated, in some sense Christians *started* with a canon in that the founder of their religion was himself a Jewish teacher who accepted the Torah as authoritative scripture from God, and who taught his followers his interpretation of it. The earliest Christians were followers of Jesus who accepted the books of the Jewish Bible (which was not yet set as a "canon," once and for all) as their own scripture. For the writers of the New Testament, including our earliest author, Paul, the "scriptures" referred to the Jewish Bible, the collection of books that God had given his people and that predicted the coming of the Messiah, Jesus.

It was not long, however, before Christians began accepting other writings as standing on a par with the Jewish scriptures. This acceptance may have had its roots in the authoritative teaching of Jesus himself, as his followers took his *interpretation* of scripture to be equal in authority to the words of scripture itself. Jesus may have encouraged this understanding by the way he phrased some of his teachings. In the Sermon on the Mount, for example, Jesus is recorded as stating laws given by God to Moses, and then giving his own more radical interpretation of them, indicating that his interpretation is authoritative. This is found in the so-called Antitheses recorded in Matthew, chapter 5. Jesus says, "You have heard it said, 'You shall not commit murder' [one of the Ten Commandments], but *I* say to you, 'whoever is even angry with a brother or sister is liable to judgment.'" What Jesus says, in his interpretation of the Law, appears to be as authoritative as the Law itself. Or Jesus says, "You have heard it said, 'You shall not commit adultery' [another of the Ten Commandments]. But *I* say to you, 'whoever looks at a woman to lust after her in his heart has already committed adultery with her.'"

On some occasions these authoritative interpretations of scripture appear, in effect, to countermand the laws of scripture themselves. For example, Jesus says, "You have heard it said, 'Whoever divorces his wife should give her a certificate of divorce' [a command found in Deut. 24:1], but *I* say to you that everyone who divorces his wife for reason other than sexual immorality, makes her commit adultery, and whoever marries a divorced woman commits adultery." It is hard to see how one can follow Moses' command to give a certificate of divorce, if in fact divorce is not an option.

In any event, Jesus's teachings were soon seen to be as authoritative as the pronouncements of Moses—that is, those of the Torah itself. This becomes even more clear later in the New Testament period, in the book of 1 Timothy, allegedly by Paul but frequently taken by scholars to have been written in his name by a later follower. In 1 Tim. 5:18 the author is urging his readers to pay those who minister among them, and supports his exhortation by quoting "the scripture." What is interesting is that he then quotes two passages, one found in the Torah ("Do not muzzle an ox that is treading," Deut. 25:4) and the other found on the lips of Jesus ("A workman is worthy of his hire"; see Luke 10:7). It appears that for this author, Jesus's words are already on a par with scripture.

Nor was it just Jesus's teachings that were being considered scriptural by these second- or third-generation Christians. So too were the writings of his apostles. Evidence comes in the final book of the New Testament to be written, 2 Peter, a book that most critical scholars believe was not actually written by Peter but by one of his followers, pseudonymously. In 2 Peter 3 the author makes reference to false teachers who twist the meaning of Paul's letters to make them say what they want them to say, "just as they do with the rest of the scriptures" (2 Pet. 3:16). It appears that Paul's letters are here being understood as scripture.

Soon after the New Testament period, certain Christian writings were being quoted as authoritative texts for the life and beliefs of the church. An outstanding example is a letter written by Polycarp, the previously mentioned bishop of Smyrna, in the early second century. Polycarp was asked by the church at Philippi to advise them, particularly with respect to a case involving one of the leaders who had evidently engaged in some form of financial mismanagement within the church (possibly embezzling church funds). Polycarp's letter to the

Philippians, which still survives, is intriguing for a number of reasons, not the least of which is its propensity to quote earlier writings of the Christians. In just fourteen brief chapters, Polycarp quotes more than a hundred passages known from these earlier writings, asserting their authority for the situation the Philippians were facing (in contrast to just a dozen quotations from the Jewish scriptures); in one place he appears to call Paul's letter to the Ephesians scripture. More commonly, he simply quotes or alludes to earlier writings, assuming their authoritative status for the community.[11]

The Role of Christian Liturgy in the Formation of the Canon

Some time before the letter of Polycarp, we know that Christians were hearing the Jewish scriptures read during their worship services. The author of 1 Timothy, for example, urges that the letter's recipient "pay close attention to [public] reading, to exhortation, and to teaching" (4:13). As we saw in the case of the letter to the Colossians, it appears that letters by Christians were being read to the gathered community as well. And we know that by the middle of the second century, a good portion of the Christian worship services involved the public reading of scripture. In a much discussed passage from the writings of the Christian intellectual and apologist Justin Martyr, for example, we get a glimpse of what a church service involved in his home city of Rome:

> On the day called Sunday, all who live in cities or in the country
> gather together to one place, and the memoirs of the apostles or the
> writings of the prophets are read, as long as time permits; then, when
> the reader has ceased, the president verbally instructs, and exhorts to
> the imitation of these good things . . . (1 Apol. 67)

It seems likely that the liturgical use of some Christian texts—for example, "the memoirs of the apostles," which are usually understood to be the Gospels—elevated their status for most Christians so that they, as much as the Jewish scriptures ("the writings of the prophets"), were considered to be authoritative.

The Role of Marcion in the Formation of the Canon

We can trace the formation of the Christian canon of scripture a bit more closely still, from the surviving evidence. At the same time that Justin was writing in the mid second century, another prominent Christian was also active in Rome, the philosopher-teacher Marcion, later declared a heretic.[12] Marcion is an intriguing figure in many ways. He had come to Rome from Asia Minor, having already made a fortune in what was evidently a shipbuilding business. Upon arriving in the Rome, he made an enormous donation to the Roman church, probably, in part, to get in its good favor. For five years he stayed in Rome, spending much of his time teaching his understanding of the Christian faith and working out its details in several writings. Arguably his most influential literary production was not something he wrote but something he edited. Marcion was the first Christian that we know of who produced an actual "canon" of scripture—that is, a collection of books that, he argued, constituted the sacred texts of the faith.

To make sense of this initial attempt to establish the canon, we need to know a bit about Marcion's distinctive teaching. Marcion was completely absorbed by the life and teachings of the apostle Paul, whom he considered to be the one "true" apostle from the early days of the church. In some of his letters, such as Romans and Galatians, Paul had taught that a right standing before God came only by faith in Christ, not by doing any of the works prescribed by the Jewish law. Marcion took this differentiation between the law of the Jews and faith in Christ to what he saw as its logical conclusion, that there was an absolute distinction between the law on the one hand and the gospel on the other. So distinct were the law and the gospel, in fact, that both could not possibly have come from the same God. Marcion concluded that the God of Jesus (and Paul) was not, therefore, the God of the Old Testament. There were, in fact, two different Gods: the God of the Jews, who created the world, called Israel to be his people, and gave them his harsh law; and the God of Jesus, who sent Christ into the world to save people from the wrathful vengeance of the Jewish creator God.

Marcion believed this understanding of Jesus was taught by Paul himself, and so, naturally, his canon included the ten letters of Paul available to him (all those in the New Testament apart from the pastoral Epistles of 1 and 2 Timothy and Titus); and since Paul sometimes referred to his "Gospel," Marcion included a Gospel in his canon, a form of what is now the Gospel of Luke. And that was all. Marcion's canon consisted of eleven books: there was no Old Testament, only one Gospel, and ten Epistles. But not only that: Marcion had come to believe that false believers, who did not have his understanding of the faith, had transmitted these eleven books by copying them, and by adding bits and pieces here and there in order to accommodate their own beliefs, including the "false" notion that the God of the Old Testament was also the God of Jesus. And so Marcion "corrected" the eleven books of his canon by editing out references to the Old Testament God, or to the creation as the work of the true God, or to the Law as something that should be followed.

As we will see, Marcion's attempt to make his sacred texts conform more closely to his teaching by actually changing them was not unprecedented. Both before and after him, copyists of the early Christian literature occasionally changed their texts to make them say what they were already thought to mean.

The "Orthodox" Canon after Marcion

Many scholars are convinced that it was precisely in opposition to Marcion that other Christians became more concerned to establish the contours of what was to become the New Testament canon. It is interesting that in Marcion's own day, Justin could speak rather vaguely about the "memoirs of the apostles" without indicating which of these books (presumably Gospels) were accepted in the churches or why, whereas some thirty years later another Christian writer, who equally opposed Marcion, took a far more authoritative stand. This was the bishop of Lyons in Gaul (modern France), Irenaeus, who wrote a five-volume work against heretics such as Marcion and the Gnostics, and who had very clear ideas about which books should be considered among the canonical Gospels.

In a frequently cited passage from his work *Against Heresies,* Irenaeus says that not just Marcion, but also other "heretics," had mistakenly assumed that only one or another of the Gospels was to be accepted as scripture: Jewish Christians who held to the ongoing validity of the Law used only Matthew; certain groups who argued that Jesus was not really the Christ accepted only the Gospel of Mark; Marcion and his followers accepted only (a form of) Luke; and a group of Gnostics called the Valentinians accepted only John. All these groups were in error, however, because

> it is not possible that the Gospels can be either more or fewer in
> number than they are. For, since there are four zones of the world
> in which we live, and four principal winds, while the Church is
> scattered throughout the world, and the pillar and ground of the
> Church is the Gospel . . . it is fitting that she should have four
> pillars . . . (Against Heresies 3.11.7)

In other words, four corners of the earth, four winds, four pillars—and necessarily, then, four Gospels.

And so, near the end of the second century there were Christians who were insisting that Matthew, Mark, Luke, and John were *the* Gospels; there were neither more nor fewer.

Debates about the contours of the canon continued for several centuries. It appears that Christians by and large were concerned to know which books to accept as authoritative so that they would (1) know which books should be read in their services of worship and, relatedly, (2) know which books could be trusted as reliable guides for what to believe and how to behave. The decisions about which books should finally be considered canonical were not automatic or problem-free; the debates were long and drawn out, and sometimes harsh. Many Christians today may think that the canon of the New Testament simply appeared on the scene one day, soon after the death of Jesus, but nothing could be farther from the truth. As it turns out, we are able to pinpoint the first time that any Christian of record listed the twenty-seven books of our New Testament as *the* books of the New Testament—neither more nor fewer. Surprising as it may seem, this Christian was writing in the second half of the fourth century, nearly three hundred years after the books of the New Testament had themselves been written. The author was the powerful bishop of Alexandria named Athanasius. In the year 367 C.E., Athanasius wrote his annual pastoral letter to the Egyptian churches under his jurisdiction, and in it he included advice concerning which books should be read as scripture in the churches. He lists our twenty-seven books, excluding all others. This is the first surviving instance of anyone affirming our set of books as the New Testament. And even Athanasius did not settle the matter. Debates continued for decades, even centuries. The books we call the New Testament were not gathered together into one canon and considered scripture, finally and ultimately, until hundreds of years after the books themselves had first been produced.

THE READERS OF CHRISTIAN WRITINGS

In the preceding section our discussion focused on the canonization of scripture. As we saw earlier, however, many kinds of books were being written and read by Christians in the early centuries, not just the books that made it into the New Testament. There were other gospels, acts, epistles, and apocalypses; there were records of persecution, accounts of martyrdom, apologies for the faith, church orders, attacks on heretics, letters of exhortation and instruction, expositions of scripture—an entire range of literature that helped define Christianity and make it the religion it came to be. It would be helpful at this stage of our discussion to ask a basic question about all this literature. Who, actually, was reading it?

In the modern world, this would seem to be a rather bizarre question. If authors are writing books for Christians, then the people reading the books would presumably be Christians. When asked about the ancient world, however, the question has special poignancy because, in the ancient world, most people could not read.

Literacy is a way of life for those of us in the modern West. We read all the time, every day. We read newspapers and magazines and books of all kinds—biographies, novels, how-to books, self-help books, diet books, religious books, philosophical books, histories, memoirs, and on and on. But our facility with written language today has little to do with reading practices and realities in antiquity.

Studies of literacy have shown that what we might think of as mass literacy is a modern phenomenon, one that appeared only with the advent of the Industrial Revolution.[13] It was only when nations could see an economic benefit in having virtually everyone able to read that they were willing to devote the massive resources—especially time, money, and human resources—needed to ensure that everyone had a basic education in literacy. In nonindustrial societies, the resources were desperately needed for other things, and literacy would not have helped either the economy or the well-being of society as a whole. As a result, until the modern period, almost all societies contained only a small minority of people who could read and write.

This applies even to ancient societies that we might associate with reading and writing—for example, Rome during the early Christian centuries, or even Greece during the classical period. The best and most influential study of literacy in ancient times, by Columbia University professor William Harris, indicates that at the very best of times and places—for example, Athens at the height of the classical period in the fifth century B.C.E.—literacy rates were rarely higher than 10–15 percent of the population. To reverse the numbers, this means that under the best of conditions, 85–90 percent of the population could not read or write. In the first Christian century, throughout the Roman Empire, the literacy rates may well have been lower.[14]

As it turns out, even defining what it means to read and write is a very complicated business. Many people can read but are unable to compose a sentence, for example. And what does it mean to read? Are people literate if they can manage to make sense of the comic strips but not the editorial page? Can people be said to be able to write if they can sign their name but cannot copy a page of text?

The problem of definition is even more pronounced when we turn to the ancient world, where the ancients themselves had difficulty defining what it meant to be literate. One of the most famous illustrative examples comes from Egypt in the second Christian century. Throughout most of antiquity, since most people could not write, there were local "readers" and "writers" who hired out their services to people who needed to conduct business that required written texts: tax receipts, legal contracts, licenses, personal letters, and the like. In Egypt, there were local officials who were assigned the task of overseeing certain governmental tasks that required writing. These assignments as local (or village) scribes were not usually sought after: as with many "official" administrative posts, the people who were required to take them were responsible for paying for the job out-of-pocket. These jobs, in other words, went to the wealthier members of the society and carried a kind of status with them, but they required the expenditure of personal funds.

The example that illustrates the problem of defining literacy involves an Egyptian scribe called Petaus, from the village of Karanis in upper Egypt. As often happened, Petaus was assigned to duties in a different village, Ptolemais Hormou, where he was given oversight of financial and agricultural affairs. In the year 184 C.E., Petaus had to respond to some complaints about another village scribe from Ptolemais Hormou, a man named Ischyrion, who had been assigned somewhere else to undertake responsibilities as a scribe. The villagers under Ischyrion's jurisdiction were upset that Ischyrion could not fulfill his obligations, because, they charged, he was "illiterate." In dealing with the dispute Petaus argued that Ischyrion wasn't illiterate at all, because he had actually signed his name to a range of official documents. In other words, for Petaus "literacy" meant simply the ability to sign one's name.

Petaus himself had trouble doing much more than that. As it turns out, we have a scrap of papyrus on which Petaus practiced his writing, on which he wrote, twelve times over, the words (in Greek) that he had to sign on official documents: "I Petaus, the village scribe, have submitted this." What is odd is that he copied the words correctly the first four times, but the fifth time he left off the first letter of the final word, and for the remaining seven times he continued to leave off the letter, indicating that he was not writing words that he knew how to write but was merely *copying* the preceding line. He evidently couldn't read even the simple words he was putting on the page. And *he* was the official local scribe![15]

If we count Petaus among the "literate" people in antiquity, how many people could actually read texts and make sense of what they said? It is impossible to come up with an exact figure, but it appears that the percentage would not be very high. There are reasons for thinking that within the Christian communities, the numbers would have been even lower than in the population at large. This is because it appears that Christians, especially early on in the movement, came for the most part from the lower, uneducated classes. There were always exceptions, of course, like the apostle Paul and the other authors whose works made it into the New Testament and who were obviously skilled writers; but for the most part, Christians came from the ranks of the illiterate.

This is certainly true of the very earliest Christians, who would have been the apostles of Jesus. In the Gospel accounts, we find that most of Jesus's disciples are simple peasants from Galilee—uneducated fishermen, for example. Two of them, Peter and John, are explicitly said to be "illiterate" in the book of Acts (4:13). The apostle

Paul indicates to his Corinthian congregation that "not many of you were wise by human standards" (1 Cor. 1:27)—which might mean that some few were well educated, but not most. As we move into the second Christian century, things do not seem to change much. As I have indicated, some intellectuals converted to the faith, but most Christians were from the lower classes and uneducated.

Evidence for this view comes from several sources. One of the most interesting is a pagan opponent of Christianity named Celsus who lived in the late second century. Celsus wrote a book called *The True Word,* in which he attacked Christianity on a number of grounds, arguing that it was a foolish, dangerous religion that should be wiped off the face of the earth. Unfortunately, we do not have *The True Word* itself; all we have are quotations from it in the writings of the famous Christian church father Origen, who lived about seventy years after Celsus and was asked to produce a reply to his charges. Origen's book *Against Celsus* survives and is our chief source of information about what the learned critic Celsus said in his book directed against the Christians.[16] One of the great features of Origen's book is that he quotes Celsus's earlier work at length, line by line, before offering his refutation of it. This allows us to reconstruct with fair accuracy Celsus's claims. One of these claims is that the Christians are ignorant lower-class people. What is striking is that in his reply, Origen does not deny it. Consider the following charges made by Celsus.

> *[The Christians'] injunctions are like this. "Let no one educated, no one wise, no one sensible draw near. For these abilities are thought by us to be evils. But as for anyone ignorant, anyone stupid, anyone uneducated, anyone who is a child, let him come boldly." (Against Celsus 3.44)*
>
> *Moreover, we see that those who display their secret lore in the market-places and go about begging would never enter a gathering of intelligent men, nor would they dare to reveal their noble beliefs in their presence; but whenever they see adolescent boys and a crowd*

*of slaves and a company of fools, they push themselves in and show off. (*Against Celsus *3.50)*

*In private houses also we see wool-workers, cobblers, laundry-workers, and the most illiterate and bucolic yokels, who would not dare to say anything at all in front of their elders and more intelligent masters. But whenever they get hold of children in private and some stupid women with them, they let out some astonishing statements, as, for example, that they must not pay any attention to their father and school teachers . . .; they say that these talk nonsense and have no understanding. . . . But, if they like, they should leave father and their schoolmasters, and go along with the women and little children who are their playfellows to the wooldresser's shop, or to the cobbler's or the washerwoman's shop, that they may learn perfection. And by saying this they persuade them. (*Against Celsus *3.56)*

Origen replies that the true Christian believers are in fact wise (and some, in fact, are well educated), but they are wise with respect to God, not with respect to things in this world. He does not deny, in other words, that the Christian community is largely made up of the lower, uneducated classes.

PUBLIC READING IN CHRISTIAN ANTIQUITY

We appear, then, to have a paradoxical situation in early Christianity. This was a bookish religion, with writings of all kinds proving to be of uppermost importance to almost every aspect of the faith. Yet most people could not read these writings. How do we account for this paradox?

In fact, the matter is not all that strange if we recall what was hinted at earlier, that communities of all kinds throughout antiquity generally used the services of the literate for the sake of the illiterate. For in the ancient world "reading" a book did not mean, usually, reading it to oneself; it meant reading it aloud, to others. One could be said to have *read* a book when in fact one had *heard* it read by others. There seems to be no way around the conclusion that books—as important as they were to the early Christian movement—were almost always read aloud in social settings, such as in settings of worship.

We should recall here that Paul instructs his Thessalonian hearers that his "letter is to be read to all of the brothers and sisters" (1 Thess. 5:27). This would have happened out loud, in community. And the author of Colossians wrote: "And when you have read this epistle, be sure that it is read in the church of the Laodiceans, and that you read the letter written to Laodicea" (Col. 4:16). Recall, too, Justin Martyr's report that "On the day called Sunday, all who live in cities or in the country gather together to one place, and the memoirs of the apostles or the writings of the prophets are read, as long as time permits" (1 *Apol.* 67). The same point is made in other early Christian writings. For example, in the book of Revelation we are told, "Blessed is the one who reads the words of the prophecy and blessed are those who hear the words" (1:3)—obviously referring to the public reading of the text. In a lesser-known book called 2 *Clement,* from the mid second century, the author indicates, in reference to his words of exhortation, "I am reading you a request to pay attention to what has been written, so that you may save yourselves and the one who is your reader" (2 Clem. 19.1).

In short, the books that were of paramount importance in early Christianity were for the most part read out loud by those who were able to read, so that the illiterate could hear, understand, and even study them. Despite the fact that early Christianity was by and large made up of illiterate believers, it was a highly literary religion.

Other key issues need to be discussed, however. If books were so important to early Christianity, if they were being read to Christian communities around the Mediterranean, how did the communities actually get those books? How were they put in circulation? This was in the days before desktop publishing, electronic means of reproduction, and even moveable type. If communities of believers obtained copies of various Christian books in circulation, how did they acquire those copies? Who was doing the copying? And most important for the ultimate subject of our investigation, how can we (or how could they) know that the copies they obtained were accurate, that they hadn't been modified in the process of reproduction?

A page from the fourth-century Codex Vaticanus, with a note in the margin (between columns one and two) in which a medieval scribe maligns a predecessor for altering the text: Fool and knave, leave the old reading, don't change it!

2

THE COPYISTS OF
THE EARLY CHRISTIAN
WRITINGS

A s we saw in chapter 1, Christianity from its very beginning was a literary religion, with books of all kinds playing a central role in the life and faith of the burgeoning Christian communities around the Mediterranean. How, then, was this Christian literature placed in circulation and distributed? The answer, of course, is that for a book to be distributed broadly, it had to be copied.

COPYING IN THE GRECO-ROMAN WORLD

The only way to copy a book in the ancient world was to do it by hand, letter by letter, one word at a time. It was a slow, painstaking process—but there was no alternative. Accustomed as we are today to seeing multiple copies of books appear on the shelves of major book chains around the country just days after they are published, we simply accept that one copy of, say, *The Da Vinci Code* will be exactly like any other copy. None of the words will ever vary—it will be exactly the same book no matter which copy we read. Not so in the ancient world. Just as books could not easily be distributed en masse (no trucks or planes or railroads), they could not be produced en masse (no printing presses). And since they had to be copied by hand, one at a time, slowly, painstakingly, most books were not mass produced. Those few that were produced in multiple copies were not all alike, for the scribes who copied texts inevitably made alterations in those texts— changing the words they copied either by accident (via a slip of the pen or other carelessness) or by design (when the scribe intentionally altered the words he copied). Anyone reading a book in antiquity could never be completely sure that he or she was reading what the author had written. The words could have been altered. In fact, they probably had been, if only just a little.

Today, a publisher releases a set number of books to the public by having them sent to bookstores. In the ancient world, since books were not mass produced and there were no publishing companies or bookstores, things were different.[1] Usually an author would write a book, and possibly have a group of friends read it or listen to it being read aloud. This would provide a chance for editing some of the book's contents. Then when the author was finished with the book, he or she would have copies made for a few friends and acquaintances. This, then, was the act of publication, when the book was no longer solely in the author's control but in the hands of others. If these others wanted extra copies—possibly to give to other family members or friends—they would have to arrange to have copies made, say, by a local scribe who made copies for a living, or by a literate slave who copied texts as part of his household duties.

We know that this process could be maddeningly slow and inac- curate, that the copies produced this way could end up being quite different from the originals. Testimony comes to us from ancient writers themselves. Here I will mention just a couple of interesting examples from the first century C.E. In a famous essay on the problem of anger, the Roman philosopher Seneca points out that there is a difference between anger directed at what has caused us harm and anger at what can do nothing to hurt us. To illustrate the latter category he mentions "certain inanimate things, such as the manuscript which we often hurl from us because it is written in too small a script or tear up because it is full of mistakes."[2] It must have been a frustrating experience, reading a text that was chock-full of "printer's errors" (i.e., copyist's errors), enough to drive one to distraction.

A humorous example comes to us from the epigrams of the witty Roman poet Martial, who, in one poem, lets his reader know

> If any poems in those sheets, reader, seem to you either too obscure or not quite good Latin, not mine is the mistake: the copyist spoiled them in his haste to complete for you his tale of verses. But if you think that not he, but I am at fault, then I will believe that you have no intelligence. "Yet, see, those are bad." As if I denied what is plain! They are bad, but you don't make better.[3]

Copying texts allowed for the possibilities of manual error; and the problem was widely recognized throughout antiquity.

COPYING IN EARLY CHRISTIAN CIRCLES

We have a number of references in early Christian texts to the practices of copying.[4] One of the most interesting comes from a popular text of the early second century called *The Shepherd* of Hermas. This book was widely read during the second to fourth Christian centuries; some Christians believed that it should be considered part of the canon of scripture. It is included as one of the books of the New Testament, for example, in one of our oldest surviving manuscripts, the famous fourth-century Codex Sinaiticus. In the book, a Christian prophet named Hermas is given a number of revelations, some of them concerning what is to come, others concerned with the personal and communal lives of Christians of the day. At an early point in the book (it is a lengthy book, longer than any of the books that made it into the

New Testament), Hermas has a vision of an elderly woman, a kind of angelic figure symbolizing the Christian church, who is reading aloud from a little book. She asks Hermas if he can announce the things he has heard to his fellow Christians. He replies that he can't remember everything she has read and asks her to "Give me the book to make a copy." She gives it to him, and he then relates that

> I took it and went away to another part of the field, where I copied the whole thing, letter by letter, for I could not distinguish between the syllables. And then, when I completed the letters of the book, it was suddenly seized from my hand; but I did not see by whom. (Shepherd 5.4)

Even though it was a small book, it must have been a difficult process copying it one letter at a time. When Hermas says that he "could not distinguish between the syllables," he may be indicating that he was not skilled in reading—that is, that he was not trained as a professional scribe, as one who could read texts fluently. One of the problems with ancient Greek texts (which would include all the earliest Christian writings, including those of the New Testament) is that when they were copied, no marks of punctuation were used, no distinction made between lowercase and uppercase letters, and, even more bizarre to modern readers, no spaces used to separate words. This kind of continuous writing is called *scriptuo continua,* and it obviously could make it difficult at times to read, let alone understand, a text. The words *godisnowhere* could mean quite different things to a theist (God is now here) and an atheist (God is nowhere);[5] and what would it mean to say *lastnightatdinnerisawabundanceonthetable?* Was this a normal or a supernormal event?

When Hermas says he could not distinguish between the syllables, he evidently means he could not read the text fluently but could recognize the letters, and so copied them one at a time. Obviously, if you don't know what you're reading, the possibilities of making mistakes in transcription multiply.

Hermas again refers to copying somewhat later in his vision. The elderly woman comes to him again and asks whether he has yet handed over the book he copied to the church leaders. He replies that he has not, and she tells him:

You have done well. For I have some words to add. Then, when I complete all the words they will be made known through you to all those who are chosen. And so, you will write two little books, sending one to Clement and the other to Grapte. Clement will send his to the foreign cities, for that is his commission. But Grapte will admonish the widows and orphans. And you will read yours in this city, with the presbyters who lead the church. (Shepherd 8.3)

And so the text he had slowly copied had some additions that he was to make; and he was to make two copies. One of these copies would go to a man named Clement, who may have been a person known from other texts to have been the third bishop of the city of Rome. Possibly this is before he became the head of the church, as it appears here that he is a foreign correspondent for the Roman Christian community. Was he a kind of official scribe who copied their texts? The other copy is to go to a woman named Grapte, who possibly was also a scribe, perhaps one who made copies of texts for some of the church members in Rome. Hermas himself is to read his copy of the book to the Christians of the community (most of whom would have been illiterate, and so unable to read the text themselves)—although how he can be expected to do so if he still can't distinguish the syllables from one another is never explained.

Here, then, we get a real-life glimpse into what copying practices were like in the early church. Presumably the situation was similar in various churches scattered throughout the Mediterranean region, even though no other church was (probably) as large as the one in Rome. A select few members were scribes for the church. Some of these scribes were more skilled than others: Clement appears to have had as one of his duties the dissemination of Christian literature;

Hermas simply does the task because on this one occasion it was as-signed to him. The copies of texts that are reproduced by these literate members of the congregation (some of them more literate than oth-ers) are then read to the community as a whole.

What more can we say about these scribes in the Christian com-munities? We don't know exactly who Clement and Grapte were, al-though we do have additional information about Hermas. He speaks of himself as a former slave (*Shepherd* 1.1). He was obviously literate, and so comparatively well educated. He was not one of the leaders of the church in Rome (he is not included among the "presbyters"), al-though later tradition claims that his brother was a man named Pius, who became bishop of the church in the mid second century.[6] If so, then possibly the family had attained a prestigious status level in the Christian community—even though Hermas had once been a slave. Since only educated people, obviously, could be literate, and since get-ting educated normally meant having the leisure and money needed to do so (unless one was trained in literacy as a slave), it appears that the early Christian scribes were the wealthier, more highly educated members of the Christian communities in which they lived.

As we have seen, *outside* the Christian communities, in the Roman world at large, texts were typically copied either by professional scribes or by literate slaves who were assigned to do such work within a house-hold. That means, among other things, that the people reproducing texts throughout the empire were not, as a rule, the people who wanted the texts. The copyists were by and large reproducing the texts for others. One of the important recent findings of scholars who study the early *Christian* scribes, on the other hand, is that just the op-posite was the case with them. It appears that the Christians copying the texts were the ones who wanted the texts—that is, they were copy-ing the texts either for their own personal and/or communal use or they were making them for the sake of others in their community.[7] In short, the people copying the early Christian texts were not, for the most part, if at all, professionals who copied texts for a living (cf. Her-

mas, above); they were simply the literate people in the Christian congregation who could make copies (since they were literate) and wanted
to do so.

Some of these people—or most of them?—may have been the
leaders of the communities. We have reason to think that the earliest
Christian leaders were among the wealthier members of the church,
in that the churches typically met in the homes of their members
(there were no church buildings, that we know of, during the first two
centuries of the church) and only the homes of the wealthier members
would have been sufficiently large to accommodate very many people,
since most people in ancient urban settings lived in tiny apartments. It
is not unreasonable to conclude that the person who provided the
home also provided the leadership of the church, as is assumed in a
number of the Christian letters that have come down to us, in which
an author will greet so-and-so and "the church that meets in his
home." These wealthier homeowners would probably have been more
educated, and so it is no surprise that they are sometimes exhorted to
"read" Christian literature to their congregations, as we have seen, for
example, in 1 Tim. 4:13: "Until I come, pay special heed to [public]
reading, to exhortation, and to teaching." Is it possible, then, that church
leaders were responsible, at least a good bit of the time, for the copying of the Christian literature being read to the congregation?

PROBLEMS WITH COPYING
EARLY CHRISTIAN TEXTS

Because the early Christian texts were not being copied by professional scribes,[8] at least in the first two or three centuries of the church,
but simply by educated members of the Christian congregations who
could do the job and were willing to do so, we can expect that in the
earliest copies, especially, mistakes were commonly made in transcription. Indeed, we have solid evidence that this was the case, as it

was a matter of occasional complaint by Christians reading those texts and trying to uncover the original words of their authors. The third-century church father Origen, for example, once registered the following complaint about the copies of the Gospels at his disposal:

> *The differences among the manuscripts have become great, either through the negligence of some copyists or through the perverse audacity of others; they either neglect to check over what they have transcribed, or, in the process of checking, they make additions or deletions as they please.*[9]

Origen was not the only one to notice the problem. His pagan opponent Celsus had, as well, some seventy years earlier. In his attack on Christianity and its literature, Celsus had maligned the Christian copyists for their transgressive copying practices:

> *Some believers, as though from a drinking bout, go so far as to oppose themselves and alter the original text of the gospel three or four or several times over, and they change its character to enable them to deny difficulties in face of criticism.* (Against Celsus 2.27)

What is striking in this particular instance is that Origen, when confronted with an *outsider*'s allegation of poor copying practices among Christians, actually denies that Christians changed the text, despite the fact that he himself decried the circumstance in his other writings. The one exception he names in his reply to Celsus involves several groups of heretics, who, Origen claims, maliciously altered the sacred texts.[10]

We have already seen this charge that heretics sometimes modified the texts they copied in order to make them stand in closer conformity with their own views, for this was the accusation leveled against the second-century philosopher-theologian Marcion, who presented his canon of eleven scriptural books only after excising those portions that contradicted his notion that, for Paul, the God of the Old Testament was not the true God. Marcion's "orthodox" opponent Irenaeus claimed that Marcion did the following:

dismembered the epistles of Paul, removing all that is said by the apostle respecting that God who made the world, to the effect that He is the Father of our Lord Jesus Christ, and also those passages from the prophetical writings which the apostle quotes, in order to teach us that they announced beforehand the coming of the Lord. (Against Heresies *1.27.2*)

Marcion was not the only culprit. Living roughly at the same time as Irenaeus was an orthodox bishop of Corinth named Dionysius who complained that false believers had unscrupulously modified his own writings, just as they had done with more sacred texts.

When my fellow-Christians invited me to write letters to them I did so. These the devil's apostles have filled with tares, taking away some things and adding others. For them the woe is reserved. Small wonder then if some have dared to tamper even with the word of the Lord himself, when they have conspired to mutilate my own humble efforts.

Charges of this kind against "heretics"—that they altered the texts of scripture to make them say what they wanted them to mean—are very common among early Christian writers. What is noteworthy, however, is that recent studies have shown that the evidence of our surviving manuscripts points the finger in the opposite direction. Scribes who were associated with the *orthodox* tradition not infrequently changed their texts, sometimes in order to eliminate the possibility of their "misuse" by Christians affirming heretical beliefs and sometimes to make them more amenable to the doctrines being espoused by Christians of their own persuasion.[11]

The very real danger that texts could be modified at will, by scribes who did not approve of their wording, is evident in other ways as well. We need always to remember that the copyists of the early Christian writings were reproducing their texts in a world in which there were not only no printing presses or publishing houses but also no such thing as copyright law. How could authors guarantee that their texts were not modified once put into circulation? The short answer is that they could not. That explains why authors would sometimes call curses down on any copyists who modified their texts without permission. We find this kind of imprecation already in one early Christian writing that made it into the New Testament, the book of Revelation, whose author, near the end of his text, utters a dire warning:

> *I testify to everyone who hears the words of the prophecy of this book: If anyone adds to them, God will add to him the plagues described in this book; and if anyone removes any of the words of the book of this prophecy, God will remove his share from the tree of life and from the holy city, as described in this book. (Rev. 22:18–19)*

This is not a threat that the reader has to accept or believe everything written in this book of prophecy, as it is sometimes interpreted; rather, it is a typical threat to *copyists* of the book, that they are not to add to or remove any of its words. Similar imprecations can be found scattered throughout the range of early Christian writings. Consider the rather severe threats uttered by the Latin Christian scholar Rufinus with respect to his translation of one of Origen's works:

> *Truly in the presence of God the Father and of the Son and of the Holy Spirit, I adjure and beseech everyone who may either transcribe or read these books, by his belief in the kingdom to come, by the mystery of the resurrection from the dead, and by that everlasting fire prepared for the devil and his angels, that, as he would not possess for an eternal inheritance that place where there is weeping and gnashing of teeth and where their fire is not quenched and their spirit does not die, he add nothing to what is written and take nothing away from it, and make no insertion or alteration, but that he compare his transcription with the copies from which he made it.*[12]

These are dire threats—hellfire and brimstone—for simply changing some words of a text. Some authors, though, were fully determined to make sure their words were transmitted intact, and no threat could be serious enough in the face of copyists who could change texts at will, in a world that had no copyright laws.

CHANGES OF THE TEXT

It would be a mistake, however, to assume that the only changes being made were by copyists with a personal stake in the wording of the text. In fact, most of the changes found in our early Christian manuscripts have nothing to do with theology or ideology. Far and away the most changes are the result of mistakes, pure and simple—slips of the pen, accidental omissions, inadvertent additions, misspelled words, blunders of one sort or another. Scribes could be incompetent: it is important to recall that most of the copyists in the early centuries were not trained to do this kind of work but were simply the literate members of their congregations who were (more or less) able and willing. Even later, starting in the fourth and fifth centuries, when Christian scribes emerged as a professional class within the church,[13] and later still when most manuscripts were copied by monks devoted to this kind of work in monasteries—even then, some scribes were less skilled than others. At all times the task could be drudgery, as is indicated in notes occasionally added to manuscripts in which a scribe would pen a kind of sigh of relief, such as "The End of the Manuscript. Thanks Be to God!"[14] Sometimes scribes grew inattentive; sometimes they were hungry or sleepy; sometimes they just couldn't be bothered to give their best effort.

Even scribes who were competent, trained, and alert sometimes made mistakes. Sometimes, though, as we have seen, they changed the text because they thought it was *supposed* to be changed. This was not just for certain theological reasons, however. There were other reasons for scribes to make an intentional change—for example, when they came across a passage that appeared to embody a mistake that needed to be corrected, possibly a contradiction found in the text, or a mistaken geographical reference, or a misplaced scriptural allusion. Thus, when scribes made intentional changes, sometimes their motives were as pure as the driven snow. But the changes were made nonetheless, and the author's original words, as a result, may have become altered and eventually lost.

An interesting illustration of the intentional change of a text is found in one of our finest old manuscripts, Codex Vaticanus (so named because it was found in the Vatican library), made in the fourth century. In the opening of the book of Hebrews there is a passage in which, according to most manuscripts, we are told that "Christ bears [Greek: PHERŌN] all things by the word of his power" (Heb. 1:3). In Codex Vaticanus, however, the original scribe produced a slightly different text, with a verb that sounded similar in Greek; here the text instead reads: "Christ manifests [Greek: PHANERŌN] all things by the word of his power." Some centuries later, a second scribe read this passage in the manuscript and decided to change the unusual word *manifests* to the more common reading *bears*—erasing the one word and writing in the other. Then, again some centuries later, a third scribe read the manuscript and noticed the alteration his predecessor had made; he, in turn, erased the word *bears* and rewrote the word *manifests*. He then added a scribal note in the margin to indicate what he thought of the earlier, second scribe. The note says: "Fool and knave! Leave the old reading, don't change it!"

I have a copy of the page framed and hanging on the wall above my desk as a constant reminder about scribes and their proclivities to change, and rechange, their texts. Obviously it is the change of a single word: so why does it matter? It matters because the only way to understand what an author wants to say is to know what his words— all his words—actually were. (Think of all the sermons preached on the basis of a single word in a text: what if the word is one the author didn't actually write?) Saying that Christ reveals all things by his word of power is quite different from saying that he keeps the universe together by his word!

COMPLICATIONS IN KNOWING
THE "ORIGINAL TEXT"

And so, all kinds of changes were made in manuscripts by the scribes who copied them. We will be looking at the types of changes in greater depth in a later chapter. For the moment, it is enough to know that the changes were made, and that they were made widely, especially in the first two hundred years in which the texts were being copied, when most of the copyists were amateurs. One of the leading questions that textual critics must deal with is how to get back to the original text—the text as the author first wrote it—given the circumstance that our manuscripts are so full of mistakes. The problem is exacerbated by the fact that once a mistake was made, it could become firmly embedded in the textual tradition, more firmly embedded, in fact, than the original.

That is to say, once a scribe changes a text—whether accidentally or intentionally—then those changes are *permanent* in his manuscript (unless, of course, another scribe comes along to correct the mistake). The next scribe who copies *that* manuscript copies those mistakes (thinking they are what the text said), and he adds mistakes of his own. The next scribe who then copies *that* manuscript copies the mistakes of both his predecessors and adds mistakes of his own, and so on. The only way mistakes get corrected is when a scribe recognizes that a predecessor has made an error and tries to resolve it. There is no guarantee, however, that a scribe who tries to correct a mistake corrects it correctly. That is, by changing what he thinks is an error, he may in fact change it incorrectly, so now there are three forms of the text: the original, the error, and the incorrect attempt to resolve the error. Mistakes multiply and get repeated; sometimes they get corrected and sometimes they get compounded. And so it goes. For centuries.

Sometimes, of course, a scribe may have more than one manuscript at hand, and can correct the mistakes in one manuscript by the correct readings of the other manuscript. This does, in fact, improve the situation significantly. On the other hand, it is also possible that a scribe will sometimes correct the *correct* manuscript in light of the wording of the incorrect one. The possibilities seem endless.

Given these problems, how can we hope to get back to anything like the original text, the text that an author actually wrote? It is an enormous problem. In fact, it is such an enormous problem that a number of textual critics have started to claim that we may as well suspend any discussion of the "original" text, because it is inaccessible to us. This may be going too far, but a concrete example or two taken from the New Testament writings can show the problems.

Examples of the Problems

For the first example, let's take Paul's letter to the Galatians. Even at the point of the original penning of the letter, we have numerous difficulties to consider, which may well make us sympathetic with those who want to give up on the notion of knowing what the "original" text was. Galatia was not a single town with a single church; it was a region in Asia Minor (modern Turkey) in which Paul had established churches. When he writes to the Galatians, is he writing to one of the churches or to all of them? Presumably, since he doesn't single out any particular town, he means for the letter to go to all of them. Does that mean that he made multiple copies of the same letter, or that he wanted the one letter to circulate to all the churches of the region? We don't know.

Suppose he made multiple copies. How did he do it? To begin with, it appears that this letter, like others by Paul, was not written by his hand but was dictated to a secretarial scribe. Evidence for this comes at the end of the letter, where Paul added a postscript in his own handwriting, so that the recipients would know that it was he who was responsible for the letter (a common technique for dictated letters in antiquity): "See with what large letters I am writing you with my own hand" (Gal. 6:11). His handwriting, in other words, was larger and probably less professional in appearance than that of the scribe to whom he had dictated the letter.[15]

Now, if Paul dictated the letter, did he dictate it word for word? Or did he spell out the basic points and allow the scribe to fill in the rest? Both methods were commonly used by letter writers in antiquity.[16] If the scribe filled in the rest, can we be assured that he filled it in exactly as Paul wanted? If not, do we actually have Paul's words, or are they the words of some unknown scribe? But let's suppose that Paul dictated the letter word for word. Is it possible that in some places the scribe wrote down the *wrong* words? Stranger things have happened. If so, then the autograph of the letter (i.e., the original) would already have a "mistake" in it, so that all subsequent copies would not be of Paul's words (in the places where his scribe got them wrong).

Suppose, though, that the scribe got all the words 100 percent correct. If multiple copies of the letter went out, can we be sure that all the copies were also 100 percent correct? It is possible, at least, that even if they were all copied in Paul's presence, a word or two here or there got changed in one or the other of the copies. If so, what if only *one* of the copies served as the copy from which all subsequent copies were made—then in the first century, into the second century and the third century, and so on? In that case, the oldest copy that provided the basis for all subsequent copies of the letter was not exactly what Paul wrote, or wanted to write.

Once the copy is in circulation—that is, once it arrives at its destination in one of the towns of Galatia—it, of course, gets copied, and mistakes get made. Sometimes scribes might intentionally change the text; sometimes accidents happen. These mistake-ridden copies get copied; and the mistake-ridden copies of the copies get copied; and so on, down the line. Somewhere in the midst of all this, the original copy (or *each* of the original copies) ends up getting lost, or worn out, or destroyed. At some point, it is no longer possible to compare a copy with the original to make sure it is "correct," even if someone has the bright idea of doing so.

What survives today, then, is not the original copy of the letter, nor one of the first copies that Paul himself had made, nor any of the copies that were produced in any of the towns of Galatia to which the letter was sent, nor any of the copies of those copies. The first reasonably complete copy we have of Galatians (this manuscript is fragmentary; i.e., it has a number of missing parts) is a papyrus called P[46] (since it was the forty-sixth New Testament papyrus to be catalogued), which dates to about 200 C.E.[17] That's approximately 150 *years* after Paul wrote the letter. It had been in circulation, being copied sometimes correctly and sometimes incorrectly, for fifteen decades before *any* copy was made that has survived down to the present day. We cannot reconstruct the copy from which P[46] was made. Was it an accurate copy? If so, how accurate? It surely had mistakes of some kind, as did the copy from which it was copied, and the copy from which that copy was copied, and so on.

In short, it is a very complicated business talking about the "original" text of Galatians. We don't have it. The best we can do is get back to an early stage of its transmission, and simply hope that what we reconstruct about the copies made at that stage—based on the copies that happen to survive (in increasing numbers as we move into the Middle Ages)—reasonably reflects what Paul himself actually wrote, or at least what he intended to write when he dictated the letter.

As a second example of the problems, let's take the Gospel of John. This Gospel is quite different from the other three Gospels of the New Testament, telling a range of stories that differ from theirs and employing a very different style of writing. Here, in John, the sayings of Jesus are long discourses rather than pithy, direct sayings; Jesus never tells a parable, for example, in John, unlike in the other three Gospels. Moreover, the events narrated in John are often found only in this Gospel: for example, Jesus's conversations with Nicodemus (in chapter 3) and with the Samaritan woman (chapter 4) or his miracles of turning water into wine (chapter 2) and raising Lazarus from the dead (chapter 10). The author's portrayal of Jesus is quite different too; unlike in the other three Gospels, Jesus spends much of his time explaining who he is (the one sent from heaven) and doing "signs" in order to prove that what he says about himself is true.

John no doubt had sources for his account—possibly a source that narrated Jesus's signs, for example, and sources that described his discourses.[18] He put these sources together into his own flowing narrative of Jesus's life, ministry, death, and resurrection. It is possible, though, that John actually produced several different versions of his Gospel. Readers have long noted, for example, that chapter 21 appears to be a later add-on. The Gospel certainly seems to come to an end in 20:30–31; and the events of chapter 21 seem to be a kind of afterthought, possibly added to fill out the stories of Jesus's resurrection appearances and to explain that when the "beloved disciple" responsible for narrating the traditions in the Gospel had died, this was not unforeseen (cf. 21:22–23).

Other passages of the Gospel also do not cohere completely with the rest. Even the opening verses 1:1–18, which form a kind of prologue to the Gospel, appear to be different from the rest. This highly celebrated poem speaks of the "Word" of God, who existed with God from the beginning and was himself God, and who "became flesh" in Jesus Christ. The passage is written in a highly poetic style not found in the rest of the Gospel; moreover, while its central themes are repeated in the rest of the narrative, some of its most important vocabulary is not. Thus, Jesus is portrayed throughout the narrative as the one who came from above, but never is he called the Word elsewhere in the Gospel. Is it possible that this opening passage came from a different source than the rest of the account, and that it was added as an appropriate beginning by the author after an earlier edition of the book had already been published?

Assume, for a second, just for the sake of the argument, that chapter 21 and 1:1–18 were not original components of the Gospel. What does that do for the textual critic who wants to reconstruct the "original" text? Which original is being constructed? All our Greek manuscripts contain the passages in question. So does the textual critic reconstruct as the original text the form of the Gospel that originally contained them? But shouldn't we consider the "original" form to be the *earlier* version, which lacked them? And if one wants to reconstruct that earlier form, is it fair to stop there, with reconstructing, say, the first edition of John's Gospel? Why not go even further and try to reconstruct the *sources* that lie behind the Gospel, such as the signs sources and the discourse sources, or even the oral traditions that lie behind them?

These are questions that plague textual critics, and that have led some to argue that we should abandon any quest for the original text— since we can't even agree on what it might *mean* to talk about the "original" of, say, Galatians or John. For my part, however, I continue to think that even if we cannot be 100 percent certain about what we can attain to, we can at least be certain that all the surviving manuscripts were copied from other manuscripts, which were themselves copied from other manuscripts, and that it is at least possible to get back to the *oldest* and *earliest* stage of the manuscript tradition for each of the books of the New Testament. All our manuscripts of Galatians, for example, evidently go back to *some* text that was copied; all our manuscripts of John evidently go back to a version of John that included the prologue and chapter 21. And so we must rest content knowing that getting back to the earliest attainable version is the best we can do, whether or not we have reached back to the "original" text. This oldest form of the text is no doubt closely (*very* closely) related to what the author originally wrote, and so it is the basis for our interpretation of his teaching.

RECONSTRUCTING THE TEXTS OF
THE NEW TESTAMENT

Similar problems, of course, apply to all our early Christian writings, both those in the New Testament and those outside it, whether gospels, acts, epistles, apocalypses, or any of the other kinds of early Christian writing. The task of the textual critic is to determine what the earliest

form of the text is for all these writings. As we will see, there are established principles for making this determination, ways of deciding
which differences in our manuscripts are mistakes, which are intentional changes, and which appear to go back to the original author.
But it's not an easy task.

The results, on the other hand, can be extremely enlightening, interesting, and even exciting. Textual critics have been able to determine with relative certainty a number of places in which manuscripts
that survive do not represent the original text of the New Testament.
For those who are not at all familiar with the field, but who know the
New Testament well (say, in English translation), some of the results
can be surprising. To conclude this chapter, I will discuss two such
passages—passages from the Gospels, in this case, that we are now
fairly certain did not originally belong in the New Testament, even
though they became popular parts of the Bible for Christians down
through the centuries and remain so today.

The Woman Taken in Adultery

The story of Jesus and the woman taken in adultery is arguably the
best-known story about Jesus in the Bible; it certainly has always been
a favorite in Hollywood versions of his life. It even makes it into Mel
Gibson's *The Passion of the Christ,* although that movie focuses only on
Jesus's last hours (the story is treated in one of the rare flashbacks).
Despite its popularity, the account is found in only one passage of the
New Testament, in John 7:53–8:12, and it appears not to have been
original even there.

The story line is familiar. Jesus is teaching in the temple, and a
group of scribes and Pharisees, his sworn enemies, approach him,
bringing with them a woman "who had been caught in the very act of
adultery." They bring her before Jesus because they want to put him
to the test. The Law of Moses, as they tell him, demands that such a
one be stoned to death; but they want to know what he has to say
about the matter. Should they stone her or show her mercy? It is a
trap, of course. If Jesus tells them to let the woman go, he will be

accused of violating the Law of God; if he tells them to stone her, he will be accused of dismissing his own teachings of love, mercy, and forgiveness.

Jesus does not immediately reply; instead he stoops to write on the ground. When they continue to question him, he says to them, "Let the one who is without sin among you be the first to cast a stone at her." He then returns to his writing on the ground, while those who have brought the woman start to leave the scene—evidently feeling convicted of their own wrongdoing—until no one is left but the woman. Looking up, Jesus says, "Woman, where are they? Is there no one who condemns you?" To which she replies, "No one, Lord." He then responds, "Neither do I condemn you. Go and sin no more."

It is a brilliant story, filled with pathos and a clever twist in which Jesus uses his wits to get himself—not to mention the poor woman—off the hook. Of course, to a careful reader, the story raises numerous questions. If this woman was caught in the act of adultery, for example, where is the man she was caught with? Both of them are to be stoned, according to the Law of Moses (see Lev. 20:10). Moreover, when Jesus wrote on the ground, what exactly was he writing? (According to one ancient tradition, he was writing the sins of the accusers, who seeing that their own transgressions were known, left in embarrassment!) And even if Jesus did teach a message of love, did he really think that the Law of God given by Moses was no longer in force and should not be obeyed? Did he think sins should not be punished at all?

Despite the brilliance of the story, its captivating quality, and its inherent intrigue, there is one other enormous problem that it poses. As it turns out, it was not originally in the Gospel of John. In fact, it was not originally part of any of the Gospels. It was added by later scribes.

How do we know this? In fact, scholars who work on the manuscript tradition have no doubts about this particular case. Later in this book we will be examining in greater depth the kinds of evidence that scholars adduce for making judgments of this sort. Here I can simply point out a few basic facts that have proved convincing to nearly all scholars of every persuasion: the story is not found in our oldest and best manuscripts of the Gospel of John;[18] its writing style is very different from what we find in the rest of John (including the stories immediately before and after); and it includes a large number of words and phrases that are otherwise alien to the Gospel. The conclusion is unavoidable: this passage was not originally part of the Gospel.

How then did it come to be added? There are numerous theories about that. Most scholars think that it was probably a well-known story circulating in the oral tradition about Jesus, which at some point was added in the margin of a manuscript. From there some scribe or other thought that the marginal note was meant to be part of the text and so inserted it immediately after the account that ends in John 7:52. It is noteworthy that other scribes inserted the account in different locations in the New Testament—some of them after John 21:25, for example, and others, interestingly enough, after Luke 21:38. In any event, whoever wrote the account, it was not John.

That naturally leaves readers with a dilemma: if this story was not originally part of John, should it be considered part of the Bible? Not everyone will respond to this question in the same way, but for most textual critics, the answer is no.

The Last Twelve Verses of Mark

The second example that we will consider may not be as familiar to the casual reader of the Bible, but it has been highly influential in the history of biblical interpretation and poses comparable problems for the scholar of the textual tradition of the New Testament. This example comes from the Gospel of Mark and concerns its ending.

In Mark's account, we are told that Jesus is crucified and then buried by Joseph of Arimathea on the day before the Sabbath (15:42–47). On the day after Sabbath, Mary Magdalene and two other women come back to the tomb in order properly to anoint the body (16:1–2). When they arrive, they find that the stone has been rolled away. Entering the tomb, they see a young man in a white robe, who tells them, "Do not

be startled! You are seeking Jesus the Nazarene, who has been crucified. He has been raised and is not here—see the place where they laid
him?" He then instructs the women to tell the disciples that Jesus is
preceding them into Galilee and that they will see him there, "just as
he told you." But the women flee the tomb and say nothing to anyone,
"for they were afraid" (16:4–8).

Then come the last twelve verses of Mark in many modern English translations, verses that continue the story. Jesus himself is said to
appear to Mary Magdalene, who goes and tells the disciples; but they
do not believe her (vv. 9–11). He then appears to two others (vv. 12–14),
and finally to the eleven disciples (the Twelve, not including Judas Is-
cariot) who are gathered together at table. Jesus upbraids them for
failing to believe, and then commissions them to go forth and proclaim his gospel "to the whole creation." Those who believe and are
baptized "will be saved," but those who do not "will be condemned."
And then come two of the most intriguing verses of the passage:

> And these are the signs that will accompany those who believe: they
> will cast out demons in my name; they will speak in new tongues; and
> they will take up snakes in their hands; and if they drink any poison,
> it will not harm them; they will place their hands upon the sick and
> heal them. (vv. 17–18)

Jesus is then taken up into heaven, and seated at the right hand of
God. And the disciples go forth into the world proclaiming the
gospel, their words being confirmed by the signs that accompany
them (vv. 19–20).

It is a terrific passage, mysterious, moving, and powerful. It is one
of the passages used by Pentecostal Christians to show that Jesus's followers will be able to speak in unknown "tongues," as happens in
their own services of worship; and it is the principal passage used by
groups of "Appalachian snake-handlers," who till this day take poi-
sonous snakes in their hands in order to demonstrate their faith in the
words of Jesus, that when doing so they will come to no harm.

But there's one problem. Once again, this passage was not originally in the Gospel of Mark. It was added by a later scribe.

In some ways this textual problem is more disputed than the passage about the woman taken in adultery, because *without* these final verses Mark has a very different, and hard to understand, ending. That doesn't mean that scholars are inclined to accept the verses, as we'll see momentarily. The reasons for taking them to be an addition are solid, almost indisputable. But scholars debate what the genuine ending of Mark actually was, given the circumstance that this ending found in many English translations (though usually marked as inauthentic) and in later Greek manuscripts is not the original.

The evidence that these verses were not original to Mark is similar in kind to that for the passage about the woman taken in adultery, and again I don't need to go into all the details here. The verses are absent from our two oldest and best manuscripts of Mark's Gospel, along with other important witnesses; the writing style varies from what we find elsewhere in Mark; the transition between this passage and the one preceding it is hard to understand (e.g., Mary Magdalene is introduced in verse 9 as if she hadn't been mentioned yet, even though she is discussed in the preceding verses; there is another problem with the Greek that makes the transition even more awkward); and there are a large number of words and phrases in the passage that are not found elsewhere in Mark. In short, the evidence is sufficient to convince nearly all textual scholars that these verses are an addition to Mark.

Without them, though, the story ends rather abruptly. Notice what happens when these verses are taken away. The women are told to inform the disciples that Jesus will precede them to Galilee and meet them there; but they, the women, flee the tomb and say nothing to anyone, "for they were afraid." And that's where the Gospel ends.

Obviously, scribes thought the ending was too abrupt. The women told no one? Then, did the disciples never learn of the resurrection? And didn't Jesus himself ever appear to them? How could *that* be the ending! To resolve the problem, scribes added an ending.[19]

Some scholars agree with the scribes in thinking that 16:8 is too abrupt an ending for a Gospel. As I have indicated, it is not that these scholars believe the final twelve verses in our later manuscripts were the original ending—they know that's not the case—but they think that, possibly, the last page of Mark's Gospel, one in which Jesus actually did meet the disciples in Galilee, was somehow lost, and that all our copies of the Gospel go back to this one truncated manuscript, without the last page.

That explanation is entirely possible. It is also possible, in the opinion of yet other scholars, that Mark did indeed mean to end his Gospel with 16:8.[20] It certainly is a shocker of an ending. The disciples never learn the truth of Jesus's resurrection because the women never tell them. One reason for thinking that this could be how Mark ended his Gospel is that some such ending coincides so well with other motifs throughout his Gospel. As students of Mark have long noticed, the disciples never do seem to "get it" in this Gospel (unlike in some of the other Gospels). They are repeatedly said not to understand Jesus (6:51–52; 8:21), and when Jesus tells them on several occasions that he must suffer and die, they manifestly fail to comprehend his words (8:31–33; 9:30–32; 10:33–40). Maybe, in fact, they never did come to understand (unlike Mark's readers, who can understand who Jesus really is from the very beginning). Also, it is interesting to note that throughout Mark, when someone comes to understand something about Jesus, Jesus orders that person to silence—and yet often the person ignores the order and spreads the news (e.g., 1:43–45). How ironic that when the women at the tomb are told not to be silent but to speak, they also ignore the order—and are silent!

In short, Mark may well have intended to bring his reader up short with this abrupt ending—a clever way to make the reader stop, take a faltering breath, and ask: *What?*

CONCLUSION

The passages discussed above represent just two out of thousands of places in which the manuscripts of the New Testament came to be changed by scribes. In both of the examples, we are dealing with additions that scribes made to the text, additions of sizable length. Although most of the changes are not of this magnitude, there are lots of significant changes (and lots more insignificant ones) in our surviving manuscripts of the New Testament. In the chapters that follow we will want to see how scholars began to discover these changes and how they developed methods for figuring out what the oldest form of the text (or the "original" text) is; we will especially like to see more examples of where this text has been changed—and how these changes affected our English translations of the Bible.

I would like to end this chapter simply with an observation about a particularly acute irony that we seem to have discovered. As we saw in chapter 1, Christianity from the outset was a bookish religion that stressed certain texts as authoritative scripture. As we have seen in this chapter, however, we don't actually have these authoritative texts. This is a textually oriented religion whose texts have been changed, surviving only in copies that vary from one another, sometimes in highly significant ways. The task of the textual critic is to try to recover the oldest form of these texts.

This is obviously a crucial task, since we can't interpret the words of the New Testament if we don't know what the words were. Moreover, as I hope should be clear by now, knowing the words is important not just for those who consider the words divinely inspired. It is important for anyone who thinks of the New Testament as a significant book. And surely everyone interested in the history, society, and culture of Western civilization thinks so, because the New Testament, if nothing else, is an enormous cultural artifact, a book that is revered by millions and that lies at the foundation of the largest religion of the world today.

*Early sixteenth century engraving of Albrecht Duerer depicting
Desiderus Erasmus, the famous humanist of Rotterdam who produced the
first published edition of the Greek New Testament.*

3

TEXTS OF THE
NEW TESTAMENT

*Editions, Manuscripts,
and Differences*

The copying practices we have considered thus far have been principally those of the first three centuries of Christianity, when most of the copyists of the Christian texts were not professionals trained for the job but simply literate Christians of this or that congregation, able to read and write and so called upon to reproduce the texts of the community in their spare time.[1] Because they were not highly trained to perform this kind of work, they were more prone to make mistakes than professional scribes would have been. This explains why our *earliest* copies of the early Christian writings tend to vary more frequently from one another and from later copies than do the later copies (say, of the high Middle Ages) from one another. Eventually a kind of professional scribal class came to be a part of the Christian intellectual landscape, and with the advent of professional scribes came more controlled copying practices, in which mistakes were made much less frequently.

Before that happened, during the early centuries of the church, Christian texts were copied in whatever location they were written or taken to. Since texts were copied *locally,* it is no surprise that different localities developed different kinds of textual tradition. That is to say, the manuscripts in Rome had many of the same errors, because they were for the most part "in-house" documents, copied from one another; they were not influenced much by manuscripts being copied in Palestine; and those in Palestine took on their own characteristics, which were not the same as those found in a place like Alexandria, Egypt. Moreover, in the early centuries of the church, some locales had better scribes than others. Modern scholars have come to recognize that the scribes in Alexandria—which was a major intellectual center in the ancient world—were particularly scrupulous, even in these early centuries, and that there, in Alexandria, a very pure form of the text of the early Christian writings was preserved, decade after decade, by dedicated and relatively skilled Christian scribes.

PROFESSIONAL CHRISTIAN SCRIBES

When did the church begin to use professional scribes to copy its texts? There are good reasons for thinking that this happened sometime near the beginning of the fourth century. Until then, Christianity was a small, minority religion in the Roman Empire, often opposed, sometimes persecuted. But a cataclysmic change occurred when the emperor of Rome, Constantine, converted to the faith about 312 C.E. Suddenly Christianity shifted from being a religion of social outcasts, persecuted by local mobs and imperial authorities alike, to being a major player in the religious scene of the empire. Not only were persecutions halted, but favors began to pour out upon the church from the greatest power in the Western world. Massive conversions resulted, as it became a popular thing to be a follower of Christ in an age in which the emperor himself publicly proclaimed his allegiance to Christianity.

More and more highly educated and trained persons converted to the faith. They, naturally, were the ones most suited to copy the texts of the Christian tradition. There are reasons to suppose that about this time Christian scriptoria arose in major urban areas.[2] A scriptorium is a place for the professional copying of manuscripts. We have hints of Christian scriptoria functioning by the early part of the fourth century. In 331 C.E. the emperor Constantine, wanting magnificent Bibles to be made available to major churches he was having built, wrote a request to the bishop of Caesarea, Eusebius,[3] to have fifty Bibles produced at imperial expense. Eusebius treated this request with all the pomp and respect it deserved, and saw that it was carried out. Obviously, an accomplishment of this magnitude required a professional scriptorium, not to mention the materials needed for making lavish copies of the Christian scriptures. We are clearly in a different age from just a century or two earlier when local churches would simply request that one of their members cobble together enough free time to make a copy of a text.

Starting in the fourth century, then, copies of scripture began to be made by professionals; this naturally curtailed significantly the number of errors that crept into the text. Eventually, as the decades grew into centuries, the copying of the Greek scriptures became the charge of monks working out of monasteries, who spent their days copying the sacred texts carefully and conscientiously. This practice continued on down through the Middle Ages, right up to the time of the invention of printing with moveable type in the fifteenth century. The great mass of our surviving Greek manuscripts come from the pens of these medieval Christian scribes who lived and worked in the East (for example, in areas that are now Turkey and Greece), known as the Byzantine Empire. For this reason, Greek manuscripts from the seventh century onward are sometimes labeled "Byzantine" manuscripts.

As I have pointed out, anyone familiar with the manuscript tradition of the New Testament knows that these Byzantine copies of the text tend to be very similar to one another, whereas the earliest copies vary significantly both among themselves and from the form of text found in these later copies. The reason for this should now be clear: it had to do with who was copying the texts (professionals) and where they were working (in a relatively constricted area). It would be a grave mistake, though, to think that because later manuscripts agree so extensively with one another, they are therefore our superior witnesses to the "original" text of the New Testament. For one must always ask: where did these medieval scribes *get* the texts they copied in so professional a manner? They got them from earlier texts, which were copies of yet earlier texts, which were themselves copies of still earlier texts. Therefore, the texts that are closest in form to the originals are, perhaps unexpectedly, the more variable and amateurish copies of early times, not the more standardized professional copies of later times.

THE LATIN VULGATE

The copying practices I have been summarizing principally involve the *eastern* part of the Roman Empire, where Greek was, and continued to be, the principal language. It was not long, however, before Christians in non-Greek-speaking regions wanted the Christian sacred texts in their own, local languages. Latin, of course, was the language of much of the western part of the empire; Syriac was spoken in Syria; Coptic in Egypt. In each of these areas, the books of the New Testament came to be translated into the indigenous languages, probably sometime in the mid to late second century. And then these translated texts were themselves copied by scribes in their locales.[4]

Particularly important for the history of the text were the translations into Latin, because a very large number of Christians in the West had this as their principal language. Problems emerged very soon, however, with the Latin translations of scripture, because there were so many of them and these translations differed broadly from one another. The problem came to a head near the end of the fourth Christian century, when Pope Damasus commissioned the greatest scholar of his day, Jerome, to produce an "official" Latin translation that could be accepted by all Latin-speaking Christians, in Rome and elsewhere, as an authoritative text. Jerome himself speaks of the plethora of available translations, and set himself to resolving the problem. Choosing one of the best Latin translations available, and comparing its text with the superior Greek manuscripts at his disposal, Jerome created a new edition of the Gospels in Latin. It may be that he, or one of his followers, was also responsible for the new edition of the other books of the New Testament in Latin.[5]

This form of the Bible in Latin—Jerome's translation—came to be known as the Vulgate (= Common) Bible of Latin-speaking Christendom. This was the Bible for the Western church, itself copied and recopied many times over. It was the book that Christians read, scholars studied, and theologians used for centuries, down to the modern period. Today there are nearly twice as many copies of the Latin Vulgate as there are Greek manuscripts of the New Testament.

The First Printed Edition of the Greek New Testament

As I have indicated, the text of the New Testament was copied in a fairly standardized form throughout the centuries of the Middle Ages, both in the East (the Byzantine text) and in the West (the Latin Vulgate). It was the invention of the printing press in the fifteenth century by Johannes Gutenberg (1400–1468) that changed everything for the reproduction of books in general and the books of the Bible in particular. By printing books with moveable type, one could guarantee that every page looked exactly like every other page, with no variations of any kind in the wording. Gone were the days when transcribers would each produce different copies of the same text by means of accidental and intentional alterations. What was set in print was set in stone. Moreover, books could be made far more rapidly: no longer did they need to be copied one letter at a time. And, as a result, they could be made much more cheaply. Scarcely anything has made a more revolutionary impact on the modern world than the printing press; the next closest thing (which may, eventually, surpass it in significance) is the advent of the personal computer.

The first major work to be printed on Gutenberg's press was a magnificent edition of the Latin (Vulgate) Bible, which took all of 1450–56 to produce.[6] In the half century that followed, some fifty editions of the Vulgate were produced at various printing houses in Europe. It may seem odd that there was no impulse to produce a copy of the *Greek* New Testament in those early years of printing. But the reason is not hard to find: it is the one already alluded to. Scholars throughout Europe—including biblical scholars—had been accustomed for nearly a thousand years to thinking that Jerome's Vulgate was *the* Bible of the church (somewhat like some modern churches assume that the King James Version is the "true" Bible). The Greek Bible was thought of as foreign to theology and learning; in the Latin West, it was thought of as belonging to the Greek Orthodox Christians, who were considered to be schismatics who had branched off from the true church. Few scholars in Western Europe could even read Greek. And so, at first, no one felt compelled to put the Greek Bible in print.

The first Western scholar to conceive the idea of producing a version of the Greek New Testament was a Spanish cardinal named Ximenes de Cisneros (1437–1517). Under his leadership, a group of scholars, including one named Diego Lopez de Zuñiga (Stunica), undertook a multivolume edition of the Bible. This was a *polyglot* edition; that is, it reproduced the text of the Bible in a variety of languages. And so, the Old Testament was represented by the original Hebrew, the Latin Vulgate, and the Greek Septuagint, side by side in columns. (What these editors thought of the superiority of the Vulgate can be seen in their comments on this arrangement in their preface: they likened it to Christ—represented by the Vulgate—being crucified between two criminals, the false Jews represented by the Hebrew and the schismatic Greeks represented by the Septuagint.)

The work was printed in a town called Alcalá, whose Latin name is Complutum. For this reason, Ximenes's edition is known as the

Complutensian Polyglot. The New Testament volume was the first to be printed (volume 5, completed in 1514); it contained the Greek text and included a Greek dictionary with Latin equivalents. But there was no plan to publish this volume separately—all six volumes (the sixth included a Hebrew grammar and dictionary, to assist in the reading of volumes 1–4) were to be published together, and this took considerable time. The entire work was finished, evidently, by 1517; but as this was a Catholic production, it needed the sanction of the pope, Leo X, before it could appear. This was finally obtained in 1520, but because of other complications, the book did not come to be distributed until 1522, some five years after Ximenes himself had died.

As we have seen, by this time there were many hundreds of Greek *manuscripts* (i.e., handwritten copies) available to Christian churches and scholars in the East. How did Stunica and his fellow editors decide which of these manuscripts to use, and which manuscripts were actually available to them? Unfortunately, these are questions that scholars have never been able to answer with confidence. In the Dedication of the work, Ximenes expresses his gratitude to Pope Leo X for Greek copies lent "from the Apostolical Library." And so the manuscripts for the edition may have come from the Vatican's holdings. Some scholars, however, have suspected that manuscripts available locally were used. About 250 years after the production of the Complutum, a Danish scholar named Moldenhawer visited Alcalá to survey their library resources in order to answer the question, but he could find no manuscripts of the Greek New Testament at all. Suspecting that the library must have had some such manuscripts at some point, he made persistent inquiries until he was finally told by the librarian that the library had indeed previously contained ancient Greek manuscripts of the New Testament, but that in 1749 all of them had been sold to a rocket maker named Toryo "as useless parchments" (but suitable for making fireworks).

Later scholars have tried to discredit this account.[7] At the very least, though, it shows that the study of the Greek manuscripts of the New Testament is not rocket science.

THE FIRST PUBLISHED EDITION OF
THE GREEK NEW TESTAMENT

Even though the Complutensian Polyglot was the first printed edition of the Greek New Testament, it was not the first published version. As we have seen, the Complutum had been printed by 1514, but it did not see the light of published day until 1522. Between those two dates an enterprising Dutch scholar, the humanist intellectual Desiderius Erasmus, both produced and published an edition of the Greek New Testament, receiving the honor, then, of editing the so-called *editio princeps* (= first published edition). Erasmus had studied the New Testament, along with other great works of antiquity, on and off for many years, and had considered at some point putting together an edition for printing. But it was only when he visited Basel in August 1514 that he was persuaded by a publisher named Johann Froben to move forward.

Both Erasmus and Froben knew that the Complutensian Polyglot was in the works, and so they made haste to publish a Greek text as quickly as possible, although other obligations prevented Erasmus from taking up the task seriously until July of 1515. At that time he went to Basel in search of suitable manuscripts that he could use as the basis of his text. He did not uncover a great wealth of manuscripts, but what he found was sufficient for the task. For the most part, he relied on a mere handful of late medieval manuscripts, which he marked up as if he were copyediting a handwritten copy for the printer; the printer took the manuscripts so marked and set his type directly from them.

It appears that Erasmus relied heavily on just one twelfth-century manuscript for the Gospels and another, also of the twelfth century, for the book of Acts and the Epistles—although he was able to consult several other manuscripts and make corrections based on their readings. For the book of Revelation he had to borrow a manuscript from his friend the German humanist Johannes Reuchlin; unfortunately, this manuscript was almost impossible to read in places, and it had lost its last page, which contained the final six verses of the book. In his haste to have the job done, in those places Erasmus simply took the Latin Vulgate and translated its text back into Greek, thereby creating some textual readings found today in no surviving Greek manuscript. And this, as we will see, is the edition of the Greek New Testament that for all practical purposes was used by the translators of the King James Bible nearly a century later.

The printing of Erasmus's edition began in October 1515 and was finished in just five months. The edition included the rather hastily gathered Greek text and a revised version of the Latin Vulgate, side by side (in the second and later editions, Erasmus included his own Latin translation of the text in lieu of the Vulgate, much to the consternation of many theologians of the day, who still considered the Vulgate to be "the" Bible of the church). The book was a large one, nearly a thousand pages. Even so, as Erasmus himself later said, it was "rushed out rather than edited" (in his Latin phrasing: *praecipitatum verius quam editum*).

It is important to recognize that Erasmus's edition was the *editio princeps* of the Greek New Testament not simply because it makes for an interesting historical tale, but even more so because, as the history of the text developed, Erasmus's editions (he made five, all based ultimately on this first rather hastily assembled one) became the standard form of the Greek text to be published by Western European printers for more than three hundred years. Numerous Greek editions followed, produced by publishers whose names are well known to scholars in this field: Stephanus (Robert Estienne), Theodore Beza, and Bonaventure and Abraham Elzevir. All these texts, however, relied more or less on the texts of their predecessors, and all those go back to the text of Erasmus, with all its faults, based on just a handful of manuscripts (sometimes just two or even one—or in parts of Revelation, none!) that had been produced relatively late in the medieval period. Printers for the most part did not search out new manuscripts that might be older and better in order to base their texts on them. Instead, they simply printed and reprinted the same text, making only minor changes.

Some of these editions, to be sure, are significant. For example, Stephanus's third edition of 1550 is notable as the first edition ever to include notes documenting differences among some of the manuscripts consulted; his fourth edition (1551) is possibly even more significant, as it is the first edition of the Greek New Testament that divides the text into verses. Until then, the text had been printed all together, with no indication of verse division. There's an amusing anecdote associated with how Stephanus did his work for this edition. His son later reported that Stephanus had decided on his verse divisions (most of which are retained for us in our English translations) while making a journey on horseback. Undoubtedly he meant that his father was "working on the road"—that is, that he entered verse numbers in the evenings at the inns in which he was staying. But since his son literally says that Stephanus made these changes "while on horseback," some wry observers have suggested that he actually did his work in transit, so that whenever his horse hit an unexpected bump, Stephanus's pen jumped, accounting for some of the rather odd verse placements that we still find in our English translations of the New Testament.

The larger point I am trying to make, however, is that all these subsequent editions—those of Stephanus included—ultimately go back to Erasmus's *editio princeps,* which was based on some rather late, and not necessarily reliable, Greek manuscripts—the ones he happened to find in Basel and the one he borrowed from his friend Reuchlin. There would be no reason to suspect that these manuscripts were particularly high in quality. They were simply the ones he could lay his hands on.

Indeed, as it turns out, these manuscripts were *not* of the best quality: they were, after all, produced some eleven hundred years after the originals! For example, the main manuscript that Erasmus used for the Gospels contained both the story of the woman taken in adultery in John and the last twelve verses of Mark, passages that did not originally form part of the Gospels, as we learned in the preceding chapter.

There was one key passage of scripture that Erasmus's source manuscripts did not contain, however. This is the account of 1 John 5:7–8, which scholars have called the Johannine Comma, found in the manuscripts of the Latin Vulgate but not in the vast majority of Greek manuscripts, a passage that had long been a favorite among Christian theologians, since it is the only passage in the entire Bible that explicitly delineates the doctrine of the Trinity, that there are three persons in the godhead, but that the three all constitute just one God. In the Vulgate, the passage reads:

> *There are three that bear witness in heaven: the Father, the Word, and the Spirit, and these three are one; and there are three that bear witness on earth, the Spirit, the water, and the blood, and these three are one.*

It is a mysterious passage, but unequivocal in its support of the traditional teachings of the church on the "triune God who is one." Without this verse, the doctrine of the Trinity must be inferred from a range of passages combined to show that Christ is God, as is the Spirit and the Father, and that there is, nonetheless, only one God. This passage, in contrast, states the doctrine directly and succinctly.

But Erasmus did not find it in his Greek manuscripts, which instead simply read: "There are three that bear witness: the Spirit, the water, and the blood, and these three are one." Where did the "Father, the Word, and the Spirit" go? They were not in Erasmus's primary manuscript, or in any of the others that he consulted, and so, naturally, he left them out of his first edition of the Greek text.

More than anything else, it was this that outraged the theologians of his day, who accused Erasmus of tampering with the text in an attempt to eliminate the doctrine of the Trinity and to devalue its corollary, the doctrine of the full divinity of Christ. In particular, Stunica, one of the chief editors of the Complutensian Polyglot, went public with his defamation of Erasmus and insisted that in future editions he return the verse to its rightful place.

As the story goes, Erasmus—possibly in an unguarded moment—agreed that he would insert the verse in a future edition of his Greek

New Testament on one condition: that his opponents produce a *Greek* manuscript in which the verse could be found (finding it in Latin manuscripts was not enough). And so a Greek manuscript was produced. In fact, it was produced for the occasion. It appears that someone copied out the Greek text of the Epistles, and when he came to the passage in question, he translated the Latin text into Greek, giving the Johannine Comma in its familiar, theologically useful form. The manuscript provided to Erasmus, in other words, was a sixteenth-century production, made to order.

Despite his misgivings, Erasmus was true to his word and included the Johannine Comma in his next edition, and in all his subsequent editions. These editions, as I have already noted, became the basis for the editions of the Greek New Testament that were then reproduced time and again by the likes of Stephanus, Beza, and the Elzevirs. These editions provided the form of the text that the translators of the King James Bible eventually used. And so familiar passages to readers of the English Bible—from the King James in 1611 onward, up until modern editions of the twentieth century—include the woman taken in adultery, the last twelve verses of Mark, and the Johannine Comma, even though *none* of these passages can be found in the oldest and superior manuscripts of the Greek New Testament. They entered into the English stream of consciousness merely by a chance of history, based on manuscripts that Erasmus just happened to have handy to him, and one that was manufactured for his benefit.

The various Greek editions of the sixteenth and seventeenth centuries were so much alike that eventually printers could claim that they were the text that was universally accepted by all scholars and readers of the Greek New Testament—as indeed they were, since there were no competitors! The most-quoted claim is found in an edition produced in 1633 by Abraham and Bonaventure Elzevir (who were uncle and nephew), in which they told their readers, in words that have since become famous among scholars, that "You now have the text that is received by all, in which we have given nothing changed or corrupted."[8] The phrasing of this line, especially the words "text that is received by all," provides us with the common phrase *Textus Receptus* (abbreviated T.R.), a term used by textual critics to refer to that form of the Greek text that is based, not on the oldest and best manuscripts, but on the form of text originally published by Erasmus and handed down to printers for more than three hundred years, until textual scholars began insisting that the Greek New Testament should be established on scientific principles based on our oldest and best manuscripts, not simply reprinted according to custom. It was the inferior textual form of the Textus Receptus that stood at the base of the earliest English translations, including the King James Bible, and other editions until near the end of the nineteenth century.

MILL'S APPARATUS OF
THE GREEK NEW TESTAMENT

The text of the Greek New Testament, then, appeared to be on solid footing to most scholars who could avail themselves of the printed editions throughout the sixteenth and seventeenth centuries. After all, nearly all the editions were the same in their wording. Occasionally, though, scholarship was devoted to finding and noting that the Greek manuscripts varied from the text as it was familiarly printed. We have seen that Stephanus, in his edition of 1550, included marginal notes identifying places of variation among several manuscripts he had looked at (fourteen altogether). Somewhat later, in the seventeenth century, editions were published by English scholars such as Brian Walton and John Fell who took the variations in the surviving (and available) manuscripts more seriously. But almost no one recognized the enormity of the problem of textual variation until the groundbreaking publication in 1707 of one of the classics in the field of New Testament textual criticism, a book that had a cataclysmic effect on the study of the transmission of the Greek New Testament, opening the floodgates that compelled scholars to take the textual situation of our New Testament manuscripts seriously.[9]

This was an edition of the Greek New Testament by John Mill, fellow of Queens College, Oxford. Mill had invested thirty years of hard work amassing the materials for his edition. The text that he printed was simply the 1550 edition of Stephanus; what mattered for Mill's publication was not the text he used, but the variant readings *from* that text that he cited in a critical apparatus. Mill had access to the readings of some one hundred Greek manuscripts of the New Testament. In addition, he carefully examined the writings of the early church fathers to see how they quoted the text—on the assumption that one could reconstruct the manuscripts available to those fathers by examining their quotations. Moreover, even though he could not read many of the other ancient languages, except for Latin, he used an earlier edition published by Walton to see where the early versions in languages such as Syriac and Coptic differed from the Greek.

On the basis of this intense thirty-year effort to accumulate materials, Mill published his text with apparatus, in which he indicated places of variation among all the surviving materials available to him. To the shock and dismay of many of his readers, Mill's apparatus isolated some thirty thousand places of variation among the surviving witnesses, thirty thousand places where different manuscripts, Patristic (= church father) citations, and versions had different readings for passages of the New Testament.

Mill was not exhaustive in his presentation of the data he had collected. He had, in fact, found far more than thirty thousand places of variation. He did not cite everything he discovered, leaving out variations such as those involving changes of word order. Still, the places he noted were enough to startle the reading public away from the complacency into which it had fallen based on the constant republication of the Textus Receptus and the natural assumption that in the T.R. one had the "original" Greek of the New Testament. Now the status of the original text was thrown wide open to dispute. If one did not know which words were original to the Greek New Testament, how could one use these words in deciding correct Christian doctrine and teaching?

The Controversy Created by
Mill's Apparatus

The impact of Mill's publication was immediately felt, although he himself did not live to see the drama play out. He died, the victim of a stroke, just two weeks after his massive work was published. His untimely death (said by one observer to have been brought on by "drinking too much coffee"!) did not prevent detractors from coming to the fore, however. The most scathing attack came three years later in a learned volume by a controversialist named Daniel Whitby, who in 1710 published a set of notes on the interpretation of the New Testament, to which he added an appendix of one hundred pages examining, in great detail, the variants cited by Mill in his apparatus. Whitby was a conservative Protestant theologian whose basic view was that even though God certainly would not prevent errors from creeping into scribal copies of the New Testament, at the same time he would never allow the text to be corrupted (i.e., altered) to the point that it could not adequately achieve its divine aim and purpose. And so he laments, "I GRIEVE therefore and am vexed that I have found so much in Mill's Prolegomena which seems quite plainly to render the standard of faith insecure, or at best to give others too good a handle for doubting."[10]

Whitby goes on to suggest that Roman Catholic scholars—whom he calls "the Papists"—would be all too happy to be able to show, on the basis of the insecure foundations of the Greek text of the New Testament, that scripture was not a sufficient authority for the faith—that is, that the authority of the church instead is paramount. As he states: "Morinus [a Catholic scholar] argued for a depravation of the Greek Text which would render its authority insecure from the variety of readings which he found in the Greek Testament of R. Stephens [= Stephanus]; what triumphs then will the Papists have over the same text when they see the variations quadrupled by Mill after sweating for thirty years at the work?"[11] Whitby proceeds to argue that, in fact, the text of the New Testament is secure, since scarcely any variant cited by

Mill involves an article of faith or question of conduct, and the vast majority of Mill's variants have no claim to authenticity.

Whitby may have intended his refutation to have its effect without anyone actually reading it; it is a turgid, dense, unappealing one hundred pages of close argumentation, which tries to make its point simply through the accumulated mass of its refutation.

Whitby's defense might well have settled the issue had it not been taken up by those who used Mill's thirty thousand places of variation precisely to the end that Whitby feared, to argue that the text of scripture could not be trusted because it was in itself so insecure. Chief among those who argued the point was the English deist Anthony Collins, a friend and follower of John Locke, who in 1713 wrote a pamphlet called *Discourse on Free Thinking*. The work was typical of early-eighteenth-century deistic thought: it urged the primacy of logic and evidence over revelation (e.g., in the Bible) and claims of the miraculous. In section 2 of the work, which deals with "Religious Questions," Collins notes, in the midst of a myriad of other things, that even the Christian clergy (i.e., Mill) have been "owning and labouring to prove the Text of the Scripture to be precarious," making reference then to Mill's thirty thousand variants.

Collins's pamphlet, which was widely read and influential, provoked a number of pointed responses, many of them dull and laborious, some of them learned and indignant. Arguably its most significant result was that it drew into the fray a scholar of enormous international reputation, the Master of Trinity College, Cambridge, Richard Bentley. Bentley is renowned for his work on classical authors such as Homer, Horace, and Terence. In a reply to both Whitby and Collins, written under the pseudonym Phileleutherus Lipsiensis (which means something like "the lover of freedom from Leipzig"—an obvious allusion to Collins's urging of "free thinking"), Bentley made the obvious point that the variant readings that Mill had accumulated could not render the foundation of the Protestant faith insecure, since the readings existed even *before* Mill had noticed them. He didn't invent them; he only pointed them out!

[I]f we are to believe not only this wise Author [Collins] but a wiser Doctor of your own [Whitby], He [Mill] was labouring *all that while,* to prove the Text of the Scripture precarious. . . . *For what is it, that your Whitbyus so inveighs and exclaims at? The Doctor's Labours, says he, make the whole Text precarious; and expose both the Reformation to the* Papists, *and Religion itself to the* Atheists. *God forbid! We'll still hope better things. For sure those* Various Readings *existed before in the several Exemplars; Dr Mill did not make and coin them, he only exhibited them to our View. If Religion therefore was true before, though such Various Readings were in being: it will be as true and consequently as safe still, though every body sees them. Depend on't; no Truth, no matter of Fact fairly laid open, can ever subvert true Religion.*[12]

Bentley, an expert in the textual traditions of the classics, goes on to point out that one would expect to find a multitude of textual variants whenever one uncovers a large number of manuscripts. If there were only one manuscript of a work, there would be *no* textual variants. Once a second manuscript is located, however, it will differ from the first in a number of places. This is not a bad thing, however, as a number of these variant readings will show where the first manuscript has preserved an error. Add a third manuscript, and you will find additional variant readings, but also additional places, as a result, where the original text is preserved (i.e., where the first two manuscripts agree in an error). And so it goes—the more manuscripts one discovers, the more the variant readings; but also the more the likelihood that somewhere among those variant readings one will be able to uncover the original text. Therefore, the thirty thousand variants uncovered by Mill do not detract from the integrity of the New Testament; they simply provide the data that scholars need to work on to establish the text, a text that is more amply documented than any other from the ancient world.

As we will see in the next chapter, this controversy over Mill's publication eventually induced Bentley to turn his remarkable powers of intellect to the problem of establishing the oldest available text of the New Testament. Before moving to that discussion, however, perhaps we should take a step back and consider where we are today vis-à-vis Mill's astonishing discovery of thirty thousand variations in the manuscript tradition of the New Testament.

OUR CURRENT SITUATION

Whereas Mill knew of or examined some one hundred Greek manuscripts to uncover his thirty thousand variations, today we know of far, far more. At last count, more than fifty-seven hundred Greek manuscripts have been discovered and catalogued. That's fifty-seven *times* as many as Mill knew about in 1707. These fifty-seven hundred include everything from the smallest fragments of manuscripts—the size of a credit card—to very large and magnificent productions, preserved in their entirety. Some of them contain only one book of the New Testament; others contain a small collection (for example, the four Gospels or the letters of Paul); a very few contain the entire New Testament.[13] There are, in addition, many manuscripts of the various early versions (= translations) of the New Testament.

These manuscripts range in date from the early second century (a small fragment called P^{52}, which has several verses from John 18) down to the sixteenth century.[14] They vary greatly in size: some are small copies that could fit in the hand, such as Coptic copy of Matthew's Gospel, called the Scheide Codex, which measures 4×5 inches; others are very large and impressive copies, among them the previously mentioned Codex Sinaiticus, which measures 15×13.5 inches, making an impressive spread when opened up completely. Some of these manuscripts are inexpensive, hastily produced copies; some were actually copied onto reused pages (a document was erased and the text of the New Testament was written over the top of the erased pages); others are enormously lavish and expensive copies, including some written on purple-dyed parchment with silver or gold ink.

As a rule, scholars speak of four kinds of Greek manuscripts.[15] (1) The oldest are *papyrus* manuscripts, written on material manufactured from the papyrus reed, a valuable but inexpensive and efficient writing material in the ancient world; they date from the second to the seventh centuries. (2) The *majuscule* (= large-lettered) manuscripts are made of parchment (= animal skins; sometimes called vellum) and are named after the large letters, somewhat like our capital letters, that are used; these date, for the most part, from the fourth to the ninth centuries. (3) *Minuscule* (= small-lettered) manuscripts are also made of parchment but are written in smaller letters that are frequently combined (without the pen leaving the page) into what looks something like the Greek equivalent of cursive writing; these date from the ninth century onward. (4) *Lectionaries* are usually minuscule in form as well, but instead of consisting of the books of the New Testament, they contain, in a set order, "readings" taken from the New Testament to be used in church each week or on each holiday (like the lectionaries used in churches today).

In addition to these Greek manuscripts, we know of about ten thousand manuscripts of the Latin Vulgate, not to mention the manuscripts of other versions, such as the Syriac, Coptic, Armenian, Old Georgian, Church Slavonic, and the like (recall that Mill had access to only a few of the ancient versions, and these he knew only through their Latin translations). In addition, we have the writings of church fathers such as Clement of Alexandria, Origen, and Athanasius among the Greeks and Tertullian, Jerome, and Augustine among the Latins—all of them quoting the texts of the New Testament in places, making it possible to reconstruct what their manuscripts (now lost, for the most part) must have looked like.

With this abundance of evidence, what can we say about the total number of variants known today? Scholars differ significantly in their estimates—some say there are 200,000 variants known, some say 300,000, some say 400,000 or more! We do not know for sure because, despite impressive developments in computer technology, no one has yet been able to count them all. Perhaps, as I indicated earlier, it is best simply to leave the matter in comparative terms. There are more variations among our manuscripts than there are words in the New Testament.

KINDS OF CHANGES IN OUR MANUSCRIPTS

If we have trouble talking about the *numbers* of changes that still survive, what can we say about the *kinds* of changes found in these manuscripts? Scholars typically differentiate today between changes that appear to have been made accidentally through scribal mistakes and those made intentionally, through some forethought. These are not hard and fast boundaries, of course, but they still seem appropriate: one can see how a scribe might inadvertently leave out a word when copying a text (an accidental change), but it is hard to see how the last twelve verses of Mark could have been added by a slip of the pen.

And so, it might be worthwhile to end this chapter with a few examples of each kind of change. I will start by pointing out some kinds of "accidental" variants.

Accidental Changes

Accidental slips of the pen[16] no doubt were exacerbated, as we have seen, by the fact that Greek manuscripts were all written in *scriptuo continua*—with no punctuation, for the most part, or even spaces between words. This means that words that looked alike were often mistaken for one another. For example, in 1 Cor. 5:8, Paul tells his readers that they should partake of Christ, the Passover lamb, and should not eat the "old leaven, the leaven of wickedness and evil." The final word, *evil,* is spelled PONĒRAS in Greek, which, it turns out, looks a lot like the word for "sexual immorality," PORNEIAS. The difference in meaning may not be overwhelming, but it is striking that in a couple of surviving manuscripts, Paul explicitly warns not against evil in general, but against sexual vice in particular.

This kind of spelling mistake was made even more likely by the circumstance that scribes sometimes abbreviated certain words to save time or space. The Greek word for "and," for example, is KAI, for which some scribes simply wrote the initial letter *K,* with a kind of downstroke at the end to indicate that it was an abbreviation. Other common abbreviations involved what scholars have called the *nomina sacra* (= sacred names), a group of words such as *God, Christ, Lord, Jesus,* and *Spirit* that were abbreviated either because they occurred so frequently or else to show that they were being paid special attention. These various abbreviations sometimes led to confusion for later scribes, who mistook one abbreviation for another or misread an abbreviation as a full word. So, for example, in Rom. 12:11, Paul urges his reader to "serve the Lord." But the word *Lord,* KURIW, was typically abbreviated in manuscripts as KW (with a line drawn over the top), which some early scribes misread as an abbreviation for KAIRW, which means "time." And so in those manuscripts, Paul exhorts his readers to "serve the time."

Similarly, in 1 Cor. 12:13, Paul points out that everyone in Christ has been "baptized into one body" and they have all "drunk of one Spirit." The word *Spirit* (PNEUMA) would have been abbreviated in most manuscripts as $\overline{\text{PMA}}$, which understandably could be—and was—misread by some scribes as the Greek word for "drink" (POMA); and so in these witnesses Paul is said to indicate that all have "drunk of one drink."

One common type of mistake in Greek manuscripts occurred when two lines of the text being copied ended with the same letters or the same words. A scribe might copy the first line of text, and then when his eye went back to the page, it might pick up on the *same* words on the *next* line, instead of the line he had just copied; he would continue copying from there and, as a result, leave out the intervening words and/or lines. This kind of mistake is called *periblepsis* (an "eye-skip") occasioned by *homoeoteleuton* (the "same endings"). I teach my students that they can lay claim to a university education when they can speak intelligently about periblepsis occasioned by homoeoteleuton.

How this works can be illustrated by the text of Luke 12:8–9, which reads:

> [8]*Whoever confesses me before humans, the son of man*
>   *will confess before the angels of God*
> [9]*But whoever denies me before humans*
>   *will be denied before the angels of God*

Our earliest papyrus manuscript of the passage leaves off all of verse 9; and it is not difficult to see how the mistake was made. The scribe copied the words "before the angels of God" in verse 8, and when his eye returned to the page, he picked up the same words in verse 9 and assumed those were the words just copied—and so he proceeded to copy verse 10, leaving out verse 9 altogether.

Sometimes this kind of error can be even more disastrous to the meaning of a text. In John 17:15, for example, Jesus says in his prayer to God about his followers:

> *I do not ask that you keep them from the*
> *world, but that you keep them from the*
> *evil one.*

In one of our best manuscripts (the fourth-century Codex Vaticanus), however, the words "world . . . from the" are omitted, so that now Jesus utters the unfortunate prayer "I do not ask that you keep them from the evil one"!

Sometimes accidental mistakes were made not because words *looked* alike, but because they *sounded* alike. This could happen, for example, when a scribe was copying a text by dictation—when one scribe would be reading from a manuscript and one or more other scribes would be copying the words into new manuscripts, as sometimes happened in scriptoria after the fourth century. If two words were pronounced the same, then the scribe doing the copying might inadvertently use the wrong one in his copy, especially if it made perfectly good (but wrong) sense. This appears to be what happened, for example, in Rev. 1:5, where the author prays to "the one who released us from our sins." The word for "released" (LUSANTI) sounds exactly like the word for "washed" (LOUSANTI), and so it is no surprise that in a number of medieval manuscripts the author prays to the one "who washed us from our sins."

Another example occurs in Paul's letter to the Romans, where Paul states that "since we have been justified by faith, we have peace with God" (Rom. 5:1). Or is that what he said? The word for "we have peace," a statement of fact, sounded exactly like the word "let us have peace," an exhortation. And so in a large number of manuscripts, including some of our earliest, Paul doesn't rest assured that he and his followers have peace with God, he urges himself and others to seek peace. This is a passage for which textual scholars have difficulty deciding *which* reading is the correct one.[17]

In other cases there is little ambiguity, because the textual change, while understandable, actually makes for nonsense instead of sense. This happens a lot, and often for some of the reasons we have been discussing. As an example, in John 5:39, Jesus tells his opponents to "search the scriptures . . . for they bear witness to me." In one early manuscript, the final verb was changed to one that sounds similar but makes no sense in the context. In that manuscript Jesus says to "search the scriptures . . . for they are sinning against me"! A second example comes from the book of Revelation, where the prophet has a vision of the throne of God, around which there "was a rainbow that looked like an emerald" (1:3). In some of our earliest manuscripts there is a change, in which, odd as it might seem, we are told that around the throne "were priests that looked like an emerald"!

Of all the many thousands of accidental mistakes made in our manuscripts, probably the most bizarre is one that occurs in a minuscule manuscript of the four Gospels officially numbered 109, which was produced in the fourteenth century.[18] Its peculiar error occurs in Luke, chapter 3, in the account of Jesus's genealogy. The scribe was evidently copying a manuscript that gave the genealogy in two columns.

For some reason, he did not copy one column at a time, but copied *across* the two columns. As a result, the names of the genealogy are thrown out of whack, with most people being called the sons of the wrong father. Worse still, the second column of the text the scribe was copying did not have as many lines as the first, so that now, in the copy he made, the father of the human race (i.e., the last one mentioned) is not God but an Israelite named Phares; and God himself is said to be the son of a man named Aram!

Intentional Changes

In some respects, the changes we have been looking at are the easiest to spot and eliminate when trying to establish the earliest form of the text. Intentional changes tend to be a bit more difficult. Precisely because they were (evidently) made deliberately, these changes tend to make *sense*. And since they make sense, there will always be critics who argue that they make the *best* sense—that is, that they are original. This is not a dispute between scholars who think the text has been altered and those who think it has not. Everyone knows that the text has been changed; the only question is which reading represents the alteration and which represents the earliest attainable form of the text. Here scholars sometimes disagree.

In a remarkable number of instances—most of them, actually—scholars by and large agree. It is perhaps useful for us here to consider an array of the *kinds* of intentional changes one finds among our manuscripts, as these can show us the reasons scribes had for making alterations.

Sometimes scribes changed their texts because they thought the text contained a factual error. This appears to be the case at the very beginning of Mark, where the author introduces his Gospel by saying, "Just as is written in Isaiah the prophet, 'Behold I am sending a messenger before your face. . . . Make straight his paths.'" The problem is that the beginning of the quotation is not from Isaiah at all but represents a combination of a passage from Exod. 23:20 and one from

Mal. 3:1. Scribes recognized that this was a difficulty and so changed the text, making it say, "Just as is written *in the prophets....*" Now there is no problem with a misattribution of the quotation. But there can be little doubt concerning what Mark originally wrote: the attribution to Isaiah is found in our earliest and best manuscripts.

On occasion the "error" that a scribe attempted to correct was not factual, but interpretive. A well-known example comes in Matt. 24:36, where Jesus is predicting the end of the age and says that "concerning that day and hour, no one knows—not the angels in heaven, nor even the Son, but only the Father." Scribes found this passage difficult: the Son of God, Jesus himself, does not know when the end will come? How could that be? Isn't he all-knowing? To resolve the problem, some scribes simply modified the text by taking out the words "nor even the Son." Now the angels may be ignorant, but the Son of God isn't.[19]

In other cases scribes changed a text not because they thought that it contained a mistake but because they wanted to circumvent a misunderstanding of it. An example is Matt. 17:12–13, in which Jesus identifies John the Baptist as Elijah, the prophet to come at the end of time:

> *"I tell you that Elijah has already come, and they did not recognize him, but did to him as much as they wished. Thus also the Son of Man is about to suffer by them." Then his disciples realized that he was speaking to them about John the Baptist.*

The potential problem is that, as it reads, the text *could* be interpreted to mean not that John the Baptist was Elijah, but that he was the Son of Man. Scribes knew full well this was not the case, and so some of them switched the text around, making the statement "his disciples realized that he was speaking to them about John the Baptist" occur *before* the statement about the Son of Man.

Sometimes scribes changed their text for more patently theological reasons, to make sure that the text could not be used by "heretics" or to ensure that it said what it was already supposed (by the scribes) to mean. There are numerous instances of this kind of change, which we will consider at greater length in a later chapter. For now I will simply point out a couple of brief examples.

In the second century there were Christians who firmly believed that the salvation brought by Christ was a completely new thing, superior to anything the world had ever seen and certainly superior to the religion of Judaism from which Christianity had emerged. Some Christians went so far as to insist that Judaism, the old religion of the Jews, had been completely circumvented by the appearance of Christ. For some scribes of this persuasion, the parable that Jesus tells of new wine and old wineskins may have seemed problematic.

> *No one places new wine in old wineskins. . . . But new wine must be placed in new wineskins. And no one who drinks the old wine wishes for the new, for they say, "The old is better." (Luke 5:38–39)*

How could Jesus indicate that the old is better than the new? Isn't the salvation he brings superior to anything Judaism (or any other religion) had to offer? Scribes who found the saying puzzling simply eliminated the last sentence, so that now Jesus says nothing about the old being better than the new.

Sometimes scribes altered their text to ensure that a favorite doctrine was duly emphasized. We find this, for example, in the account of Jesus's genealogy in Matthew's Gospel, which starts with the father of the Jews, Abraham, and traces Jesus's line from father to son all the way down to "Jacob, who was the father of Joseph, the husband of Mary, from whom was born Jesus, who is called the Christ" (Matt. 1:16). As it stands, the genealogy already treats Jesus as an exceptional case in that he is not said to be the "son" of Joseph. For some scribes, however, that was not enough, and so they changed the text to read "Jacob, who was the father of Joseph, to whom being betrothed the virgin Mary gave birth to Jesus, who is called the Christ." Now Joseph is not even called Mary's husband, but only her betrothed, and she is clearly stated to be a virgin—an important point for many early scribes!

On occasion scribes modified their texts not because of theology but for liturgical reasons. As the ascetic tradition strengthened in early Christianity, it is not surprising to find this having an impact on scribal changes to the text. For example, in Mark 9, when Jesus casts out a demon that his disciples had been unable to budge, he tells them, "This kind comes out only by prayer" (Mark 9:29). Later scribes made the appropriate addition, in view of their own practices, so that now Jesus indicates that "This kind comes out only by prayer and fasting."

One of the best-known liturgical changes to the text is found in Luke's version of the Lord's Prayer. The prayer is also found in Matthew, of course, and it is that longer, Matthean form that was, and is, most familiar to Christians.[20] By comparison, Luke's version sounds hopelessly truncated.

> *Father, hallowed be your name. May your kingdom come. Give us each day our daily bread. And forgive our sins, for we forgive our debtors. And do not lead us into temptation. (Luke 11:2–4)*

Scribes resolved the problem of Luke's shortened version by adding the petitions known from the parallel passage in Matt. 6:9–13, so that now, as in Matthew, the prayer reads:

> *Our Father who is in heaven, hallowed be your name. May your kingdom come and your will be done, on earth as it is in heaven. Give us each day our daily bread. And forgive us our debts as we forgive our debtors. And do not lead us into temptation, but deliver us from evil.*

This scribal tendency to "harmonize" passages in the Gospels is ubiquitous. Whenever the same story is told in different Gospels, one scribe or another is likely to have made sure that the accounts are perfectly in harmony, eliminating differences by strokes of their pens.

Sometimes scribes were influenced not by parallel passages but by oral traditions then in circulation about Jesus and the stories told about him. We have already seen this in a big way in the case of the woman taken in adultery and the last twelve verses of Mark. In smaller cases as well, we can see how oral traditions affected the written texts of the Gospels. One outstanding example is the memorable story in John 5 of Jesus healing an invalid by the pool of Bethzatha. We are told at the beginning of the story that a number of people—invalids, blind, lame, and paralyzed—lay beside this pool, and that Jesus singled out one man, who had been there for thirty-eight years, for healing. When he asks the man if he would like to be healed, the man replies that there is no one who can place him in the pool, so that "when the water is troubled" someone always beats him into it.

In our oldest and best manuscripts there is no explanation for why this man would *want* to enter the pool once the waters became disturbed, but the oral tradition supplied the lack in an addition to verses 3–4 found in many of our later manuscripts. There we are told that "an angel would at times descend into the pool and disturb the water; and the first to descend after the water was disturbed would be healed."[21] A nice touch to an already intriguing story.

CONCLUSION

We could go on nearly forever talking about specific places in which the texts of the New Testament came to be changed, either accidentally or intentionally. As I have indicated, the examples are not just in the hundreds but in the thousands. The examples given are enough to convey the general point, however: there are lots of differences among our manuscripts, differences created by scribes who were reproducing their sacred texts. In the early Christian centuries, scribes were amateurs and as such were more inclined to alter the texts they copied—or more prone to alter them accidentally—than were scribes in the later periods who, starting in the fourth century, began to be professionals.

It is important to see what kinds of changes, both accidental and intentional, scribes were susceptible of making, because then it is easier to spot the changes and we can eliminate some of the guesswork involved in determining which form of the text represents an alteration and which represents its earliest form. It is also important to see how modern scholars have devised methods for making this kind of determination. In the next chapter we will trace some of that story, starting from the time of John Mill and carrying it down to the present, seeing the methods that have developed for reconstructing the text of the New Testament and for recognizing the ways that it came to be changed in the process of its transmission.

The final page of the Gospel of John in the famous Codex Sinaiticus,
found in the nineteenth century by the determined discoverer of manuscripts,
Tischendorf, in St. Catherine's monastery on Mount Sinai.

4

THE QUEST FOR ORIGINS

Methods and Discoveries

As we have seen, long before Mill published his edition of the Greek New Testament with its notation of thirty thousand places of variation among the surviving witnesses, some (few) scholars had recognized that there was a problem with the New Testament text. Already in the second century, the pagan critic Celsus had argued that Christians changed the text at will, as if drunk from a drinking bout; his opponent Origen speaks of the "great" number of differences among the manuscripts of the Gospels; more than a century later Pope Damasus was so concerned about the varieties of Latin manuscripts that he commissioned Jerome to produced a standardized translation; and Jerome himself had to compare numerous copies of the text, both Greek and Latin, to decide on the text that he thought was originally penned by its authors.

The problem lay dormant, however, through the Middle Ages and down to the seventeenth century, when Mill and others started to deal with it seriously.[1] While Mill was in the process of compiling the data for his landmark edition of 1707, another scholar was also assiduously working on the problem of the New Testament text; this scholar was not English, however, but French, and he was not a Protestant but a Catholic. Moreover, his view was precisely the one that many English Protestants feared would result from a careful analysis of the New Testament text, namely that the wide-ranging variations in the tradition showed that Christian faith could not be based solely on scripture (the Protestant Reformation doctrine of *sola scriptura*), since the text was unstable and unreliable. Instead, according to this view, the Catholics must be right that faith required the apostolic tradition preserved in the (Catholic) church. The French author who pursued these thoughts in a series of significant publications was Richard Simon (1638–1712).

RICHARD SIMON

Although Simon was principally a Hebrew scholar, he worked on the textual tradition of both the Old and the New Testaments. His magisterial study, *A Critical History of the Text of the New Testament,* appeared in 1689 while Mill was still laboring to uncover variants in the textual tradition; Mill had access to this work and, in the opening discussion of his 1707 edition, acknowledges its erudition and importance for his own investigations even while disagreeing with its theological conclusions.

Simon's book is devoted not to uncovering every available variant reading but to discussing textual differences in the tradition, in order to show the uncertainty of the text in places and to argue, at times, for the superiority of the Latin Bible, still held to be the authoritative text by Catholic theologians. He is all too familiar with key textual problems. He discusses at length, for example, a number of the ones we have examined ourselves to this point: the woman taken in adultery, the last twelve verses of Mark, and the Johannine Comma (which explicitly affirms the doctrine of the Trinity). Throughout his discussion he strives to show that it was Jerome who provided the church with a text that could be used as the basis for theological reflection. As he says in the preface to part 1 of his work:

> *St. Jerome has done the Church no small Service, in Correcting and Reviewing the ancient Latin Copies, according to the strictest Rules of Criticism. This we endeavor to demonstrate in this work, and that the most ancient Greek Exemplars of the New Testament are not the best, since they are suited to those Latin Copies, which St. Jerome found so degenerous as to need an Alteration.*[2]

This is at heart a clever argument, which we will meet again: the oldest Greek manuscripts are unreliable because they are precisely the degenerate copies that Jerome had to revise in order to establish the superior text; surviving Greek copies produced before Jerome's day, even though they may be our earliest copies, are not to be trusted.

As clever as the argument is, it has never won widespread support among textual critics. In effect, it is simply a declaration that our oldest surviving manuscripts cannot be trusted, but the revision of those manuscripts can. On what grounds, though, did Jerome revise his text? On the grounds of earlier manuscripts. Even he trusted the earlier record of the text. For us not to do likewise would be a giant step backward—even given the diversity of the textual tradition in the early centuries.

In any event, in pursuing his case, Simon argues that *all* manuscripts embody textual alterations, but especially the Greek ones (here we may have more polemic against "Greek schismatics" from the "true" church).

> *There would not be at this day any Copy even of the New Testament, either Greek, Latin, Syriack or Arabick, that might be truly called authentick, because there is not one, in whatsoever Language it be written, that is absolutely exempt from Additions. I might also avouch,*

that the Greek Transcribers have taken a very great liberty in writing their Copies, as shall be proved in another place.[3]

Simon's theological agenda for such observations is clear throughout his long treatise. At one point he asks rhetorically:

Is it possible . . . that God hath given to his church Books to serve her for a Rule, and that he hath at the same time permitted that the first Originals of these Books should be lost ever since the beginning of the Christian Religion?[4]

His answer, of course, is no. The scriptures do provide a foundation for the faith, but it is not the books themselves that ultimately matter (since they have, after all, been changed over time), but the interpretation of these books, as found in the apostolic tradition handed down through the (Catholic) church.

Although the Scriptures are a sure Rule on which our Faith is founded, yet this Rule is not altogether sufficient of itself; it is necessary to know, besides this, what are the Apostolical Traditions; and we cannot learn them but from the Apostolical Churches, who have preserved the true Sense of Scriptures.[5]

Simon's anti-Protestant conclusions become even clearer in some of his other writings. For example, in a work dealing with the "principal commentators on the New Testament," he is forthright in stating:

The great changes that have taken place in the manuscripts of the Bible . . . since the first originals were lost, completely destroy the principle of the Protestants . . ., who only consult these same manuscripts of the Bible in the form they are today. If the truth of religion had not lived on in the Church, it would not be safe to look for it now in books that have been subjected to so many changes and that in so many matters were dependent on the will of the copyists.[6]

This kind of intellectually rigorous attack on the Protestant understanding of scripture was taken quite seriously in the halls of academe. Once Mill's edition appeared in 1707, Protestant biblical scholars were driven by the nature of their materials to reconsider and defend their understanding of the faith. They could not, of course, simply do away with the notion of *sola scriptura*. For them, the words of the Bible continued to convey the authority of the Word of God. But how does one deal with the circumstance that in many instances we don't know what those words were? One solution was to develop methods of textual criticism that would enable modern scholars to reconstruct the original words, so that the foundation of faith might once again prove to be secure. It was this theological agenda that lay behind much of the effort, principally in England and Germany, to devise competent and reliable methods of reconstructing the original words of the New Testament from the numerous, error-ridden copies of it that happened to survive.

RICHARD BENTLEY

As we have seen, Richard Bentley, the classical scholar and Master of Trinity College, Cambridge, turned his renowned intellect to the problems of the New Testament textual tradition in response to the negative reactions elicited by the publication of Mill's Greek New Testament with its massive collection of textual variation among the manuscripts.[7] Bentley's response to the deist Collins, *A Reply to a Treatise of Free-Thinking,* proved to be very popular and went through eight editions. His overarching view was that thirty thousand variations in the Greek New Testament were not too many to expect from a textual tradition endowed with such a wealth of materials, and that Mill could scarcely be faulted for undermining the truth of the Christian religion when he had not invented these places of variation but simply observed them.

Eventually Bentley himself became interested in working on the New Testament textual tradition, and once he turned his mind to it, he concluded that he could in fact make significant progress in establishing the original text in the majority of places where textual variation existed. In a 1716 letter to a patron, Archbishop Wake, he stated the premise of a proposed new edition of the Greek Testament: he would be able, by careful analysis, to restore the text of the New Testament to its state at the time of the Council of Nicea (early fourth century), which would have been the form of the text promulgated in the preceding centuries by the great textual scholar of antiquity, Origen, many centuries *before* the vast majority of textual variations (Bentley believed) had come to corrupt the tradition.

Bentley was never one given over to false modesty. As he claims in this letter:

> *I find I am able (what some thought impossible) to give an edition of the Greek Testament exactly as it was in the best exemplars at the time of the Council of Nice; so that there shall not be twenty words, nor even particles, difference . . . so that that book which, by the present management, is thought the most uncertain, shall have a testimony of certainty above all other books whatever, and an end be put at once to all Various Lections [i.e., variant readings] now and hereafter.*[8]

Bentley's method of proceeding was rather straightforward. He had decided to collate (i.e., to compare in detail) the text of the most important Greek manuscript of the New Testament in England, the early-fifth-century Codex Alexandrinus, with the oldest available copies of the Latin Vulgate. What he found was a wide range of remarkable coincidences of readings, in which these manuscripts agreed time and again with each other but *against* the bulk of Greek manuscripts transcribed in the Middle Ages. The agreements extended even to such matters as word order, where the various manuscripts differed. Bentley was convinced, then, that he could edit both the Latin Vulgate and the Greek New Testament to arrive at the most ancient forms of these texts, so that there would be scarcely any doubt concerning their earliest reading. Mill's thirty thousand places of variation would thereby become a near irrelevancy to those invested in the authority of the text. The logic behind the method was simple: if, in fact, Jerome used the best Greek manuscripts available for editing his text, then by comparing the oldest manuscripts of the Vulgate (to ascertain Jerome's original text) with the oldest manuscripts of the Greek New Testament (to ascertain which were the ones used by Jerome), one could determine what the best texts of Jerome's day had looked like—and skip over more than a thousand years of textual transmission in which the text came to be repeatedly changed. Moreover, since Jerome's text would have been that of his predecessor Origen, one could rest assured that this was the very best text available in the earliest centuries of Christianity.

And so, Bentley draws what for him was the ineluctable conclusion:

> *By taking two thousand errors out of the Pope's Vulgate, and as many out of the Protestant Pope Stephens' [i.e., the edition of Stephanus— the T.R.] I can set out an edition of each in columns, without using any book under nine hundred years old, that shall so exactly agree word for word, and, what at first amazed me, order for order, that no two tallies nor two indentures can agree better.*[9]

Spending further time in collating manuscripts, and in examining the collations made by others, only increased Bentley's confidence in his ability to do the job, to do it right, and to do it once and for all. In 1720 he published a pamphlet entitled *Proposals for Printing* designed to bring in support for his project by acquiring a number of financial subscribers. In it he lays out his proposed method of reconstructing the text and argues for its incomparable accuracy.

> *The author believes that he has retrieved (except in very few places) the true exemplar of Origen. . . . And he is sure, that the Greek and Latin MSS., by their mutual assistance, do so settle the original text to the smallest nicety, as cannot be performed now in any Classic author whatever: and that out of a labyrinth of thirty thousand various readings, that crowd the pages of our present best editions, all put upon equal credit to the offence of many good persons; this clue so leads and extricates us, that there will scarce be two hundred out of so many thousands that can deserve the least consideration.*[10]

Paring down the significant variants from Mill's thirty thousand to a mere two hundred is obviously a major advance. Not everyone, however, was sure that Bentley could produce the goods. In an anonymous tractate written in response to the *Proposals* (this was an age of controversialists and pamphleteers), which discussed the pamphlet paragraph by paragraph, Bentley was attacked for his program and was said, by his anonymous opponent, to have "neither talents nor materials proper for the work he had undertaken."[11]

Bentley took this, as one can imagine, as a slur on his (self-acknowledged) great talents and responded in kind. Unfortunately, he mistook the identity of his opponent, who was actually a Cambridge scholar named Conyers Middleton, for another, John Colbatch, and wrote a vitriolic reply, naming Colbatch and, as was the style in those days, calling him names. Such controversial pamphlets are a marvel to behold in our own day of subtle polemics; there was nothing subtle about personal grievance in those days. Bentley remarks that "We need go no further than this paragraph for a specimen of the greatest malice and impudence, that any scribbler out of the dark committed to paper."[12] And throughout his reply he provides a smattering of rather graphic terms of abuse, calling Colbatch (who in fact had nothing to do with the pamphlet in question) a cabbage-head, insect, worm, maggot, vermin, gnawing rat, snarling dog, ignorant thief, and mountebank.[13] Ah, those were the days.

Once Bentley was alerted to the real identity of his opponent, he was naturally a bit embarrassed about barking up the wrong tree, but he continued his self-defense, and both sides had more than one volley left in the exchange. These defenses hampered the work itself, of course, as did other factors, including Bentley's onerous obligations as an administrator of his college at Cambridge, his other writing projects, and certain disheartening setbacks, which included his failure to obtain an exemption on import duties for the paper he wanted to use for the edition. In the end, his proposals for printing the Greek New Testament, with the text not of late corrupted Greek manuscripts (like those lying behind the Textus Receptus) but of the earliest possible attainable text, came to naught. After his death, his nephew was forced to return the sums that had been collected by subscription, bringing closure to the entire affair.

JOHANN ALBRECHT BENGEL

From France (Simon) to England (Mill, Bentley), and now to Germany, textual problems of the New Testament were occupying the leading biblical scholars of the day in major areas of European Christendom. Johann Albrecht Bengel (1687–1752) was a pious Lutheran pastor and professor who early in his life became deeply disturbed by the presence of such a large array of textual variants in the manuscript tradition of the New Testament, and was particularly thrown off as a twenty-year-old by the publication of Mill's edition and its thirty thousand places of variation. These were seen as a major challenge to Bengel's faith, rooted as it was in the very words of scripture. If these words were not certain, what of the faith based on them?

Bengel spent much of his academic career working on this problem, and as we will see, he made significant headway in finding solutions to it. First, though, we need to look briefly at Bengel's approach to the Bible.[14]

Bengel's religious commitments permeated his life and thought. One can get a sense of the seriousness with which he approached his faith from the title of the inaugural lecture he delivered when appointed a junior tutor at the new theological seminary in Denkendorf: "De certissima ad veram eruditonem perveniendi ratione per studium pietatis" (The diligent pursuit of piety is the surest method of attaining sound learning).

Bengel was a classically trained, extremely careful interpreter of the biblical text. He is possibly best known as a biblical commentator: he wrote extensive notes on every book of the New Testament, exploring grammatical, historical, and interpretive issues at length, in expositions that were clear and compelling—and still worth reading today. At the heart of this work of exegesis was a trust in the words of scripture. This trust went so far that it took Bengel in directions that today might seem a shade bizarre. Thinking that all the words of scripture were inspired—including the words of the prophets and the book of Revelation—Bengel became convinced that God's great involvement with human affairs was nearing a climax, and that biblical prophecy indicated that his own generation was living near the end of days. He, in fact, believed he knew when the end would come: it would be about a century in the future, in 1836.

Bengel was not taken aback by verses such as Matt. 24:36, which says that "of that day and hour no one knows, not the angels in heaven, nor even the Son, but the Father only." Careful interpreter that he was, Bengel points out that here Jesus speaks in the present tense: in his own *day* Jesus could say "no one knows," but that doesn't mean that at a later time no one would know. By studying the biblical prophecies, in fact, later Christians could come to know. The papacy was the Antichrist, the freemasons may have represented the false "prophet" of Revelation, and the end was but a century away (he was writing in the 1730s).

> *The Great Tribulation, which the primitive church looked for from the future Antichrist, is not arrived, but is very near; for the predictions of the Apocalypse, from the tenth to the fourteenth chapter, have been fulfilling for many centuries; and the principal point stands clearer and clearer in view, that within another hundred years, the great expected change of things may take place. . . . Still, let the remainder stand, especially the great termination which I anticipate for 1836.* [15]

Clearly, the predictors of doom in our own age—the Hal Lindsays (author of *The Late Great Planet Earth*) and the Timothy LaHays (co-author of the *Left Behind* series)—have had their predecessors, just as they will have their successors, world without end.

For our purposes here, Bengel's quirky interpretations of prophecy matter because they were rooted in knowing the precise words of scripture. If the number of the Antichrist were not 666 but, say, 616, that would have a profound effect. Since the words matter, it matters that we have the words. And so Bengel spent a good deal of his research time exploring the many thousands of variant readings available in our manuscripts, and in his attempt to get beyond the alterations of later scribes back to the texts of the original authors, he came up with several breakthroughs in methodology.

The first is a criterion he devised that more or less summed up his approach to establishing the original text whenever the wording was in doubt. Scholars before him, such Simon and Bentley, had tried to devise criteria of evaluation for variant readings. Some others, whom we have not discussed here, devised long lists of criteria that might prove helpful. After intense study of the matter (Bengel studied *everything* intensely), Bengel found that he could summarize the vast majority of proposed criteria in a simple four-word phrase: "Proclivi scriptioni praestat ardua"—*the more difficult reading is preferable to the easier one.* The logic is this: when scribes changed their texts, they were more likely to try to improve them. If they saw what they took to be a mistake, they corrected it; if they saw two accounts of the same story told differently, they harmonized them; if they encountered a text that stood at odds with their own theological opinions, they altered it. In every instance, to know what the oldest (or even "original") text said, preference should be given not to the reading that has corrected the mistake, harmonized the account, or improved its theology, but to just the opposite one, the reading that is "harder" to explain. In every case, the more difficult reading is to be preferred.[16]

The other breakthrough that Bengel made involves not so much the mass of readings we have at our disposal as the mass of documents that contain them. He noticed that documents that are copied from one another naturally bear the closest resemblance to the exemplars from which they were copied and to other copies made from the same exemplars. Certain manuscripts are more like some other manuscripts than others are. All the surviving documents, then, can be arranged in a kind of genealogical relationship, in which there are groups of documents that are more closely related to one another than they are to other documents. This is useful to know, because in theory one could set up a kind of family tree and trace the lineage of documents back to their source. It is a bit like finding a mutual ancestor between you and a person in another state with the same last name.

Later, we will see more fully how grouping witnesses into families developed into a more formal methodological principle for helping the textual critic establish the original text. For now, it is enough to note that it was Bengel who first had the idea. In 1734 he published his great edition of the Greek New Testament, which printed for the most part the Textus Receptus but indicated places in which he thought he had uncovered superior readings to the text.

JOHANN J. WETTSTEIN

One of the most controversial figures in the ranks of biblical scholarship in the eighteenth century was J. J. Wettstein (1693–1754). At a young age Wettstein became enthralled with the question of the text of the New Testament and its manifold variations, and pursued the subject in his early studies. The day after his twentieth birthday, on March 17, 1713, he presented a thesis at the University of Basel on "The Variety of Readings in the Text of the New Testament." Among other things, the Protestant Wettstein argued that variant readings "can have no weakening effect on the trustworthiness or integrity of the Scriptures." The reason: God has "bestowed this book once and for all on the world as an instrument for the perfection of human character. It contains all that is necessary to salvation both for belief and conduct." Thus, variant readings may affect minor points in scripture, but the basic message remains intact no matter which readings one notices.[17]

In 1715 Wettstein went to England (as part of a literary tour) and was given full access to the Codex Alexandrinus, which we have already heard about in relation to Bentley. One portion of the manuscript particularly caught Wettstein's attention: it was one of those tiny matters with enormous implications. It involved the text of a key passage in the book of 1 Timothy.

The passage in question, 1 Tim. 3:16, had long been used by advocates of orthodox theology to support the view that the New Testament itself calls Jesus God. For the text, in most manuscripts, refers to Christ as "God made manifest in the flesh, and justified in the Spirit." As I pointed out in chapter 3, most manuscripts abbreviate sacred names (the so-called *nomina sacra*), and that is the case here as well, where the Greek word *God* (ΘΕΟΣ) is abbreviated in two letters, theta and sigma (ΘΣ), with a line drawn over the top to indicate that it is an abbreviation. What Wettstein noticed in examining Codex Alexandrinus was that the line over the top had been drawn in a different ink from the surrounding words, and so appeared to be from a *later* hand (i.e., written by a later scribe). Moreover, the horizontal line in the middle of the first letter, Θ, was not actually a part of the letter but was a line that had bled through from the other side of the old vellum. In other words, rather than being the abbreviation (theta–sigma) for "God" (ΘΣ), the word was actually an omicron and a sigma (ΟΣ), a different word altogether, which simply means "who." The original reading of the manuscript thus did not speak of Christ as "God made manifest in the flesh" but of Christ "*who* was made manifest in the flesh." According to the ancient testimony of the Codex Alexandrinus, Christ is no longer explicitly called God in this passage.

As Wettstein continued his investigations, he found other passages typically used to affirm the doctrine of the divinity of Christ that in fact represented textual problems; when these problems are resolved on text-critical grounds, in most instances references to Jesus's divinity are taken away. This happens, for example, when the famous Johannine Comma (1 John 5:7–8) is removed from the text. And it happens in a passage in Acts 20:28, which in many manuscripts speaks of "the Church of God, which he obtained by his own blood." Here again, Jesus appears to be spoken of as God. But in Codex Alexandrinus and some other manuscripts, the text instead speaks of "the Church of the Lord, which he obtained by his own blood." Now Jesus is called the Lord, but he is not explicitly identified as God.

Alerted to such difficulties, Wettstein began thinking seriously about his own theological convictions, and became attuned to the problem that the New Testament rarely, if ever, actually calls Jesus God. And he began to be annoyed with his fellow pastors and teachers in his home city of Basel, who would sometimes confuse language about God and Christ—for example, when talking of the Son of God as if he were the Father, or addressing God the Father in prayer and speaking of "your sacred wounds." Wettstein thought that more precision was needed when speaking about the Father and the Son, since they were not the same.

Wettstein's emphasis on such matters started raising suspicions among his colleagues, suspicions that were confirmed for them when, in 1730, Wettstein published a discussion of the problems of the Greek New Testament in anticipation of a new edition that he was preparing. Included among the specimen passages in his discussion were some of these disputed texts that had been used by theologians to establish the biblical basis for the doctrine of the divinity of Christ. For Wettstein, these texts in fact had been altered precisely in order to incorporate that perspective: the original texts could not be used in support of it.

This raised quite a furor among Wettstein's colleagues, many of whom became his opponents. They insisted to the Basel city council that Wettstein not be allowed to publish his Greek New Testament, which they labeled "useless, uncalled for, and even dangerous work"; and they maintained that "Deacon Wettstein is preaching what is unorthodox, is making statements in his lectures opposed to the teaching of the Reformed Church, and has in hand the printing of a Greek New Testament in which some dangerous innovations very suspect of

Socinianism [a doctrine that denied the divinity of Christ] will appear."[18] Called to account for his views before the university senate, he
was found to have "rationalistic" views that denied the plenary inspiration of scripture and the existence of the devil and demons, and that
focused attention on scriptural obscurities.

He was removed from the Christian diaconate and compelled to
leave Basel; and so he set up residence in Amsterdam, where he continued his work. He later claimed that all the controversy had forced
a delay of twenty years in the publication of his edition of the Greek
New Testament (1751–52).

Even so, this was a magnificent edition, still of value to scholars
today, more than 250 years later. In it Wettstein does print the Textus
Receptus, but he also amasses a mind-boggling array of Greek, Roman,
and Jewish texts that parallel statements found in the New Testament
and can help illuminate their meaning. He also cites a large number
of textual variants, adducing as evidence some twenty-five majuscule
manuscripts and some 250 minuscules (nearly three times the number
available to Mill), arranging them in a clear fashion by referring to
each majuscule with a different capital letter and using arabic numer-
als to denote the minuscule manuscripts—a system of reference that
became standard for centuries and is still, in essence, widely used
today.

Despite the enormous value of Wettstein's edition, the textual theory lying behind it is usually seen as completely retrograde. Wettstein
ignored the advances in method made by Bentley (for whom he had
once worked, collating manuscripts) and Bengel (whom he considered an enemy) and maintained that the ancient Greek manuscripts
of the New Testament could not be trusted because, in his view, they
had all been altered in conformity with the Latin witnesses. There is
no evidence of this having happened, however, and the end result of
using it as a major criterion of evaluation is that when one is deciding
on a textual variant, the best procedure purportedly is not to see what
the oldest witnesses say (these, according to the theory, are farthest removed from the originals!), but to see what the more recent ones (the

Greek manuscripts of the Middle Ages) say. No leading scholar of the text subscribes to this bizarre theory.

KARL LACHMANN

After Wettstein there were a number of textual scholars who made greater or lesser contributions to the methodology for determining the oldest form of the biblical text in the face of an increasing number of manuscripts (as these were being discovered) that attest variation, scholars such as J. Semler and J. J. Griesbach. In some ways, though, the major breakthrough in the field did not come for another eighty years, with the inauspicious-looking but revolutionary publication of a comparatively thin edition of the Greek New Testament by the German philologist Karl Lachmann (1793–1851).[19]

Early on in his work, Lachmann decided that the textual evidence was simply not adequate to determine what the original authors wrote. The earliest manuscripts that he had access to were those of the fourth or fifth centuries—hundreds of years after the originals had been produced. Who could predict the vicissitudes of transmission that had occurred between the penning of the autographs and the production of the earliest surviving witnesses some centuries later? Lachmann therefore set for himself a simpler task. The Textus Receptus, he knew, was based on the manuscript tradition of the twelfth century. He could improve upon that—by eight hundred years—by producing an edition of the New Testament as it would have appeared at about the end of the *fourth* century. The surviving manuscripts in Greek, along with the manuscripts of Jerome's Vulgate and the quotations of the text in such writers as Irenaeus, Origen, and Cyprian, would at the very least allow that. And so that is what he did. Relying on a handful of early majuscule manuscripts plus the oldest Latin manuscripts and the patristic quotations of the text, he chose not simply to edit the Textus Receptus wherever necessary (the tack followed by his predecessors who were dissatisfied with the T.R.), but to abandon the T.R. completely and to establish the text anew, on his own principles.

Thus, in 1831 he produced a new version of the text, not based on the T.R. This was the first time anyone had dared to do so. It had taken more than three hundred years, but finally the world was given an edition of the Greek New Testament that was based exclusively on ancient evidence.

Lachmann's aim of producing a text as it would have been known in the late fourth century was not always understood, and even when understood it was not always appreciated. Many readers thought that Lachmann was claiming to present the "original" text and objected that in doing so he had, on principle, avoided almost all the evidence (the later textual tradition, which contains an abundance of manuscripts). Others noted the similarity of his approach to that of Bentley, who also had the idea of comparing the earliest Greek and Latin manuscripts to determine the text of the fourth century (which Bentley took, however, to be the text known to Origen in the early third century); as a result, Lachmann was sometimes called Bentley's Ape. In reality, though, Lachmann had broken through the unhelpful custom established among printers and scholars alike of giving favored status to the T.R., a status it surely did not deserve, since it was printed and reprinted not because anyone felt that it rested on a secure textual basis but only because its text was both customary and familiar.

LOBEGOTT FRIEDRICH CONSTANTINE VON TISCHENDORF

While scholars like Bentley, Bengel, and Lachmann were refining the methodologies that were to be used in examining the variant readings of New Testament manuscripts, new discoveries were regularly being made in old libraries and monasteries, both East and West. The nineteenth-century scholar who was most assiduous in discovering biblical manuscripts and publishing their texts had the interesting name Lobegott Friedrich Constantine von Tischendorf (1815–1874). He was called Lobegott (German for "Praise God") because before he was born, his mother had seen a blind man and succumbed to the superstitious belief that this would cause her child to be born blind. When he was born completely healthy, she dedicated him to God by giving him this unusual first name.

Tischendorf was an inordinately ardent scholar who saw his work on the text of the New Testament as a sacred, divinely ordained task. As he once wrote his fiancée, while still in his early twenties: "I am confronted with a sacred task, the struggle to regain the original form of the New Testament."[20] This sacred task he sought to fulfill by locating every manuscript tucked away in every library and monastery that he could find. He made several trips around Europe and into the "East" (meaning what we would call the Middle East), finding, transcribing, and publishing manuscripts wherever he went. One of his earliest and best-known successes involved a manuscript that was already known but that no one had been able to read. This is the Codex Ephraemi Rescriptus, housed at the Bibliothèque Nationale in Paris. The codex was originally a fifth-century Greek manuscript of the New Testament, but it had been erased in the twelfth century so that its vellum pages could be reused to record some sermons by the Syriac church father Ephraim. Since the pages had not been erased thoroughly, some of the underwriting could still be seen, although not clearly enough to decipher most of the words—even though several fine scholars had done their best. By Tischendorf's time, however, chemical reagents had been discovered that could help bring out the underwriting. Applying these reagents carefully, and plodding his way slowly through the text, Tischendorf could make out its words, and so produced the first successful transcription of this early text, gaining for himself something of a reputation among those who cared about such things.

Some such people were induced to provide financial support for Tischendorf's journeys to other lands in Europe and the Middle East to locate manuscripts. By all counts, his most famous discovery involves one of the truly great manuscripts of the Bible still available, Codex Sinaiticus. The tale of its discovery is the stuff of legend, although we have the account direct from Tischendorf's own hand.

Tischendorf had made a journey to Egypt in 1844, when not yet thirty years of age, arriving on camelback eventually at the wilderness monastery of Saint Catherine. What happened there on May 24, 1844, is still best described in his own words:

> It was at the foot of Mount Sinai, in the Convent of St Catherine, that I discovered the pearl of all my researches. In visiting the monastery in the month of May 1844, I perceived in the middle of the great hall a large and wide basket full of old parchments; and the librarian who was a man of information told me that two heaps of papers like these, mouldered by time, had been already committed to the flames. What was my surprise to find amid this heap of papers a considerable number of sheets of a copy of the Old Testament in Greek, which seemed to me to be one of the most ancient that I had ever seen. The authorities of the monastery allowed me to possess myself of a third of these parchments, or about forty three sheets, all the more readily as they were designated for the fire. But I could not get them to yield up possession of the remainder. The too lively satisfaction which I had displayed had aroused their suspicions as to the value of the manuscript. I transcribed a page of the text of Isaiah and Jeremiah, and enjoined on the monks to take religious care of all such remains which might fall their way.[21]

Tischendorf attempted to retrieve the rest of this precious manuscript but could not persuade the monks to part with it. Some nine years later he made a return trip and could find no trace of it. Then in 1859 he set out once again, now under the patronage of Czar Alexander II of Russia, who had an interest in all things Christian, especially Christian antiquity. This time Tischendorf found no trace of the manuscript until the last day of his visit. Invited into the room of the convent's steward, he discussed with him the Septuagint (the Greek

Old Testament), and the steward told him, "I too have read a Septuagint." He proceeded to pull from the corner of his room a volume
wrapped in a red cloth. Tischendorf continues:

> *I unrolled the cover, and discovered, to my great surprise, not only*
> *those very fragments which, fifteen years before, I had taken out of the*
> *basket, but also other parts of the Old Testament, the New Testament*
> *complete, and in addition, the Epistle of Barnabas and a part of the*
> *Pastor of Hermas. Full of joy, which this time I had the self-command*
> *to conceal from the steward and the rest of the community, I asked, as*
> *if in a careless way, for permission to take the manuscript into my*
> *sleeping chamber to look over it more at leisure.*[22]

Tischendorf immediately recognized the manuscript for what it
was—the earliest surviving witness to the text of the New Testament:
"the most precious Biblical treasure in existence—a document whose
age and importance exceeded that of all the manuscripts which I had
ever examined." After complicated and prolonged negotiations, in
which Tischendorf not so subtly reminded the monks of his patron,
the Czar of Russia, who would be overwhelmed with the gift of such
a rare manuscript and would no doubt reciprocate by bestowing certain financial benefactions on the monastery, Tischendorf eventually
was allowed to take the manuscript back to Leipzig, where at the expense of the Czar he prepared a lavish four-volume edition of it that
appeared in 1862 on the one-thousandth anniversary of the founding
of the Russian empire.[23]

After the Russian revolution, the new government, needing money
and not being interested in manuscripts of the Bible, sold Codex
Sinaiticus to the British Museum for £100,000; it is now part of the
permanent collection of the British Library, prominently displayed in
the British Library's manuscript room.

This was, of course, just one of Tischendorf's many contributions
to the field of textual studies.[24] Altogether he published twenty-two
editions of early Christian texts, along with eight separate editions of

the Greek New Testament, the eighth of which continues to this day to be a treasure trove of information concerning the attestation of Greek and versional evidence for this or that variant reading. His productivity as a scholar can be gauged by the bibliographical essay written on his behalf by a scholar named Caspar René Gregory: the list of Tischendorf's publications takes up eleven solid pages.[25]

BROOKE FOSS WESTCOTT AND FENTON JOHN ANTHONY HORT

More than anyone else from the eighteenth and nineteenth centuries, it is to two Cambridge scholars, Brooke Foss Westcott (1825–1901) and Fenton John Anthony Hort (1828–1892), that modern textual critics owe a debt of gratitude for developing methods of analysis that help us deal with the manuscript tradition of the New Testament. Since their famous work of 1881, *The New Testament in the Original Greek,* these have been the names that all scholars have had to contend with—in affirming their basic insights, or in tinkering with the details of their claims, or in setting up alternative approaches in view of Westcott and Hort's well-defined and compelling system of analysis. The strength of the analysis owes more than a little to the genius of Hort in particular.

Westcott and Hort's publication appeared in two volumes, one of which was an actual edition of the New Testament based on their twenty-eight years of joint labor in deciding which was the original text wherever variations appeared in the tradition; the other was an exposition of the critical principles they had followed in producing their work. The latter was written by Hort and represents an inordinately closely reasoned and compelling survey of the materials and methods available to scholars wanting to undertake the tasks of textual criticism. The writing is dense; not a word is wasted. The logic is compelling; not an angle has been overlooked. This is a great book, which in many ways is *the* classic in the field. I do not allow my graduate students to go through their studies without mastering it.

In some ways, the problems of the text of the New Testament absorbed the interests of Westcott and Hort for most of their publishing lives. Already as a twenty-three-year-old, Hort, who had been trained in the classics and was not at first aware of the textual situation of the New Testament, wrote in a letter to his friend John Ellerton:

> *I had no idea till the last few weeks of the importance of texts, having read so little Greek Testament, and dragged on with the villainous Textus Receptus. . . . So many alterations on good MS [manuscript] authority made things clear not in a vulgar, notional way, but by giving a deeper and fuller meaning. . . . Think of that vile Textus Receptus leaning entirely on late MSS [manuscripts]; it is a blessing there are such early ones.*[26]

Only a couple of years later, Westcott and Hort had decided to edit a new edition of the New Testament. In another letter to Ellerton on April 19, 1853, Hort relates:

> *I have not seen anybody that I know except Westcott, whom . . . I visited for a few hours. One result of our talk I may as well tell you. He and I are going to edit a Greek text of the N.T. some two or three years hence, if possible. Lachmann and Tischendorf will supply rich materials, but not nearly enough. . . . Our object is to supply clergymen generally, schools, etc., with a portable Greek Testament, which shall not be disfigured with Byzantine [i.e., medieval] corruptions.*[27]

Hort's sanguine expectation that this edition would not take long to produce is still in evidence in November of that year, when he indicates that he hopes Westcott and he can crank out their edition "in little more than a year."[28] As soon as work began on the project, however, the hopes for a quick turnaround faded. Some nine years later Hort, in a letter written to bolster up Westcott, whose spirits were flagging with the prospect of what still lay ahead, urged:

The work has to be done, and never can be done satisfactorily . . .
without vast labour, a fact of which hardly anybody in Europe
except ourselves seems conscious. For a great mass of the readings,
if we separate them in thought from the rest, the labour is wholly dis-
proportionate. But believing it to be absolutely impossible to draw a
line between important and unimportant readings, I should hesitate
to say the entire labour is disproportionate to the worth of fixing the
entire text to the utmost extent now practicable. It would, I think,
be utterly unpardonable for us to give up our task.[29]

They were not to give up the task, but it became more intricate and involved as time passed. In the end, it took the two Cambridge scholars twenty-eight years of almost constant work to produce their text, along with an Introduction that came from the pen of Hort.

The work was well worth it. The Greek text that Westcott and Hort produced is remarkably similar to the one still widely used by scholars today, more than a century later. It is not that no new manuscripts have been discovered, or that no theoretical advances have been made, or that no differences of opinion have emerged since Westcott and Hort's day. Yet, even with our advances in technology and methodology, even with the incomparably greater manuscript resources at our disposal, our Greek texts of today bear an uncanny resemblance to the Greek text of Westcott and Hort.

It would not serve my purpose here to enter a detailed discussion of the methodological advances that Westcott and Hort made in establishing the text of the Greek New Testament.[30] The area in which their work has perhaps proved most significant is in the grouping of manuscripts. Since Bengel had first recognized that manuscripts could be gathered together in "family" groupings (somewhat like drawing up genealogies of family members), scholars had attempted to isolate various groups of witnesses into families. Westcott and Hort were very much involved in this endeavor as well. Their view of the matter was based on the principle that manuscripts belong in the same family line whenever they agree with one another in their wording. That is, if two manuscripts have the same wording of a verse, it must be because the two manuscripts ultimately go back to the same source—either the original manuscript or a copy of it. As the principle is sometimes stated, *Identity of reading implies identity of origin.*

One can then establish family groups based on textual agreements among the various surviving manuscripts. For Westcott and Hort there were four major families of witnesses: (1) the *Syrian* text (what other scholars have called the Byzantine text), which comprises most of the late medieval manuscripts; these are numerous but not particularly close in wording to the original text; (2) the *Western* text, made up of manuscripts that could be dated very early—the archetypes must have been around sometime in the second century at the latest; these manuscripts, however, embody the wild copying practices of scribes in that period before the transcription of texts had become the business of professionals; (3) the *Alexandrian* text, which was derived from Alexandria, where the scribes were trained and careful but occasionally altered their texts to make them grammatically and stylistically more acceptable, thereby changing the wording of the originals; and (4) the *Neutral* text, which consisted of manuscripts that had not undergone any serious change or revision in the course of their transmission but represented most accurately the texts of the originals.

The two leading witnesses of this Neutral text, in Westcott and Hort's opinion, were Codex Sinaiticus (the manuscript discovered by Tischendorf) and, even more so, Codex Vaticanus, discovered in the Vatican library. These were the two oldest manuscripts available to Westcott and Hort, and in their judgment they were far superior to any other manuscripts, because they represented the so-called Neutral text.

Many things have changed in nomenclature since Westcott and Hort's day: scholars no longer talk about a Neutral text, and most realize that *Western text* is a misnomer, since wild copying practices were found in the East as well as in the West. Moreover, Westcott and

Hort's system has been overhauled by subsequent scholars. Most modern scholars, for example, think that the Neutral and Alexandrian texts are the *same:* it is just that some manuscripts are better representatives of this text than are others. Then, too, significant manuscript discoveries, especially discoveries of papyri, have been made since their day.[31] Even so, Westcott and Hort's basic methodology continues to play a role for scholars trying to decide where in our surviving manuscripts we have later alterations and where we can find the earliest stage of the text.

As we will see in the next chapter, this basic methodology is relatively simple to understand, once it is laid out clearly. Applying it to textual problems can be interesting and even entertaining, as we work to see which variant readings in our manuscripts represent the words of the text as produced by their authors and which represent changes made by later scribes.

An eleventh-century image of Christ's cruxification, with the symbolic
representations of the Gospel writers in the four corners: an angel (Matthew),
an eagle (John), a lion (Mark), and a bull (Luke).

5

ORIGINALS THAT
MATTER

I n this chapter we will examine the methods that scholars have devised to identify the "original" form of the text (or at least the
"oldest attainable" form) and the form of the text that represents a
later scribal alteration. After laying out these methods, I will illustrate
how they can be used by focusing on three textual variants found in
our manuscript tradition of the New Testament. I have chosen these
three because each of them is critical for interpreting the book it is in;
what is more, none of these variant readings is reflected in most of our
modern English translations of the New Testament. That is to say, in
my judgment the translations available to most English readers are
based on the *wrong* text, and having the wrong text makes a real difference for the interpretation of these books.

First, however, we should consider the methods scholars have developed for making decisions about which textual readings are original and which represent later changes made by scribes. As we will see,
establishing the earliest form of the text is not always a simple matter;
it can be a demanding exercise.

MODERN METHODS OF TEXTUAL CRITICISM

The majority of textual critics today would call themselves *rational eclecticists* when it comes to making decisions about the oldest form of the text. This means that they "choose" (the root meaning of *eclectic*) from among a variety of textual readings the one that best represents the oldest form of the text, using a range of (rational) textual arguments. These arguments are based on evidence that is usually classified as either external or internal in nature.[1]

External Evidence

Arguments based on external evidence have to do with the surviving manuscript support for one reading or another. Which manuscripts attest the reading? Are those manuscripts reliable? Why are they reliable or not reliable?

In thinking about the manuscripts supporting one textual variant over another, one might be tempted simply to count noses, so to speak, in order to see which variant reading is found in the most surviving witnesses. Most scholars today, however, are not at all convinced that the majority of manuscripts necessarily provide the best available text. The reason for this is easy to explain by way of an illustration.

Suppose that after the original manuscript of a text was produced, two copies were made of it, which we may call *A* and *B*. These two copies, of course, will differ from each other in some ways—possibly major and probably minor. Now suppose that *A* was copied by one other scribe, but *B* was copied by fifty scribes. Then the original manuscript, along with copies *A* and *B*, were lost, so that all that remains in the textual tradition are the fifty-one second-generation copies, one made from *A* and fifty made from *B*. If a reading found in the fifty manuscripts (from *B*) differs from a reading found in the one (from *A*), is the former necessarily more likely to be the original reading? No, not at all—even though by counting noses, it is found in fifty times as many witnesses. In fact, the ultimate difference in support for that reading is not fifty manuscripts to one. It is a difference of one to one (*A* against *B*). The mere question of numbers of manuscripts supporting one reading over another, therefore, is not particularly germane to the question of which reading in our surviving manuscripts represents the original (or oldest) form of the text.[2]

Scholars are by and large convinced, therefore, that other considerations are far more important in determining which reading is best considered the oldest form of the text. One other consideration is the *age* of the manuscripts that support a reading. It is far more likely that the oldest form of the text will be found in the oldest surviving manuscripts—on the premise that the text gets changed more frequently with the passing of time. This is not to say that one can blindly follow the oldest manuscripts in every instance, of course. This is for two reasons, the one a matter of logic and the other a matter of history. In terms of logic, suppose a manuscript of the fifth century has one reading, but a manuscript of the eighth century has a different one. Is the reading found in the fifth-century manuscript necessarily the older form of the text? No, not necessarily. What if the fifth-century manuscript had been produced from a copy of the fourth century, but the eighth-century manuscript had been produced from one of the third century? In that case, the eighth-century manuscript would preserve the older reading.

The second, historical, reason that one cannot simply look at what the oldest manuscript reads, with no other considerations, is that, as we have seen, the earliest period of textual transmission was also the least controlled. This is when nonprofessional scribes, for the most part, were copying our texts—and making lots of mistakes in their copies.

And so, age does matter, but it cannot be an absolute criterion. This is why most textual critics are *rational* eclecticists. They believe that they have to look at a range of arguments for one reading or another, not simply count the manuscripts or consider only the verifiably oldest ones. Still, at the end of the day, if the *majority* of our *earliest* manuscripts support one reading over another, surely that combination of factors should be seen as carrying some weight in making a textual decision.

Another feature of the external evidence is the geographical range of manuscripts in support of one reading over another. Suppose a reading is found in a number of manuscripts, but all these manuscripts can be shown to have originated, say, in Rome, whereas a wide range of other manuscripts from, say, Egypt, Palestine, Asia Minor, and Gaul all represent some other reading. In that case, the textual critic might suspect that the one reading was a "local" variant (the copies in Rome all having the same mistake) and that the other reading is the one that is older and more likely to preserve the original text.

Probably the most important external criterion that scholars follow is this: for a reading to be considered "original," it normally should be found in the best manuscripts and the best groups of manuscripts. This is a rather tricky assessment, but it works this way: some manuscripts can be shown, on a variety of grounds, to be superior to others. For example, whenever internal evidence (discussed below) is virtually decisive for a reading, these manuscripts almost always have that reading, whereas other manuscripts (usually, as it turns out, the later manuscripts) have the alternative reading. The principle involved here states that if some manuscripts are known to be superior in readings when the oldest form is obvious, they are more likely to be superior also in readings for which internal evidence is not as clear. In a way, it is like having witnesses in a court of law or knowing friends whose word you can trust. When you *know* that a person is prone to lying, then you can never be sure that he or she is to be trusted; but if you know that a person is completely reliable, then you can trust that person even when he or she is telling you something you can't otherwise verify.

The same applies to groups of witnesses. We saw in chapter 4 that Westcott and Hort developed Bengel's idea that manuscripts could be grouped into textual families. Some of these textual groupings, as it turns out, are more to be trusted than others, in that they preserve the oldest and best of our surviving witnesses and, when tested, are shown to provide superior readings. In particular, most rational eclecticists think that the so-called Alexandrian text (this includes Hort's "Neutral" text), originally associated with the careful copying practices of the Christian scribes in Alexandria, Egypt, is the superior form of text available, and in most cases provides us with the oldest or "original" text, wherever there is variation. The "Byzantine" and "Western" texts, on the other hand, are less likely to preserve the best readings, when they are not also supported by Alexandrian manuscripts.

Internal Evidence

Textual critics who consider themselves rational eclecticists choose from a range of readings based on a number of pieces of evidence. In addition to the external evidence provided by the manuscripts, two kinds of internal evidence are typically used. The first involves what are called *intrinsic* probabilities—probabilities based on what the author of the text was himself most likely to have written. We are able to study, of course, the writing style, the vocabulary, and the theology of an author. When two or more variant readings are preserved among our manuscripts, and one of them uses words or stylistic features otherwise not found in that author's work, or if it represents a point of view that is at variance with what the author otherwise embraces, then it is unlikely that that is what the author wrote—especially if another attested reading coincides perfectly well with the author's writing elsewhere.

The second kind of internal evidence is called *transcriptional* probability. This asks, not which reading an author was likely to have written, but which reading a *scribe* was likely to have created. Ultimately, this kind of evidence goes back to Bengel's idea that the "more difficult" reading is more likely to be original. This is premised on the idea that scribes are more likely to try to correct what they take to be mistakes, to harmonize passages that they regard as contradictory, and to bring the theology of a text more into line with their own theology. Readings that might seem, on the surface, to contain a "mistake," or lack of harmony, or peculiar theology, are therefore more likely to have been changed by a scribe than are "easier" readings. This criterion is sometimes expressed as: *The reading that best explains the existence of the others is more likely to be original.*[3]

I have been laying out the various external and internal forms of evidence that textual critics consider, not because I expect everyone reading these pages to master these principles and start applying them to the manuscript tradition of the New Testament, but because it is important to recognize that, when we try to decide what the original text was, a range of considerations must be taken into account and a lot of judgment calls have to be made. There are times when the various pieces of evidence are at odds with one another, for example, when the more difficult reading (transcriptional probabilities) is not well attested in the early manuscripts (external evidence), or when the more difficult reading does not coincide with the writing style of the author otherwise (intrinsic probabilities).

In short, determining the original text is neither simple nor straightforward! It requires a lot of thought and careful sifting of the evidence, and different scholars invariably come to different conclusions—not only about minor matters that have no bearing on the meaning of a passage (such as the spelling of a word or a change of word order in Greek that can't even be replicated in English translation), but also about matters of major importance, matters that affect the interpretation of an entire book of the New Testament.

To illustrate the importance of some textual decisions, I turn now to three textual variants of the latter sort, where the determination of the original text has a significant bearing on how one understands the message of some of the New Testament authors.[4] As it turns out, in each of these cases I think most English translators have chosen the wrong reading and so present a translation not of the original text but of the text that scribes created when they altered the original. The first of these texts comes from Mark and has to do with Jesus's becoming angry when a poor leper pleads with him to be healed.

MARK AND AN ANGRY JESUS

The textual problem of Mark 1:41 occurs in the story of Jesus healing a man with a skin disease.[5] The surviving manuscripts preserve verse 41 in two different forms; both readings are shown here, in brackets.

> [39]*And he came preaching in their synagogues in all of Galilee and casting out the demons.* [40]*And a leper came to him beseeching him and saying to him, "If you wish, you are able to cleanse me."* [41]*And [* feeling compassion (Greek: SPLANGNISTHEIS)/becoming angry (Greek: ORGISTHEIS)*], reaching out his hand, he touched him and said, "I wish, be cleansed."* [42]*And immediately the leprosy went out from him, and he was cleansed.* [43]*And rebuking him severely, immediately he cast him out;* [44]*and said to him, "See that you say nothing to anyone, but go, show yourself to the priest and offer for your cleansing that which Moses commanded as a witness to them."* [45]*But when he went out he began to preach many things and to spread the word, so that he [Jesus] was no longer able to enter publicly into a city.*

Most English translations render the beginning of verse 41 so as to emphasize Jesus's love for this poor outcast leper: "feeling compassion" (or the word could be translated "moved with pity") for him. In doing so, these translations are following the Greek text found in most of our manuscripts. It is certainly easy to see why compassion might be called for in the situation. We don't know the precise nature of the man's disease—many commentators prefer to think of it as a scaly skin disorder rather than the kind of rotting flesh that we commonly associate with leprosy. In any event, he may well have fallen under the injunctions of the Torah that forbade "lepers" of any sort to live normal lives; they were to be isolated, cut off from the public, considered unclean (Leviticus 13–14). Moved with pity for such a one, Jesus reaches out a tender hand, touches his diseased flesh, and heals him.

The simple pathos and unproblematic emotion of the scene may well account for translators and interpreters, as a rule, not considering the alternative text found in some of our manuscripts. For the wording of one of our oldest witnesses, called Codex Bezae, which is supported by three Latin manuscripts, is at first puzzling and wrenching. Here, rather than saying that Jesus felt *compassion* for the man, the text indicates that he became *angry*. In Greek it is a difference between the words SPLANGNISTHEIS and ORGISTHEIS. Because of its attestation in both Greek and Latin witnesses, this other reading is generally conceded by textual specialists to go back at least to the second century. Is it possible, though, that this is what Mark himself wrote?

As we have already seen, we are never completely safe in saying that when the vast majority of manuscripts have one reading and only a couple have another, the majority are right. Sometimes a few manuscripts appear to be right even when all the others disagree. In part, this is because the vast majority of our manuscripts were produced hundreds and hundreds of years after the originals, and they themselves were copied not from the originals but from other, much later copies. Once a change made its way into the manuscript tradition, it could be perpetuated until *it* became more commonly transmitted than the original wording. In this case, both readings we are considering appear to be very ancient. Which one is original?

If Christian readers today were given the choice between these two readings, no doubt almost everyone would choose the one more commonly attested in our manuscripts: Jesus felt pity for this man, and so he healed him. The other reading is hard to figure out: what would it *mean* to say that Jesus felt angry? Isn't this in itself sufficient ground for assuming that Mark must have written that Jesus felt compassion?

On the contrary, the fact that one of the readings makes such good sense and is easy to understand is precisely what makes some scholars suspect that it is wrong. For, as we have seen, scribes also would have preferred the text to be nonproblematic and simple to understand. The question to be asked is this: which is more likely, that a scribe copying this text would change it to say that Jesus became wrathful instead of compassionate, or to say that Jesus became compassionate instead of wrathful? Which reading better explains the existence of the other? When seen from this perspective, the latter is obviously more likely. The reading that indicates Jesus became angry is the "more difficult" reading and therefore more likely to be "original."

There is even better evidence than this speculative question of which reading the scribes were more likely to invent. As it turns out, we don't have any Greek manuscripts of Mark that contain this passage until the end of the fourth century, nearly three hundred years after the book was produced. But we do have two authors who copied this story within *twenty years* of its first production.

Scholars have long recognized that Mark was the first Gospel to be written, and that both Matthew and Luke used Mark's account as a source for their own stories about Jesus.[6] It is possible, then, to examine Matthew and Luke to see how they changed Mark, wherever they tell the same story but in a (more or less) different way. When we do this, we find that Matthew and Luke have both taken over this story from Mark, their common source. It is striking that Matthew and Luke are almost word for word the same as Mark in the leper's request and in Jesus's response in verses 40–41. Which word, then, do they use to describe Jesus's reaction? Does he become compassionate or angry? Oddly enough, Matthew and Luke both omit the word altogether.

If the text of Mark available to Matthew and Luke had described Jesus as feeling compassion, why would each of them have omitted the word? Both Matthew and Luke describe Jesus as compassionate elsewhere, and whenever Mark has a story in which Jesus's compassion is explicitly mentioned, one or the other of them retains this description in his own account.[7]

What about the other option? What if both Matthew and Luke read in Mark's Gospel that Jesus became angry? Would they have been inclined to eliminate *that* emotion? There are, in fact, other occasions on which Jesus becomes angry in Mark. In each instance, Matthew and Luke have modified the accounts. In Mark 3:5 Jesus looks around "with anger" at those in the synagogue who are watching to see if he will heal the man with the withered hand. Luke has the verse almost the same as Mark, but he removes the reference to Jesus's anger. Matthew completely rewrites this section of the story and says nothing of Jesus's wrath. Similarly, in Mark 10:14 Jesus is aggravated at his disciples (a different Greek word is used) for not allowing people to bring their children to be blessed. Both Matthew and Luke have the story, often verbally the same, but *both* delete the reference to Jesus's anger (Matt. 19:14; Luke 18:16).

In sum, Matthew and Luke have no qualms about describing Jesus as compassionate, but they never describe him as angry. Whenever one of their sources (Mark) did so, they both independently rewrote the term out of their stories. Thus, whereas it is difficult to understand why they would have removed "feeling compassion" from the account of Jesus's healing of the leper, it is altogether easy to see why they might have wanted to remove "feeling anger." Combined with the circumstance that the latter term is attested in a very ancient stream of our manuscript tradition and that scribes would have been unlikely to create it out of the much more readily comprehensible "feeling compassion," it is becoming increasingly evident that Mark, in fact, described Jesus as angry when approached by the leper to be healed.

One other point must be emphasized before we move on. I have indicated that whereas Matthew and Luke have difficulty ascribing anger to Jesus, Mark has no problem doing so. Even in the story under consideration, *apart* from the textual problem of verse 41, Jesus does not treat this poor leper with kid gloves. After he heals him, he "severely rebukes him" and "throws him out." These are literal renderings of the Greek words, which are usually softened in translation. They are harsh terms, used elsewhere in Mark always in contexts of violent conflict and aggression (e.g., when Jesus casts out demons). It is difficult to see why Jesus would harshly upbraid this person and cast him out if he feels compassion for him; but if he is angry, perhaps it makes better sense.

At what, though, would Jesus be angry? This is where the relationship of text and interpretation becomes critical. Some scholars who have preferred the text that indicates that Jesus "became angry" in this passage have come up with highly improbable interpretations. Their goal in doing so appears to be to exonerate the emotion by making Jesus look compassionate even though they realize that the text says he became angry.[8] One commentator, for example, argues that Jesus is angry with the state of the world that is full of disease; in other words, he loves the sick but hates the sickness. There is no textual basis for the interpretation, but it does have the virtue of making Jesus look good. Another interpreter argues that Jesus is angry because this leprous person had been alienated from society, overlooking the facts that the text says nothing about the man being an outsider and that, and even if it assumes he was, it would not have been the fault of Jesus's society but of the Law of God (specifically the book of Leviticus). Another argues that, in fact, *that* is what Jesus was angry about, that the Law of Moses forces this kind of alienation. This interpretation ignores the fact that at the conclusion of the passage (v. 44) Jesus affirms the Law of Moses and urges the former leper to observe it.

All these interpretations have in common the desire to exonerate Jesus's anger and the decision to bypass the text in order to do so. Should we opt to do otherwise, what might we conclude? It seems to me that there are two options, one that focuses on the immediate literary context of the passage and the other, on its broader context.

First, in terms of the more immediate context, how is one struck by the portrayal of Jesus in the opening part of Mark's Gospel? Bracketing for a moment our own preconceptions of who Jesus was and simply reading this particular text, we have to admit that Jesus does not come off as the meek-and-mild, soft-featured, good shepherd of the stain-glassed window. Mark begins his Gospel by portraying Jesus as a physically and charismatically powerful authority figure who is not to be messed with. He is introduced by a wild-man prophet in the wilderness; he is cast out from society to do battle in the wilderness with Satan and the wild beasts; he returns to call for urgent repentance in the face of the imminent coming of God's judgment; he rips his followers away from their families; he overwhelms his audiences with his authority; he rebukes and overpowers demonic forces that can completely subdue mere mortals; he refuses to accede to popular demand, ignoring people who plead for an audience with him. The only story in this opening chapter of Mark that hints at personal compassion is the healing of Simon Peter's mother-in-law, sick in bed. But even that compassionate interpretation may be open to question. Some wry observers have noted that after Jesus dispels her fever, she rises to serve them, presumably bringing them their evening meal.

Is it possible that Jesus is being portrayed in the opening scenes of Mark's Gospel as a powerful figure with a strong will and an agenda of his own, a charismatic authority who doesn't like to be disturbed? It would certainly make sense of his response to the healed leper, whom he harshly rebukes and then casts out.

There is another explanation, though. As I've indicated, Jesus does get angry elsewhere in Mark's Gospel. The next time it happens is in chapter 3, which involves, strikingly, another healing story. Here Jesus is explicitly said to be angry at Pharisees, who think that he has no authority to heal the man with the crippled hand on the Sabbath.

In some ways, an even closer parallel comes in a story in which Jesus's anger is not explicitly mentioned but is nonetheless evident. In Mark 9, when Jesus comes down from the Mount of Transfiguration with Peter, James, and John, he finds a crowd around his disciples and a desperate man in their midst. The man's son is possessed by a demon, and he explains the situation to Jesus and then appeals to him: "If you are able, have pity on us and help us." Jesus fires back an angry response, "If you are able? Everything is possible to the one who believes." The man grows even more desperate and pleads, "I believe, help my unbelief." Jesus then casts out the demon.

What is striking in these stories is that Jesus's evident anger erupts when someone doubts his willingness, ability, or divine authority to heal. Maybe this is what is involved in the story of the leper as well. As in the story of Mark 9, someone approaches Jesus gingerly to ask: "If you are *willing* you are able to heal me." Jesus becomes angry. *Of course* he's willing, just as he is able and authorized. He heals the man and, still somewhat miffed, rebukes him sharply and throws him out.

There's a completely different feel to the story, given this way of construing it, a construal based on the text as Mark appears to have written it. Mark, in places, portrays an angry Jesus.[9]

LUKE AND AN IMPERTURBABLE JESUS

Unlike Mark, the Gospel of Luke never explicitly states that Jesus becomes angry. In fact, here Jesus never appears to become disturbed at all, in any way. Rather than an angry Jesus, Luke portrays an imperturbable Jesus. There is only one passage in this Gospel in which Jesus appears to lose his composure. And that, interestingly enough, is in a passage whose authenticity is hotly debated among textual scholars.[10]

The passage occurs in the context of Jesus's prayer on the Mount of Olives just before he is betrayed and arrested (Luke 22:39–46). After enjoining his disciples to "pray, lest you enter into temptation," Jesus leaves them, bows to his knees, and prays, "Father, if it be your will, remove this cup from me. Except not my will, but yours be done." In a large number of manuscripts the prayer is followed by the account, found nowhere else among our Gospels, of Jesus's heightened agony and so-called bloody sweat: "And an angel from heaven appeared to him, strengthening him. And being in agony he began to pray yet more fervently, and his sweat became like drops of blood falling to the ground" (vv. 43–44). The scene closes with Jesus rising from prayer and returning to his disciples to find them asleep. He then repeats his initial injunction for them to "pray, lest you enter into temptation." Immediately Judas arrives with the crowds, and Jesus is arrested.

One of the intriguing features of the debate about this passage is the balance of arguments back and forth over whether the disputed verses (vv. 43–44) were written by Luke or were instead inserted by a later scribe. The manuscripts that are known to be earliest and that are generally conceded to be the best (the "Alexandrian" text) do not, as a rule, include the verses. So perhaps they are a later, scribal addition. On the other hand, the verses are found in several other early witnesses and are, on the whole, widely distributed throughout the entire manuscript tradition. So were they added by scribes who wanted them in or deleted by scribes who wanted them out? It is difficult to say on the basis of the manuscripts themselves.

Some scholars have proposed that we consider other features of the verses to help us decide. One scholar, for example, has claimed that the vocabulary and style of the verses are very much like what is found in Luke otherwise (this is an argument based on "intrinsic probabilities"): for example, appearances of angels are common in Luke, and several words and phrases found in the passage occur in other places in Luke but nowhere else in the New Testament (such as the verb for "strengthen"). The argument hasn't proved convincing to everyone, however, since most of these "characteristically Lukan" ideas, constructions, and phrases are either formulated in *uncharacteristically* Lukan ways (e.g., angels never appear elsewhere in Luke without speaking) or are common in Jewish and Christian texts outside the New Testament. Moreover, there is an inordinately high concentration of *unusual* words and phrases in these verses: for example, three of the key words (*agony, sweat,* and *drops*) occur nowhere else in Luke, nor are they found in Acts (the second volume that the same author wrote). At the end of the day, it's difficult to decide about these verses on the basis of their vocabulary and style.

Another argument scholars have used has to do with the literary structure of the passage. In a nutshell, the passage appears to be deliberately structured as what scholars have called a *chiasmus.* When a passage is chiastically structured, the first statement of the passage corresponds to the last one; the second statement corresponds to the second to last; the third to the third to last, and so on. In other words, this is an intentional design; its purpose is to focus attention on the center of the passage as its key. And so here:

Jesus (a) tells his disciples to "pray lest you enter into temptation" (v. 40). He then (b) leaves them (v. 41a) and (c) kneels to pray (v. 41b).

The center of the passage is (d) Jesus's prayer itself, a prayer bracketed by his two requests that God's will be done (v. 42). Jesus then (*c*) rises from prayer (v. 45a), (*b*) returns to his disciples (v. 45b), and (*a*) finding them asleep, once again addresses them in the same words, telling them to "pray lest you enter into temptation" (vv. 45c–46).

The mere presence of this clear literary structure is not really the point. The point is how the chiasmus contributes to the meaning of the passage. The story begins and ends with the injunction to the disciples to pray so as to avoid entering into temptation. Prayer has long been recognized as an important theme in the Gospel of Luke (more so than in the other Gospels); here it comes into special prominence. For at the very center of the passage is Jesus's own prayer, a prayer that expresses his desire, bracketed by his greater desire that the Father's will be done (vv. 41c–42). As the center of the chiastic structure, this prayer supplies the passage's point of focus and, correspondingly, the key to its interpretation. This is a lesson on the importance of prayer in the face of temptation. The disciples, despite Jesus's repeated request to them to pray, fall asleep instead. Immediately the crowd comes to arrest Jesus. And what happens? The disciples, who have failed to pray, *do* "enter into temptation"; they flee the scene, leaving Jesus to face his fate alone. What about Jesus, the one who *has* prayed before the coming of his trial? When the crowd arrives, he calmly submits to his Father's will, yielding himself up to the martyrdom that has been prepared for him.

Luke's Passion narrative, as has long been recognized, is a story of Jesus's martyrdom, a martyrdom that functions, as do many others, to set an example to the faithful of how to remain firm in the face of death. Luke's martyrology shows that only prayer can prepare one to die.

What happens, though, when the disputed verses (vv. 43–44) are injected into the passage? On the literary level, the chiasmus that focuses the passage on Jesus's prayer is absolutely destroyed. Now the center of the passage, and hence its focus, shifts to Jesus's agony, an agony so terrible as to require a supernatural comforter for strength to bear it. It is significant that in this longer version of the story, Jesus's prayer does not produce the calm assurance that he exudes throughout the rest of the account; indeed, it is only after he prays "yet more fervently" that his sweat takes on the appearance of great drops of blood falling to the ground. My point is not simply that a nice literary structure has been lost, but that the entire focus of attention shifts to Jesus in deep and heartrending agony and in need of miraculous intervention.

This in itself may not seem like an insurmountable problem, until one realizes that nowhere else in Luke's Gospel is Jesus portrayed in this way. Quite the contrary, Luke has gone to great lengths to counter precisely the view of Jesus that these verses embrace. Rather than entering his passion with fear and trembling, in anguish over his coming fate, the Jesus of Luke goes to his death calm and in control, confident of his Father's will until the very end. It is a striking fact, of particular relevance to our textual problem, that Luke could produce this image of Jesus only by eliminating traditions that contradicted it from his sources (e.g., the Gospel according to Mark). Only the longer text of Luke 22:43–44 stands out as anomalous.

A simple comparison with Mark's version of the story at hand is instructive in this regard (understanding that Mark was Luke's source—which he changed to create his own distinctive emphases). For Luke has completely omitted Mark's statement that Jesus "began to be distressed and agitated" (Mark 14:33), as well as Jesus's own comment to his disciples, "My soul is deeply troubled, even unto death" (Mark 14:34). Rather than falling to the ground in anguish (Mark 14:35), Luke's Jesus bows to his knees (Luke 22:41). In Luke, Jesus does not ask that the hour might pass from him (cf. Mark 14:35); and rather than praying three times for the cup to be removed (Mark 14:36, 39, 41), he asks only once (Luke 22:42), prefacing his prayer, only in Luke, with the important condition, "If it be your will." And so, while Luke's source, the Gospel of Mark, portrays Jesus in anguish as he prays in the garden, Luke has completely remodeled the scene to show Jesus at peace in the face of death. The only exception is the account of Jesus's "bloody sweat," an account absent from our earliest and best witnesses. Why would Luke have gone to such lengths to eliminate Mark's portrayal of an anguished Jesus if in fact Jesus's anguish were the point of his story?

It is clear that Luke does not share Mark's understanding that Jesus was in anguish, bordering on despair. Nowhere is this more evident than in their subsequent accounts of Jesus's crucifixion. Mark portrays Jesus as silent on his path to Golgotha. His disciples have fled; even the faithful women look on only "from a distance." All those present deride him—passers-by, Jewish leaders, and both robbers. Mark's Jesus has been beaten, mocked, deserted, and forsaken, not just by his followers but finally by God himself. His only words in the entire proceeding come at the very end, when he cries aloud, "Eloi, Eloi, lema sabachthani" (My God, my God, why have *you* forsaken me?). He then utters a loud cry and dies.

This portrayal, again, stands in sharp contrast to what we find in Luke. In Luke's account, Jesus is far from silent, and when he speaks, he shows that he is still in control, trustful of God his Father, confident of his fate, concerned for the fate of others. En route to his crucifixion, according to Luke, when Jesus sees a group of women bewailing his misfortune, he tells them not to weep for him, but for themselves and their children, because of the disaster that is soon to befall them (23:27–31). While being nailed to the cross, rather than being silent, he prays to God, "Father, forgive them, for they don't know what they are doing" (23:34). On the cross, in the throes of his passion, Jesus engages in an intelligent conversation with one of the robbers crucified beside him, assuring him that they will be together that day in paradise (23:43). Most telling of all, rather than uttering his pathetic cry of dereliction at the end, Luke's Jesus, in full confidence of his standing before God, commends his soul to his loving Father: "Father, into your hands I commend my spirit" (24:46).

It would be difficult to overestimate the significance of these changes that Luke made in his source (Mark) for understanding our textual problem. At no point in Luke's Passion narrative does Jesus lose control; never is he in deep and debilitating anguish over his fate. He is in charge of his own destiny, knowing what he must do and what will happen to him once he does it. This is a man who is at peace with himself and tranquil in the face of death.

What, then, shall we say about our disputed verses? These are the only verses in the entire Gospel of Luke that undermine this clear portrayal. Only here does Jesus agonize over his coming fate; only here does he appear out of control, unable to bear the burden of his destiny. Why would Luke have totally eliminated all remnants of Jesus's agony elsewhere if he meant to emphasize it in yet stronger terms here? Why remove compatible material from his source, both before and after the verses in question? It appears that the account of Jesus's "bloody sweat," not found in our earliest and best manuscripts, is not original to Luke but is a scribal addition to the Gospel.[11]

HEBREWS AND A FORSAKEN JESUS

Luke's portrayal of Jesus stands in contrast not only to that of Mark, but also to that of other New Testament authors, including the unknown author of the Epistle to the Hebrews, who appears to presuppose knowledge of passion traditions in which Jesus was terrified in the face of death and died with no divine succor or support, as can be seen in the resolution of one of the most interesting textual problems of the New Testament.[12]

The problem occurs in a context that describes the eventual subjugation of all things to Jesus, the Son of Man. Again, I have placed in brackets the textual variants in question.

For when [God] subjects to him all things, he leaves nothing that is not subjected to him. But we do not yet see all things subjected to him. But we do see Jesus, who, having been made for a little while lower than the angels, was crowned with glory and honor on account of his suffering of death, so that [by the grace of God/apart from God] he might taste death for everyone. (Heb. 2:8–9)

Although almost all the surviving manuscripts state that Jesus died for all people "by the grace of God" (CHARITI THEOU), a couple of others state, instead, that he died "apart from God" (CHŌRIS THEOU). There are good reasons for thinking that the latter, however, was the original reading of the Epistle to the Hebrews.

I don't need to go into the intricacies of the manuscript support for the reading "apart from God" except to say that even though it occurs in only two documents of the tenth century, one of these (Ms. 1739) is known to have been produced from a copy that was at least as ancient as our earliest manuscripts. Of yet greater interest, the early-third-century scholar Origen tells us that this was the reading of the majority of manuscripts of his own day. Other evidence also suggests its early popularity: it was found in manuscripts known to Ambrose and Jerome in the Latin West, and it is quoted by a range of church writers down to the eleventh century. And so, despite the fact that it is not widely attested among our surviving manuscripts, the reading was at one time supported by strong external evidence.

When one turns from external to internal evidence, there can be no doubt concerning the superiority of this poorly attested variant. We have already seen that scribes were far more likely to make a reading that was hard to understand easier, rather than make an easy reading harder. This variant provides a textbook case of the phenomenon. Christians in the early centuries commonly regarded Jesus's death as the supreme manifestation of God's grace. To say, though, that Jesus died "apart from God" could be taken to mean any number of things, most of them unpalatable. Since scribes must have created one of these readings out of the other, there is little question concerning which of the two is more likely the corruption.

But was the alteration deliberate? Advocates of the more commonly attested text ("grace of God") have naturally had to claim that the change was not made on purpose (otherwise their favored text would almost certainly be the modification). By virtue of necessity, then, they have devised alternative scenarios to explain the *accidental* origin of the more difficult reading. Most commonly, it is simply supposed that because the words in question are similar in appearance (XARITI/ XWRIS), a scribe inadvertently mistook the word *grace* for the preposition *apart from*.

This view, however, seems a shade unlikely. Is a negligent or absentminded scribe likely to have changed his text by writing a word used *less* frequently in the New Testament ("apart from") or one used *more* frequently ("grace," four times as common)? Is he likely to have created a phrase that occurs nowhere else in the New Testament ("apart from God") or one that occurs more than twenty times ("by the grace of God")? Is he likely to have produced a statement, even by accident, that is bizarre and troubling or one that is familiar and easy? Surely, it's the latter: readers typically mistake unusual words for common ones and simplify what is complex, especially when their minds have partially strayed. Thus, even a theory of carelessness supports the less-attested reading ("apart from God") as original.

The most popular theory among those who think that the phrase *apart from God* is not original is that the reading was created as a marginal note: a scribe read in Heb. 2:8 that "all things" are to be subjected to the lordship of Christ, and immediately thought of 1 Cor. 15:27:

> *"For all things will be subjected under his [Christ's] feet." But when it says that "all things will be subjected," it is clear that it means all things* except *for the one who subjected them [i.e., God himself is not among the things subjected to Christ at the end].*

According to this theory, the scribe copying Hebrews 2 wanted it to be clear here as well that when the text indicates that everything is to be subjected to Christ, this does not include God the Father. To protect the text from misconstrual, the scribe then inserted an explanatory note in the margin of Heb. 2:8 (as a kind of cross-reference to 1 Cor. 15:27), pointing out that nothing is left unsubjected to Christ, "except for God." This note was subsequently transferred by a later, inattentive, scribe into the text of the next verse, Heb. 2:9, where he thought it belonged.

Despite the popularity of the solution, it is probably too clever by half, and requires too many dubious steps to work. There is no manuscript that attests *both* readings in the text (i.e., the correction in the margin or text of verse 8, where it would belong, *and* the original text of verse 9). Moreover, if a scribe thought that the note was a marginal correction, why did he find it in the margin next to verse 8 rather than verse 9? Finally, if the scribe who created the note had done so in reference to 1 Corinthians, would he not have written "except for God" (EKTOS THEOU—the phrase that actually occurs in the 1 Corinthians passage) rather than "apart from God" (CHŌRIS THEOU—a phrase not found in 1 Corinthians)?

In sum, it is extremely difficult to account for the phrase *apart from God* if the phrase *by the grace of God* was the original reading of Heb. 2:9. At the same time, whereas a *scribe* could scarcely be expected to have said that Christ died "apart from God," there is every reason to think that this is precisely what the author of Hebrews said. For this less-attested reading is also more consistent with the theology of Hebrews ("intrinsic probabilities"). Never in this entire Epistle does the word *grace* (CHARIS) refer to Jesus's death or to the benefits of salvation that accrue as a result of it. Instead, it is consistently connected with the gift of salvation that is *yet* to be bestowed upon the believer by the goodness of God (see especially Heb. 4:16; also 10:29; 12:15; 13:25). To be sure, Christians historically have been more influenced by other New Testament authors, notably Paul, who saw Jesus's sacrifice on the cross as the supreme manifestation of the grace of God. But Hebrews does not use the term in this way, even though scribes who thought that this author was Paul may not have realized that.

On the other hand, the statement that Jesus died "apart from God"—enigmatic when taken in isolation—makes compelling sense in its broader literary context in the book of Hebrews. Whereas this author never refers to Jesus's death as a manifestation of divine "grace," he repeatedly emphasizes that Jesus died a fully human, shameful death, totally removed from the realm whence he came, the realm of God; his sacrifice, as a result, was accepted as the perfect expiation for sin. Moreover, God did not intervene in Jesus's passion and did nothing to minimize his pain. Thus, for example, Heb. 5:7 speaks of Jesus, in the face of death, beseeching God with loud cries and tears. In 12:2 he is said to endure the "shame" of his death, not because God sustained him, but because he hoped for vindication. Throughout this Epistle, Jesus is said to experience human pain and death, like other human beings "in every respect." His was not an agony attenuated by special dispensation.

Yet more significant, this is a major theme of the immediate context of Heb. 2:9, which emphasizes that Christ lowered himself below the angels to share fully in blood and flesh, experience human sufferings, and die a human death. To be sure, his death is known to bring salvation, but the passage says not a word about God's grace as manifest in Christ's work of atonement. It focuses instead on Christology, on Christ's condescension into the transitory realm of suffering and death. It is as a full human being that Jesus experiences his passion, apart from any succor that might have been his as an exalted being. The work he began at his condescension he completes in his death, a death that had to be "apart from God."

How is it that the reading "apart from God," which can scarcely be explained as a scribal alteration, conforms to the linguistic preferences, style, and theology of the Epistle to the Hebrews, while the alternative reading "by the grace of God," which would have caused scribes no difficulties at all, stands at odds both with what Hebrews says about the death of Christ and with the way it says it? Heb. 2:9 appears originally to have said that Jesus died "apart from God," forsaken, much as he is portrayed in the Passion narrative of Mark's Gospel.

CONCLUSION

In each of the three cases we have considered, there is an important textual variant that plays a significant role in how the passage in question is interpreted. It is obviously important to know whether Jesus was said to feel compassion or anger in Mark 1:41; whether he was calm and collected or in deep distress in Luke 22:43–44; and whether he was said to die by God's grace or "apart from God" in Heb. 2:9. We could easily look at other passages as well, to get the sense of how important it is to know the words of an author if we want to interpret his message.

But there is far more to the textual tradition of the New Testament than merely establishing what its authors actually wrote. There is also the question of *why* these words came to be changed, and how these changes affect the meanings of their writings. This question of the modification of scripture in the early Christian church will be the subject of the next two chapters, as I try to show how scribes who were not altogether satisfied with what the New Testament books said modified their words to make them more clearly support orthodox Christianity and more vigorously oppose heretics, women, Jews, and pagans.

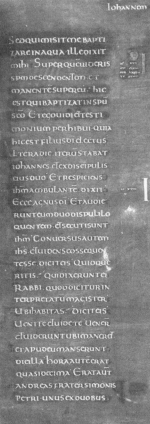

A page from the Gospel of John from one of the most extravagant biblical manuscripts of the tenth century: written on purple vellum with silver ink.

6

THEOLOGICALLY
MOTIVATED ALTERATIONS
OF THE TEXT

Textual criticism involves more than simply determining the original text. It also entails seeing how that text came to be modified over time, both through scribal slips and as scribes made deliberate modifications. The latter, the intentional changes, can be highly significant, not because they necessarily help us understand what the original authors were trying to say, but because they can show us something about how the authors' texts came to be interpreted by the scribes who reproduced them. By seeing how scribes altered their texts, we can discover clues about what these scribes thought was important in the text, and so we can learn more about the history of the texts as they came to be copied and recopied over the centuries.

The thesis of this chapter is that sometimes the texts of the New Testament were modified for theological reasons. This happened whenever the scribes copying the texts were concerned to ensure that the texts said what they wanted them to say; sometimes this was because of theological disputes raging in the scribes' own day. To make sense of this kind of change, we need to understand something about theological disputes in the early centuries of Christianity—the centuries in which most alterations of scripture were made, before the widespread appearance of "professional" scribes.

THE THEOLOGICAL CONTEXT OF
THE TRANSMISSION OF THE TEXTS

We know a good deal about Christianity during the second and third centuries—the time, say, between the completion of the writing of the New Testament books and the conversion of the Roman emperor Constantine to the religion, which, as we have seen, changed everything.[1] These two centuries were particularly rich in theological diversity among the early Christians. In fact, the theological diversity was so extensive that groups calling themselves Christian adhered to beliefs and practices that most Christians today would insist were not Christian at all.[2]

In the second and third centuries there were, of course, Christians who believed that there was only one God, the Creator of all there is. Other people who called themselves Christian, however, insisted that there were two different gods—one of the Old Testament (a God of wrath) and one of the New Testament (a God of love and mercy). These were not simply two different facets of the same God: they were actually two different gods. Strikingly, the groups that made these claims—including the followers of Marcion, whom we have already met—insisted that their views were the true teachings of Jesus and his apostles. Other groups, for example, of Gnostic Christians, insisted that there were not just two gods, but twelve. Others said thirty. Others still said 365. All these groups claimed to be Christian, insisting that their views were true and had been taught by Jesus and his followers.

Why didn't these other groups simply read their New Testaments to see that their views were wrong? It is because there *was* no New

Testament. To be sure, all the books of the New Testament had been written by this time, but there were lots of other books as well, also claiming to be by Jesus's own apostles—other gospels, acts, epistles, and apocalypses having very different perspectives from those found in the books that eventually came to be called the New Testament. The New Testament itself emerged out of these conflicts over God (or the gods), as one group of believers acquired more converts than all the others and decided which books should be included in the canon of scripture. During the second and third centuries, however, there was no agreed-upon canon—and no agreed-upon theology. Instead, there was a wide range of diversity: diverse groups asserting diverse theologies based on diverse written texts, all claiming to be written by apostles of Jesus.

Some of these Christian groups insisted that God had created this world; others maintained that the true God had not created this world (which is, after all, an evil place), but that it was the result of a cosmic disaster. Some of these groups insisted that the Jewish scriptures were given by the one true God; others claimed that the Jewish scriptures belong to the inferior God of the Jews, who was not the one true God. Some of these groups insisted that Jesus Christ was the one Son of God who was both completely human and completely divine; other groups insisted that Christ was completely human and not at all divine; others maintained that he was completely divine and not at all human; and yet others asserted that Jesus Christ was two things—a divine being (Christ) and a human being (Jesus). Some of these groups believed that Christ's death brought about the salvation of the world; others maintained that Christ's death had nothing to do with the salvation of this world; yet other groups insisted that Christ had never actually died.

Each and every one of these viewpoints—and many others besides—were topics of constant discussion, dialogue, and debate in the early centuries of the church, while Christians of various persuasions tried to convince others of the truth of their own claims. Only one group eventually "won out" in these debates. It was this group that decided what the Christian creeds would be: the creeds would affirm that there is only one God, the Creator; that Jesus his Son is both human and divine; and that salvation came by his death and resurrection. This was also the group that decided which books would be included in the canon of scripture. By the end of the fourth century, most Christians agreed that the canon was to include the four Gospels, Acts, the letters of Paul, and a group of other letters such as 1 John and 1 Peter, along with the Apocalypse of John. And who had been copying these texts? Christians from the congregations themselves, Christians who were intimately aware of and even involved in the debates over the identity of God, the status of the Jewish scriptures, the nature of Christ, and the effects of his death.

The group that established itself as "orthodox" (meaning that it held what it considered to be the "right belief") then determined what future Christian generations would believe and read as scripture. What should we call the "orthodox" views before they became the majority opinion of all Christians? Possibly it is best to call them proto-orthodox. That is to say, they represented the views of the "orthodox" Christians before this group had won its disputes by the early fourth century or so.

Did these disputes affect the scribes as they reproduced their scriptures? In this chapter I will be arguing that they did. To make the point, I will restrict myself to just one aspect of the ongoing theological disputes in the second and third centuries, the question over the nature of Christ. Was he human? Was he divine? Was he both? If he was both, was he two separate beings, one divine and one human? Or was he one being who was simultaneously human and divine? These are questions that were eventually resolved in the creeds that were formulated and then handed down even till today, creeds that insist that there is "one Lord Jesus Christ" who is both fully God and fully man. Before these determinations came to be made, there were widespread disagreements, and these disputes affected our texts of scripture.[3]

To illustrate this point I will consider three areas of the dispute over Christ's nature, looking at ways in which the texts of the books that were to become the New Testament came to be changed by (no doubt) well-meaning scribes, who intentionally altered their texts in order to make them more amenable to their own theological views, and less amenable to the views of their theological opponents. The first area I will consider involves the claim made by some Christians that Jesus was so fully human that he could not be divine. This was the view of a group of Christians that scholars today call the adoptionists. My contention is that Christian scribes who opposed adoptionistic views of Jesus modified their texts in places in order to stress their view that Jesus was not just human, but also divine. We might call these modifications antiadoptionistic alterations of scripture.

Antiadoptionistic Alterations of the Text

Early Christian Adoptionists

We know of a number of Christian groups from the second and third centuries that had an "adoptionistic" view of Christ. This view is called adoptionist because its adherents maintained that Jesus was not divine but a full flesh-and-blood human being whom God had "adopted" to be his son, usually at his baptism.[4]

One of the best-known early Christian groups who held to an adoptionistic Christology was a sect of Jewish-Christians known as the Ebionites. We aren't sure why they were given this name. It may have originated as a self-designation based on the Hebrew term *Ebyon,* which means "poor." These followers of Jesus may have imitated the original band of Jesus's disciples in giving up everything because of their faith, and so taking upon themselves voluntary poverty for the sake of others.

Wherever their name came from, the views of this group are clearly reported in our early records, principally written by their enemies who saw them as heretics. These followers of Jesus were, like him, Jews; where they differed from other Christians was in their insistence that to follow Jesus one *had* to be a Jew. For men, this meant becoming circumcised. For men and women, it meant following the Jewish law given by Moses, including kosher food laws and the observance of Sabbath and Jewish festivals.

In particular, it was their understanding of Jesus as the Jewish messiah that set these Christians apart from others. For since they were strict monotheists—believing that only One could be God—they insisted that Jesus was not himself divine, but was a human being no different in "nature" from the rest of us. He was born from the sexual union of his parents, Joseph and Mary, born like everyone else (his mother was not a virgin), and reared, then, in a Jewish home. What made Jesus different from all others was that he was more righteous in following the Jewish law; and because of his great righteousness, God adopted him to be his son at his baptism, when a voice came from heaven announcing that he was God's son. From that moment on, Jesus felt called to fulfill the mission God had allotted him—dying on the cross, as a righteous sacrifice for the sins of others. This he did in faithful obedience to his calling; God then honored this sacrifice by raising Jesus from the dead and exalting him up to heaven, where he still waits before returning as the judge of the earth.

According to the Ebionites, then, Jesus did not preexist; he was not born of a virgin; he was not himself divine. He was a special, righteous man, whom God had chosen and placed in a special relationship to himself.

In response to these adoptionistic views, proto-orthodox Christians insisted that Jesus was not "merely" human, but that he was actually divine, in some sense God himself. He was born of a virgin, he was more righteous than anyone else because he was different by nature, and at his baptism God did not *make* him his son (via adoption) but merely affirmed that he was his son, as he had been from eternity past.

How did these disputes affect the texts of scripture that were in circulation in the second and third centuries, texts being copied by nonprofessional scribes who were themselves involved to a greater or lesser degree in the controversies? There are very few, if any, variant readings that appear to have been created by scribes who held to an adoptionistic point of view. The reason for this lack of evidence should not be surprising. If an adoptionistic Christian *had* inserted his views into the texts of scripture, surely they would have been corrected by later scribes who took a more orthodox line. What we do find, however, are instances in which texts have been altered in such a way as to oppose an adoptionistic Christology. These changes emphasize that Jesus was born of a virgin, that he was not adopted at his baptism, and that he was himself God.

Antiadoptionist Changes of the Text

We have, in fact, already seen one textual variation related to this christological controversy, in our discussion in chapter 4 of the textual researches of J. J. Wettstein. Wettstein examined the Codex Alexandrinus, now in the British Library, and determined that in 1 Tim. 3:16, where most later manuscripts speak of Christ as "God made manifest in the flesh," this early manuscript originally spoke, instead, of Christ "who was made manifest in the flesh." The change is very slight in Greek—it is the difference between a theta and an omicron, which look very much alike (ΘΣ and ΟΣ). A later scribe had altered the original reading, so that it no longer read "who" but "God" (made manifest in the flesh). In other words, this later corrector changed the text in such a way as to stress Christ's divinity. It is striking to realize that the same correction occurred in four of our other early manuscripts of 1 Timothy, all of which have had correctors change the text in the same way, so that it now explicitly calls Jesus "God." This became the text of the vast majority of later Byzantine (i.e., medieval) manuscripts—and then became the text of most of the early English translations.

Our earliest and best manuscripts, however, speak of Christ "who" was made manifest in the flesh, without calling Jesus, explicitly, God. The change that came to dominate the medieval manuscripts, then, was made in order to emphasize Jesus's divinity in a text that was ambiguous about it, at best. This would be an example of an antiadoptionistic change, a textual alteration made to counter a claim that Jesus was fully human but not himself divine.

Other antiadoptionistic changes took place in the manuscripts that record Jesus's early life in the Gospel of Luke. In one place we are told that when Joseph and Mary took Jesus to the Temple and the holy man Simeon blessed him, "his father and mother were marveling at what was said to him" (Luke 2:33). His father? How could the text call Joseph Jesus's father if Jesus had been born of a virgin? Not surprisingly, a large number of scribes changed the text to eliminate the potential problem, by saying "Joseph and his mother were marveling. . . ." Now the text could not be used by an adoptionist Christian in support of the claim that Joseph was the child's father.

A similar phenomenon happens a few verses later in the account of Jesus as a twelve-year-old in the Temple. The story line is familiar: Joseph, Mary, and Jesus attend a festival in Jerusalem, but then when the rest of the family heads home in the caravan, Jesus remains behind, unbeknownst to them. As the text says, "his parents did not know about it." But why does the text speak of his *parents* when Joseph is not really his father? A number of textual witnesses "correct" the problem by having the text read, "Joseph and his mother did not know it." And again, some verses later, after they return to Jerusalem to hunt high and low for Jesus, Mary finds him, three days later, in the Temple. She upbraids him: "Your father and I have been looking for you!" Once again, some scribes solved the problem—this time by simply altering the text to read "We have been looking for you!"

One of the most intriguing antiadoptionist variants among our manuscripts occurs just where one might expect it, in an account of Jesus's baptism by John, the point at which many adoptionists insisted Jesus had been chosen by God to be his adopted son. In Luke's Gospel, as in Mark, when Jesus is baptized, the heavens open up, the Spirit descends upon Jesus in the form of a dove, and a voice comes from heaven. But the manuscripts of Luke's Gospel are divided concerning what exactly the voice said. According to most of our manuscripts, it spoke the same words one finds in Mark's account: "You are my beloved Son in whom I am well pleased" (Mark 1:11; Luke 3:23). In one early Greek manuscript and several Latin ones, however, the voice says something strikingly different: "You are my Son, today I have begotten you." *Today* I have begotten you! Doesn't that suggest that his day of baptism is the day on which Jesus has become the Son of God? Couldn't this text be used by an adoptionist Christian to make the point that Jesus became the Son of God at this time? As this is such an interesting variant, we might do well to give it a more extended consideration, as a further illustration of the complexities of the problems that textual critics face.

The first issue to resolve is this: which of these two forms of the text is original, and which represents the alteration? The vast majority of Greek manuscripts have the first reading ("You are my beloved Son in whom I am well pleased"); and so one might be tempted to see the other reading as the alteration. The problem in this case is that the verse was quoted a lot by early church fathers in the period before most of our manuscripts were produced. It is quoted in the second and third centuries everywhere from Rome, to Alexandria, to North Africa, to Palestine, to Gaul, to Spain. And in almost every instance, it is the *other* form of the text that is quoted ("Today I have begotten you").

Moreover, this is the form of text that is more *unlike* what is found in the parallel passage in Mark. As we have seen, scribes typically try to harmonize texts rather than take them out of harmony; it is therefore the form of the text that *differs* from Mark that is more likely to be original to Luke. These arguments suggest that the less-attested reading—"Today I have begotten you"—is indeed the original, and that it came to be changed by scribes who feared its adoptionistic overtones.

Some scholars have taken the opposite view, however, by arguing that Luke could not have had the voice at the baptism say "Today I have begotten you" because it is already clear *before* this point in Luke's narrative that Jesus is the Son of God. Thus, in Luke 1:35, before Jesus's birth, the angel Gabriel announces to Jesus's mother that "the Holy Spirit shall come upon you and the Power of the Most High will overshadow you, therefore the one who is to be born of you shall be called holy, the Son of God." For Luke himself, in other words, Jesus already *was* the Son of God at his birth. According to this argument, Jesus could not be said to have become the Son of God at his baptism—and so the more widely attested reading, "You are my beloved Son in whom I am well pleased," is probably original.

The difficulty with this line of thinking—as persuasive as it is at first glance—is that it overlooks how Luke generally uses designations of Jesus throughout his work (including not just the Gospel but also the second volume of his writing, the book of Acts). Consider, for example, what Luke says about Jesus as the "Messiah" (which is the Hebrew word for the Greek term *Christ*). According to Luke 2:11, Jesus was *born* as the Christ, but in one of the speeches in Acts, Jesus is said to have become the Christ at his baptism (Acts 10:37–38); in another passage Luke states that Jesus became the Christ at his resurrection (Acts 2:38). How can all these things be true? It appears that for Luke, it was important to emphasize the key moments of Jesus's existence, and to stress these as vital for Jesus's identity (e.g., as Christ). The same applies to Luke's understanding of Jesus as the "Lord." He is said to have been born the Lord in Luke 2:11; and he is called the Lord while living, in Luke 10:1; but Acts 2:38 indicates that he *became* the Lord at his resurrection.

For Luke, Jesus's identity as Lord, Christ, and Son of God is important. But the time at which it happened, evidently, is not. Jesus is all these things at crucial points of his life—birth, baptism, and resurrection, for example.

It appears, then, that originally in Luke's account of Jesus's baptism, the voice came from heaven to declare "You are my Son, today I have begotten you." Luke probably did not mean that to be interpreted adoptionistically, since, after all, he had already narrated an account of Jesus's virgin birth (in chapters 1–2). But later Christians reading Luke 3:22 may have been taken aback by its potential implications, as it seems open to an adoptionistic interpretation. To prevent anyone from taking the text that way, some proto-orthodox scribes changed the text to make it stand in complete conformity with the text of Mark 1:11. Now, rather than being said to have been begotten by God, Jesus is simply affirmed: "You are my beloved Son in whom I am well pleased." This is, in other words, another antiadoptionistic change of the text.

We will conclude this part of the discussion by looking at one other such change. Like 1 Tim. 3:16, this one involves a text in which a scribe has made an alteration to affirm in very strong terms that Jesus is to be understood completely as God. The text occurs in the Gospel of John, a Gospel that more than any of the others that made it into the New Testament already goes a long way toward identifying Jesus himself as divine (see, e.g., John 8:58; 10:30; 20:28). This identification is made in a particularly striking way in a passage in which the original text is hotly disputed.

The first eighteen verses of John are sometimes called its Prologue. Here is where John speaks of the "Word of God" who was "in the beginning with God" and who "was God" (vv. 1–3). This Word of God made all things that exist. Moreover, it is God's mode of communication to the world; the Word is how God manifests himself to others. And we are told that at one point the "Word became flesh and dwelt among us." In other words, God's own Word became a human being (v. 14). This human being was "Jesus Christ" (v. 17). According to this understanding of things, then, Jesus Christ represents the "incarnation" of God's own Word, who was with God in the beginning and was himself God, through whom God made all things.

The Prologue then ends with some striking words, which come in two variant forms: "No one has seen God at any time, but *the unique Son/the unique God* who is in the bosom of Father, that one has made him known" (v. 18).

The textual problem has to do with the identification of this "unique" one. Is he to be identified as the "unique God in the bosom of the Father" or as the "unique Son in the bosom of the Father"? It must be acknowledged that the first reading is the one found in the manuscripts that are the oldest and generally considered to be the best—those of the Alexandrian textual family. But it is striking that it is rarely found in manuscripts *not* associated with Alexandria. Could it be a textual variant created by a scribe in Alexandria and popularized there? If so, that would explain why the vast majority of manuscripts from everywhere else have the other reading, in which Jesus is not called the unique God, but the unique Son.

There are other reasons for thinking that the latter reading is, in fact, the correct one. The Gospel of John uses this phrase "the unique Son" (sometimes mistranslated as "only begotten Son") on several other occasions (see John 3:16, 18); nowhere else does it speak of Christ as "the unique God." Moreover, what would it even *mean* to call Christ that? The term *unique* in Greek means "one of a kind." There can be only one who is one of a kind. The term *unique God* must refer to God the Father himself—otherwise he is not unique. But if the term refers to the Father, how can it be used of the Son? Given the fact that the more common (and understandable) phrase in the Gospel of John is "the unique Son," it appears that that was the text originally written in John 1:18. This itself is still a highly exalted view of Christ— he is the "unique Son who is in the bosom of the Father." And he is the one who explains God to everyone else.

It appears, though, that some scribes—probably located in Alexandria—were not content even with this exalted view of Christ, and so they made it even more exalted, by transforming the text. Now Christ is not merely God's unique Son, he is the unique God himself! This too, then, appears to be an antiadoptionistic change of the text made by proto-orthodox scribes of the second century.

ANTIDOCETIC ALTERATIONS OF THE TEXT

Early Christian Docetists

Standing at the opposite end of the theological spectrum from the Jewish-Christian Ebionites and their adoptionistic Christology were groups of Christians known as docetists.[5] The name comes from the Greek word DOKEŌ, which means "to seem" or "to appear." Docetists maintained that Jesus was not a full flesh-and-blood human being. He was instead completely (and only) divine; he only "seemed" or "appeared" to be a human being, to feel hunger, thirst, and pain, to bleed, to die. Since Jesus was God, he could not really be a man. He simply came to earth in the "appearance" of human flesh.

Probably the best-known docetist from the early centuries of Christianity was the philosopher-teacher Marcion. We know a good deal about Marcion because proto-orthodox church fathers such as Irenaeus and Tertullian considered his views a real threat, and so wrote extensively about them. In particular, we still have a five-volume work by Tertullian called *Against Marcion* in which Marcion's understanding of the faith is detailed and attacked. From this polemical tractate we are able to discern the major features of Marcion's thought.

As we have seen,[6] Marcion appears to have taken his cues from the apostle Paul, whom he considered to be the one true follower of Jesus. In some of his letters Paul differentiates between the Law and the gospel, insisting that a person is made right with God by faith in Christ (the gospel), not by performing the works of the Jewish law. For Marcion, this contrast between the gospel of Christ and the Law of Moses was absolute, so much so that the God who gave the Law obviously could not be the one who gave the salvation of Christ. They were, in other words, two different gods. The God of the Old Testament was the one who created this world, chose Israel to be his people, and gave them his harsh Law. When they break his Law (as they all do), he punishes them with death. Jesus came from a greater God, sent to save people from the wrathful God of the Jews. Since he did not belong to this other God, who created the material world, Jesus himself obviously could not be part of this material world. That means, then, that he could not actually have been born, that he did not have a material body, that he did not really bleed, that he did not really die. All these things were an appearance. But since Jesus appeared to die—an apparently perfect sacrifice—the God of the Jews accepted this death as payment for sins. Anyone who believes in it will be saved from this God.

Proto-orthodox authors such as Tertullian objected strenuously to this theology, insisting that if Christ was not an actual human being, he could not save other human beings, that if he did not actually shed blood, his blood could not bring salvation, that if he did not actually die, his "apparent" death would do nobody any good. Tertullian and others, then, took a strong stand that Jesus—while still divine (despite what the Ebionites and other adoptionists said)—was nonetheless fully human. He had flesh and blood; he could feel pain; he really bled; he really died; he really, physically, was raised from the dead; and he really, physically, ascended to heaven, where he is now waiting to return, physically, in glory.

Antidocetic Changes of the Text

The debate over docetic Christologies affected the scribes who copied the books that eventually became the New Testament. To illustrate this point I will examine four textual variants in the final chapters of the Gospel of Luke, which, as we have seen, was the one Gospel that Marcion accepted as canonical scripture.[7]

The first involves a passage we also considered in chapter 5—the account of Jesus's "sweating blood." As we saw there, the verses in question were probably not original to Luke's Gospel. Recall that the passage describes events that take place immediately before Jesus's arrest, when he leaves his disciples to go off by himself to pray, asking that the cup of his suffering be removed from him, but praying that God's "will be done." Then, in some manuscripts, we read the disputed verses: "And an angel from heaven appeared to him, strengthening him. And being in agony he began to pray yet more fervently, and his sweat became like drops of blood falling to the ground" (vv. 43–44).

I argued in chapter 5 that verses 43–44 disrupt the structure of this passage in Luke, which is otherwise a chiasmus that focuses attention on Jesus's prayer for God's will to be done. I also suggested that the verses contain a theology completely unlike that otherwise found in

Luke's Passion narrative. Everywhere else, Jesus is calm and in control of his situation. Luke, in fact, has gone out of his way to *remove* any indication of Jesus's agony from the account. These verses, then, not only are missing from important and early witnesses, they also run counter to the portrayal of Jesus facing his death otherwise found in Luke's Gospel.

Why, though, did scribes add them to the account? We are now in a position to answer that question. It is notable that these verses are alluded to three times by proto-orthodox authors of the mid to late second century (Justin Martyr, Irenaeus of Gaul, and Hippolytus of Rome); and what is more intriguing still, each time they are mentioned it is in order to counter the view that Jesus was not a real human being. That is, the deep anguish that Jesus experiences according to these verses was taken to show that he really was a human being, that he really could suffer like the rest of us. Thus, for example, the early Christian apologist Justin, after observing that "his sweat fell down like drops of blood while he was praying," claims that this showed "that the Father wished his Son really to undergo such sufferings for our sakes," so that we "may not say that he, being the Son of God, did not feel what was happening to him and inflicted on him."[8]

In other words, Justin and his proto-orthodox colleagues understood that the verses showed in graphic form that Jesus did not merely "appear" to be human: he really was human, in every way. It seems likely, then, that since, as we have seen, these verses were not originally part of the Gospel of Luke, they were added for an antidocetic purpose, because they portrayed so well the real humanity of Jesus.

For proto-orthodox Christians, it was important to emphasize that Christ was a real man of flesh and blood because it was precisely the sacrifice of his flesh and the shedding of his blood that brought salvation—not in appearance but in reality. Another textual variant in Luke's account of Jesus's final hours emphasizes this reality. It occurs in the account of Jesus's last supper with his disciples. In one of our oldest Greek manuscripts, as well as in several Latin witnesses, we are told:

And taking a cup, giving thanks, he said, "Take this and divide it among yourselves, for I say to you that I will not drink from the fruit of the vine from now on, until the kingdom of God comes." And taking bread, giving thanks, he broke it and gave it to them, saying, "This is my body. But behold, the hand of the one who betrays me is with me at the table." (Luke 22:17–19)

In most of our manuscripts, however, there is an addition to the text, an addition that will sound familiar to many readers of the English Bible, since it has made its way into most modern translations. Here, after Jesus says "This is my body," he continues with the words "'which has been given for you; do this in remembrance of me'; And the cup likewise after supper, saying 'this cup is the new covenant in my blood which is shed for you.'"

These are the familiar words of the "institution" of the Lord's Supper, known in a very similar form also from Paul's first letter to the Corinthians (1 Cor. 11:23–25). Despite the fact that they are familiar, there are good reasons for thinking that these verses were not originally in Luke's Gospel but were added to stress that it was Jesus's broken body and shed blood that brought salvation "for you." For one thing, it is hard to explain why a scribe would have *omitted* the verses if they were original to Luke (there is no homoeoteleuton, for example, that would explain an omission), especially since they make such clear and smooth sense when they are added. In fact, when the verses are taken away, most people find that the text sounds a bit truncated. The unfamiliarity of the truncated version (without the verses) may have been what led scribes to add the verses.

Moreover, it should be noted that the verses, as familiar as they are, do not represent Luke's own understanding of the death of Jesus. For it is a striking feature of Luke's portrayal of Jesus's death—this may sound strange at first—that he *never*, anywhere else, indicates that the death itself is what brings salvation from sin. Nowhere in Luke's entire two-volume work (Luke and Acts), is Jesus's death said to be "for you." In fact, on the two occasions in which Luke's source (Mark) indicates that it was by Jesus's death that salvation came (Mark

10:45; 15:39), Luke *changed* the wording of the text (or eliminated it). Luke, in other words, has a different understanding of the way in which Jesus's death leads to salvation than does Mark (and Paul, and other early Christian writers).

It is easy to see Luke's own distinctive view by considering what he has to say in the book of Acts, where the apostles give a number of speeches in order to convert others to the faith. In none of these speeches, though, do the apostles indicate that Jesus's death brings atonement for sins (e.g., in chapters 3, 4, 13). It is not that Jesus's death is unimportant. It is *extremely* important for Luke—but not as an atonement. Instead, Jesus's death is what makes people realize their guilt before God (since he died even though he was innocent). Once people recognize their guilt, they turn to God in repentance, and then he forgives their sins.

Jesus's death for Luke, in other words, drives people to repentance, and it is this repentance that brings salvation. But not according to these disputed verses that are missing from some of our early witnesses: here Jesus's death is portrayed as an atonement "for you."

Originally the verses appear not to have been part of Luke's Gospel. Why, then, were they added? In a later dispute with Marcion, Tertullian emphasized:

> *Jesus declared plainly enough what he meant by the bread, when he called the bread his own body. He likewise, when mentioning the cup and making the new testament to be sealed in his blood, affirms the reality of his body. For no blood can belong to a body which is not a body of flesh. Thus from the evidence of the flesh we get a proof of the body, and a proof of the flesh from the evidence of the blood.*
> (Against Marcion 4, 40)

It appears that the verses were added to stress Jesus's real body and flesh, which he really sacrificed for the sake of others. This may not have been Luke's own emphasis, but it certainly was the emphasis of the proto-orthodox scribes who altered their text of Luke in order to counter docetic Christologies such as that of Marcion.[9]

. . .

Another verse that appears to have been added to Luke's Gospel by proto-orthodox scribes is Luke 24:12, which occurs just after Jesus has been raised from the dead. Some of Jesus's women followers go to the tomb, find that he is not there, and are told that he has been raised. They go back to tell the disciples, who refuse to believe them because it strikes them as a "silly tale." Then, in many manuscripts, occurs the account of 24:12: "But Peter, rising up, ran to the tomb, and stooping down he saw the linen cloths alone, and he returned home marveling at what had happened."

There are excellent reasons for thinking that this verse was not originally part of Luke's Gospel. It contains a large number of stylistic features found nowhere else in Luke, including most of the key words of the text, for example, "stooping down" and "linen cloths" (a different word was used for Jesus's burial cloths earlier in the account). Moreover, it is hard to see why someone would want to remove this verse, if it actually formed part of the Gospel (again, there is no homoeoteleuton, etc., to account for an accidental omission). As many readers have noted, the verse sounds very much like a summary of an account in the Gospel of John (20:3–10), where Peter and the "beloved disciple" race to the tomb and find it empty. Could it be that someone has added a similar account, in summary fashion, to Luke's Gospel?

If so, it is a striking addition, because it supports so well the proto-orthodox position that Jesus was not simply some kind of phantasm but had a real, physical body. Moreover, this was recognized by the chief apostle, Peter, himself. Thus, rather than letting the story of the empty tomb remain a "silly tale" of some untrustworthy women, the text now shows that the story was not just believable but true: as verified by none other than Peter (a trustworthy *man,* one might suppose). Even more important, the verse stresses the physical nature of the resurrection, because the only thing left in the tomb is the physical proof of the resurrection: the linen cloths that had covered Jesus's body. This was a fleshly resurrection of a real person. The importance of this point is made, once again, by Tertullian:

Now if [Christ's] death be denied, because of the denial of his flesh, there will be no certainty of his resurrection. For he rose not, for the very same reason that he died not, even because he possessed not the reality of the flesh, to which as death accrues, so does resurrection likewise. Similarly, if Christ's resurrection be nullified, ours also is destroyed. (Against Marcion 3, 8)

Christ must have had a real fleshly body, which was really raised, physically, from the dead.

Not only did Jesus physically suffer and die, and physically come to be raised: for the proto-orthodox he was also physically exalted to heaven. A final textual variant to consider comes at the end of Luke's Gospel, after the resurrection has occurred (but on the same day). Jesus has spoken to his followers for the last time, and then departs from them:

And it happened that while he was blessing them, he was removed from them; and they returned into Jerusalem with great joy. (Luke 24:51–52)

It is interesting to note, however, that in some of our earliest witnesses—including the Alexandrian manuscript Codex Sinaiticus—there is an addition to the text.[10] After it indicates that "he was removed from them," in these manuscripts it states "and he was taken up into heaven." This is a significant addition because it stresses the physicality of Jesus's departure at his ascension (rather than the bland "he was removed"). In part, this is an intriguing variant because the same author, Luke, in his second volume, the book of Acts, *again* narrates Jesus's ascension into heaven, but explicitly states that it took place "forty days" after the resurrection (Acts 1:1–11).

This makes it difficult to believe that Luke wrote the phrase in question in Luke 24:51—since surely he would not think Jesus ascended to heaven on the day of his resurrection if he indicates at the beginning of his second volume that he ascended forty days later. It is noteworthy, too, that the key word in question ("was taken up") never occurs anywhere else in either the Gospel of Luke or the book of Acts.

Why might someone have added these words? We know that proto-orthodox Christians wanted to stress the real, physical nature of Jesus's departure from earth: Jesus physically left, and will physically return, bringing with him physical salvation. This they argued against docetists, who maintained that it was all only an appearance. It may be that a scribe involved in these controversies modified his text in order to stress the point.

ANTISEPARATIONIST ALTERATIONS OF THE TEXT

Early Christian Separationists

A third area of concern to proto-orthodox Christians of the second and third centuries involved Christian groups who understood Christ not as only human (like the adoptionists) and not as only divine (like the docetists) but as two beings, one completely human and one completely divine.[11] We might call this a "separationist" Christology because it divided Jesus Christ into two: the man Jesus (who was completely human) and the divine Christ (who was completely divine). According to most proponents of this view, the man Jesus was temporarily indwelt by the divine being, Christ, enabling him to perform his miracles and deliver his teachings; but before Jesus's death, the Christ abandoned him, forcing him to face his crucifixion alone.

This separationist Christology was most commonly advocated by groups of Christians that scholars have called Gnostic.[12] The term Gnosticism comes from the Greek word for knowledge, *gnosis*. It is applied to a wide range of groups of early Christians who stressed the importance of secret knowledge for salvation. According to most of these groups, the material world we live in was not the creation of the one true God. It came about as a result of a disaster in the divine realm, in which one of the (many) divine beings was for some mysterious reason excluded from the heavenly places; as a result of her fall from divinity the material world came to be created by a lesser deity, who captured her and imprisoned her in human bodies here on earth. Some human beings thus have a spark of the divine within them, and they need to learn the truth of who they are, where they came from, how they got here, and how they can return. Learning this truth will lead to their salvation.

This truth consists of secret teachings, mysterious "knowledge" (*gnosis*), which can only be imparted by a divine being from the heavenly realm. For Christian Gnostics, Christ is this divine revealer of the truths of salvation; in many Gnostic systems, the Christ came into the man Jesus at his baptism, empowered him for his ministry, and then at the end left him to die on the cross. That is why Jesus cried out, "My God, my God, why have you forsaken me?" For these Gnostics, the Christ literally *had* forsaken Jesus (or "left him behind"). After Jesus's death, though, he raised him from the dead as a reward for his faithfulness, and continued through him to teach his disciples the secret truths that can lead to salvation.

Proto-orthodox Christians found this teaching offensive on just about every level. For them, the material world is not an evil place that resulted from a cosmic disaster, but is the good creation of the one true God. For them, salvation comes by faith in Christ's death and resurrection, not by learning the secret *gnosis* that can illuminate the truth of the human condition. And most important for our purposes here, for them, Jesus Christ is not two beings, but one being, both divine and human, at one and the same time.

Antiseparationist Changes of the Text

The controversies over separationist Christologies played some role in the transmission of the texts that were to become the New Testament. We have seen one instance already in a variant we considered in chapter 5, Hebrews 2:9, in which Jesus was said, in the original text of the letter, to have died "apart from God." In that discussion, we saw that most scribes had accepted the variant reading, which indicated that Christ died "by the grace of God," even though that was not the text that the author originally wrote. But we did not consider at any length the question of why scribes might have found the original text potentially dangerous and therefore worth modifying. Now, with this brief background to Gnostic understandings of Christ, the change makes better sense. For according to separationist Christologies, Christ really did die "apart from God," in that it was at his cross that the divine element that had indwelt him removed itself, so that Jesus died alone. Aware that the text could be used to support such a view, Christian scribes made a simple but profound change. Now rather than indicating that his death came apart from God, the text affirmed that Christ's death was "by the grace of God." This, then, is an antiseparationist alteration.

A second intriguing example of the phenomenon occurs almost exactly where one might expect to find it, in a Gospel account of Jesus's crucifixion. As I have already indicated, in Mark's Gospel Jesus is silent throughout the entire proceeding of his crucifixion. The soldiers crucify him, the passers-by and Jewish leaders mock him, as do the two criminals who are crucified with him; and he says not a word—until the very end, when death is near, and Jesus cries out the words taken from Psalm 22: "Eloi, Eloi, lema sabachthani," which translated means "My God, my God, why have you forsaken me?" (Mark 15:34).

It is interesting to note that according to the proto-orthodox writer Irenaeus, Mark was the Gospel of choice for those "who separated Jesus from the Christ"—that is, for Gnostics who embraced a separationist Christology.[13] We have solid evidence to suggest that some Gnostics took this last saying of Jesus literally, to indicate that it was at this point that the divine Christ departed from Jesus (since divinity cannot experience mortality and death). The evidence comes from Gnostic documents that reflect on the significance of this moment in Jesus's life. Thus, for example, the apocryphal Gospel of Peter, which some have suspected of having a separationist Christology, quotes the words in a slightly different form, "My power, O power, you have left me!" Even more striking is the Gnostic text known as the Gospel of Philip, in which the verse is quoted and then given a separationist interpretation:

"My God, my God, why O Lord have you forsaken me?" For it was
on the cross that he said these words, for it was there that he was
divided.

Proto-orthodox Christians knew of both these Gospels and their
interpretations of this climactic moment of Jesus's crucifixion. It is
perhaps no great surprise, then, that the text of Mark's Gospel was
changed by some scribes in a way that would have circumvented this
Gnostic explanation. In one Greek manuscript and several Latin witnesses, Jesus is said not to call out the traditional "cry of dereliction"
from Psalm 22, but instead to cry out, "My God, my God, why have
you mocked me?"

This change of the text makes for an interesting reading—and
one particularly suited to its literary context. For as already indicated,
nearly everyone else in the story has mocked Jesus at this point—the
Jewish leaders, the passers-by, and both robbers. Now, with this variant reading, even God *himself* is said to have mocked Jesus. In despair,
Jesus then utters a loud cry and dies. This is a powerful scene, filled
with pathos.

Nonetheless the reading is not original, as shown by the circumstance that it is lacking in nearly all our oldest and best witnesses (including those of the Alexandrian text) as well as by the fact that it does
not correspond to the Aramaic words Jesus actually utters (*lema*
sabachthani—which mean "why have you forsaken me," not "why
have you mocked me").

Why, then, did scribes alter the text? Given its usefulness for those
arguing in favor of a separationist Christology, there can be little
question why. Proto-orthodox scribes were concerned that the text
not be used against them by their Gnostic opponents. They made an
important, and contextually suitable change, so that now rather than
abandoning Jesus, God is said to have mocked him.

As a final example of a variant of this kind, made in order to counter
a separationist Christology, we might consider a passage that occurs in
the Epistle of 1 John. In the oldest form of the text of 4:2–3, we are told:

By this you know the Spirit of God. Every spirit that confesses that Jesus Christ has come in the flesh is from God; and every spirit that does not confess Jesus is not from God. This is the spirit of the anti-Christ.

This is a clear, straightforward passage: only those who acknowledge that Jesus really came in the flesh (as opposed, say, to accepting the docetist view) belong to God; those who do not acknowledge this are opposed to Christ (anti-Christs). But there is an interesting textual variant that occurs in the second half of the passage. Instead of referring to the one "that does not confess Jesus," several witnesses refer instead to the one "that looses Jesus." What does that mean—*looses* Jesus—and why did this textual variant make its way into some manuscripts?

To start with, I should stress that it is not in very *many* manuscripts. In fact, among the Greek witnesses it occurs only in the margin of one tenth-century manuscript (Ms. 1739). But this, as we have seen, is a remarkable manuscript because it appears to have been copied from one of the fourth century, and its marginal notes record the names of church fathers who had different readings for certain parts of the text. In this particular instance, the marginal note indicates that the reading "looses Jesus" was known to several late-second- and early-third-century church fathers, Irenaeus, Clement, and Origen. Moreover, it appears in the Latin Vulgate. Among other things, this shows that the variant was popular during the time in which proto-orthodox Christians were debating with Gnostics over matters of Christology.

Still, the variant probably cannot be accepted as the "original" text, given its sparse attestation—it is not found, for example, in any of our earliest and best manuscripts (in fact, not in any Greek manuscript except for this one marginal note). Why, though, would it have been created by a Christian scribe? It appears to have been created to provide a "biblical" attack on separationist Christologies, in which Jesus and Christ are divided from each other into separate entities, or as this variant would have it, in which Jesus is "loosed" from the Christ. Anyone who supports such a view, the textual variant suggests, is not from God, but is in fact an anti-Christ. Once again, then, we have a variant that was generated in the context of the christological disputes of the second and third centuries.

CONCLUSION

One of the factors contributing to scribes' alterations of their texts was their own historical context. Christian scribes of the second and third centuries were involved with the debates and disputes of their day, and occasionally these disputes affected the reproduction of the texts over which the debates raged. That is, scribes occasionally altered their texts to make them say what they were already believed to mean.

This is not necessarily a bad thing, since we can probably assume that most scribes who changed their texts often did so either semiconsciously or with good intent. The reality, though, is that once they altered their texts, the words of the texts quite literally became different words, and these altered words necessarily affected the interpretations of the words by later readers. Among the reasons for these alterations were the theological disputes of the second and third centuries, as scribes sometimes modified their texts in light of the adoptionistic, docetic, and separationist Christologies that were vying for attention in the period.

Other historical factors were also at work, factors relating less to theological controversy and more to social conflicts of the day, conflicts involving such things as the role of women in early Christian churches, the Christian opposition to Jews, and the Christian defense against attacks by pagan opponents. In the next chapter we will see how these other social conflicts affected the early scribes who reproduced the texts of scripture in the centuries before the copying of texts became the province of professional scribes.

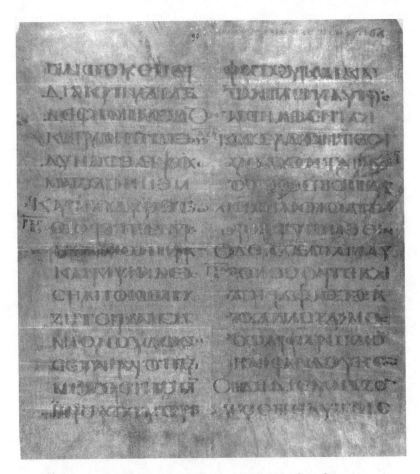

*One of the earliest copies of the Gospel of Matthew, from
the sixth century, written in Greek letters on papyrus.*

7

THE SOCIAL WORLDS
OF THE TEXT

I t is probably safe to say that the copying of early Christian texts was by and large a "conservative" process. The scribes—whether non-professional scribes in the early centuries or professional scribes of the Middle Ages—were intent on "conserving" the textual tradition they were passing on. Their ultimate concern was not to modify the tradition, but to preserve it for themselves and for those who would follow them. Most scribes, no doubt, tried to do a faithful job in making sure that the text they reproduced was the same text they inherited.

Nonetheless, changes came to be made in the early Christian texts. Scribes would sometimes—lots of times—make accidental mistakes, by misspelling a word, leaving out a line, or simply bungling the sentences they were supposed to be copying; and on occasion they changed the text deliberately, making a "correction" to the text, which in fact turned out to be an alteration of what the text's author had originally written. We examined in the preceding chapter one kind of intentional change—changes relating to some of the theological controversies raging in the second and third centuries, when most of the changes of our textual tradition were made. I do not want to convey the false impression that this kind of theological change of the text happened every time a scribe sat down to copy a passage. It happened on occasion. And when it happened, it had a profound effect on the text.

In this chapter, we will look at other contextual factors that led, on occasion, to the alteration of the text. In particular, we will be examining three kinds of disputes that were evident in the early Christian communities: one internal dispute, about the role of women in the church, and two external disputes, one with non-Christian Jews and the other with antagonistic pagans. We will see in each case that, on scattered occasions, these disputes also played a role in the transmission of the texts that scribes (themselves involved in the disputes) were reproducing for their communities.

WOMEN AND THE TEXTS OF SCRIPTURE

Debates over the role of women in the church did not play an enormous role in the transmission of the texts of the New Testament, but they did play a role, in interesting and important passages. To make sense of the kinds of textual changes that were made, we need some background on the nature of these debates.[1]

Women in the Early Church

Modern scholars have come to recognize that disputes over the role of women in the early church occurred precisely because women *had* a role—often a significant and publicly high profile role. Moreover, this was the case from the very beginning, starting with the ministry of Jesus himself. It is true that Jesus's closest followers—the twelve disciples—were all men, as would be expected of a Jewish teacher in first-century Palestine. But our earliest Gospels indicate that Jesus was also accompanied by women on his travels, and that some of these women provided for him and his disciples financially, serving as patrons for his itinerant preaching ministry (see Mark 15:40–51; Luke 8:1–3). Jesus is said to have engaged in public dialogue with women and to have ministered to them in public (Mark 7:24–30; John 4:1–42). In particular, we are told that women accompanied Jesus during his final trip to Jerusalem, where they were present at his crucifixion and where they alone remained faithful to him at the end, when the male disciples had fled (Matt. 27:55; Mark 15:40–41). Most significant of all, each of our Gospels indicates that it was women—Mary Magdalene alone, or with several companions—who discovered his empty tomb and so were the first to know about and testify to Jesus's resurrection from the dead (Matt. 28:1–10; Mark 16:1–8; Luke 23:55–24:10; John 20:1–2).

It is intriguing to ask what it was about Jesus's message that particularly attracted women. Most scholars remain convinced that Jesus proclaimed the coming Kingdom of God, in which there would be no more injustice, suffering, or evil, in which all people, rich and poor, slave and free, men and women, would be on equal footing. This obviously proved particularly attractive as a message of hope to those who in the present age were underprivileged—the poor, the sick, the outcast. And the women.[2]

In any event, it is clear that even after his death, Jesus's message continued to be attractive to women. Some of Christianity's early opponents among the pagans, including, for example, the late-second-century critic Celsus, whom we have met before, denigrated the religion on the grounds that it was made up largely of children, slaves, and women (i.e., those of no social standing in society at large). Strikingly, Origen, who wrote the Christian response to Celsus, did not deny the charge but tried to turn it against Celsus in an attempt to show that God can take what is weak and invest it with strength.

But we do not need to wait until the late second century to see that women played a major role in the early Christian churches. We already get a clear sense of this from the earliest Christian writer whose works have survived, the apostle Paul. The Pauline letters of the New Testament provide ample evidence that women held a prominent place in the emerging Christian communities from the earliest of times. We might consider, for example, Paul's letter to the Romans, at the end of which he sends greetings to various members of the Roman congregation (chapter 16). Although Paul names more men than women here, it is clear that women were seen as in no way inferior to their male counterparts in the church. Paul mentions Phoebe, for example, who is a deacon (or minister) in the church of Cenchreae, and Paul's own patron, whom he entrusts with the task of carrying his letter to Rome (vv. 1–2). And there is Prisca, who along with her husband, Aquila, is responsible for missionary work among the Gentiles and who supports a Christian congregation in her home (vv. 3–4: notice that she is mentioned first, ahead of her husband). Then there is Mary, a colleague of Paul's who works among the Romans (v. 6); there are also Tryphaena, Tryphosa, and Persis, women whom Paul calls his "co-workers" in the gospel (vv. 6, 12). And there are Julia and the mother of Rufus and the sister of Nereus, all of whom appear to have a high profile in the community (vv. 13, 15). Most impressive of all, there is Junia, a woman whom Paul calls "foremost among the apostles" (v. 7). The apostolic band was evidently larger than the list of twelve men with whom most people are familiar.

Women, in short, appear to have played a significant role in the churches of Paul's day. To some extent, this high profile was unusual in the Greco-Roman world. And it may have been rooted, as I have argued, in Jesus's proclamation that in the coming Kingdom there would be equality of men and women. This appears to have been Paul's message as well, as can be seen, for example, in his famous declaration in Galatians:

> *For as many of you as were baptized into Christ have put on Christ. There is neither Jew nor Greek, neither slave nor free; there is not male and female; for all of you are one in Jesus Christ. (Gal. 3:27–28)*

The equality in Christ may have manifested itself in the actual worship services of the Pauline communities. Rather than being silent "hearers of the word," women appear to have been actively involved in the weekly fellowship meetings, participating, for example, by praying and prophesying, much as the men did (1 Corinthians 11).

At the same time, to modern interpreters it may appear that Paul did not take his view of the relationship of men and women in Christ to what could be thought of as its logical conclusion. He did require, for example, that when women prayed and prophesied in church they do so with their heads covered, to show that they were "under authority" (1 Cor. 11:3–16, esp. v. 10). In other words, Paul did not urge a social revolution in the relationship of men and women—just as he did not urge the abolition of slavery, even though he maintained that in Christ there "is neither slave nor free." Instead he insisted that since "the time is short" (until the coming of the Kingdom), everyone should be content with the roles they had been given, and that no one should seek to change their status—whether slave, free, married, single, male, or female (1 Cor. 7:17–24).

At best, then, this can be seen as an ambivalent attitude toward the role of women: they were equal in Christ and were allowed to participate in the life of the community, but as *women,* not as *men* (they were, for example, not to remove their veils and so appear as men, without an "authority" on their head). This ambivalence on Paul's part had an interesting effect on the role of women in the churches after his day. In some churches it was the equality in Christ that was emphasized; in others it was the need for women to remain subservient to men. And so in some churches women played very important, leadership roles; in others, their roles were diminished and their voices quieted. Reading later documents associated with Paul's churches, after his death, we can see that disputes arose about the roles women should play; eventually there came an effort to suppress the role of women in the churches altogether.

This becomes evident in a letter that was written in Paul's name. Scholars today are by and large convinced that 1 Timothy was not written by Paul but by one of his later, second-generation followers.[3] Here, in one of the (in)famous passages dealing with women in the New Testament, we are told that women must not be allowed to teach men because they were created inferior, as indicated by God himself in the Law; God created Eve second, for the sake of man; and a woman (related to Eve) must not therefore lord it over a man (related to Adam) through her teaching. Furthermore, according to this author, everyone knows what happens when a woman does assume the role of teacher: she is easily duped (by the devil) and leads the man astray. So, women are to stay at home and maintain the virtues appropriate to women, bearing children for their husbands and preserving their modesty. As the passage itself reads:

> Let a woman learn in silence with full submission. I permit no woman to teach or to have authority over a man; she is to keep silent. For Adam was formed first, then Eve; and Adam was not deceived, but the woman was deceived and became a transgressor. Yet she will be saved through childbearing, provided they continue in faith and love and holiness, with modesty. (1 Tim. 2:11–15)

This seems a long way from Paul's view that "in Christ there is . . . not male and female." As we move into the second century, the battle lines appear clearly drawn. There are some Christian communities that stress the importance of women and allow them to play significant roles in the church, and there are others that believe women must be silent and subservient to the men of the community.

The scribes who were copying the texts that later became scripture were obviously involved in these debates. And on occasion the debates made an impact on the text being copied, as passages were changed to reflect the views of the scribes who were reproducing them. In almost every instance in which a change of this sort occurs, the text is changed in order to limit the role of women and to minimize their importance to the Christian movement. Here we can consider just a few examples.

Textual Alterations Involving Women

One of the most important passages in the contemporary discussion of the role of women in the church is found in 1 Corinthians 14. As represented in most of our modern English translations, the passage reads as follows.

> [33]*For God is not a God of confusion but of peace. As in all the churches of the saints,* [34]*let the women keep silent. For it is not permitted for them to speak, but to be in subjection, just as the law says.* [35]*But if they wish to learn anything, let them ask their own husbands at home. For it is shameful for a woman to speak in church.* [36]*What! Did the word go forth only from you, or has it reached you alone?*

The passage appears to be a clear and straightforward injunction for women not to speak (let alone teach!) in the church, very much like the passage from 1 Timothy 2. As we have seen, however, most scholars are convinced that Paul did not write the 1 Timothy passage, because it occurs in a letter that appears to have been written instead by a second-generation follower of Paul in his name. No one doubts, however, that Paul wrote 1 Corinthians. But there *are* doubts about this passage. For as it turns out, the verses in question (vv. 34–35) are shuffled around in some of our important textual witnesses. In three Greek manuscripts and a couple of Latin witnesses, they are found not here, after verse 33, but later, after verse 40. That has led some scholars to surmise that the verses were not written by Paul but originated as a kind of marginal note added by a scribe, possibly under the influence of 1 Timothy 2. The note was then inserted in different places of the text by various scribes—some placing the note after verse 33 and others inserting it after verse 40.

There are good reasons for thinking that Paul did not originally write these verses. For one thing, they do not fit well into their immediate context. In this part of 1 Corinthians 14, Paul is addressing the issue of prophecy in the church, and is giving instructions to Christian prophets concerning how they are to behave during the Christian services of worship. This is the theme of verses 26–33, and it is the theme again of verses 36–40. If one removes verses 34–35 from their context, the passage seems to flow seamlessly as a discussion of the role of Christian prophets. The discussion of women appears, then, as intrusive in its immediate context, breaking into instructions that Paul is giving about a different matter.

Not only do the verses seem intrusive in the context of chapter 14, they also appear anomalous with what Paul explicitly says elsewhere in 1 Corinthians. For earlier in the book, as we have already noticed, Paul gives instructions to women speaking in the church: according to chapter 11, when they pray and prophesy—activities that were always done aloud in the Christian services of worship—they are to be sure to wear veils on their heads (11:2–16). In *this* passage, which no one doubts Paul wrote, it is clear that Paul understands that women both can and do speak in church. In the disputed passage of chapter 14, however, it is equally clear that "Paul" forbids women from speaking at all. It is difficult to reconcile these two views—either Paul allowed women to speak (with covered heads, chapter 11) or not (chapter 14). As it seems unreasonable to think that Paul would flat out contradict himself within the short space of three chapters, it appears that the verses in question do not derive from Paul.

And so on the basis of a combination of evidence—several manuscripts that shuffle the verses around, the immediate literary context, and the context within 1 Corinthians as a whole—it appears that Paul did not write 1 Cor. 14:34–35. One would have to assume, then, that these verses are a scribal alteration of the text, originally made, perhaps, as a marginal note and then eventually, at an early stage of the copying of 1 Corinthians, placed in the text itself. The alteration was no doubt made by a scribe who was concerned to emphasize that women should have no public role in the church, that they should be silent and subservient to their husbands. This view then came to be incorporated into the text itself, by means of a textual alteration.[4]

We might consider briefly several other textual changes of a similar sort. One occurs in a passage I have already mentioned, Romans 16, in which Paul speaks of a woman, Junia, and a man who was presumably her husband, Andronicus, both of whom he calls "foremost among the apostles" (v. 7). This is a significant verse, because it is the only place in the New Testament in which a woman is referred to as an apostle. Interpreters have been so impressed by the passage that a large number of them have insisted that it cannot mean what it says, and so have translated the verse as referring *not* to a woman named Junia but to a *man* named Junias, who along with his companion Andronicus is praised as an apostle. The problem with this translation is that whereas Junia was a common name for a woman, there is no evidence in the ancient world for "Junias" as a man's name. Paul is referring to a woman named Junia, even though in some modern English Bibles (you may want to check your own!) translators continue to refer to this female apostle as if she were a man named Junias.[5]

Some scribes also had difficulty with ascribing apostleship to this otherwise unknown woman, and so made a very slight change in the text to circumvent the problem. In some of our manuscripts, rather than saying "Greet Andronicus and Junia, my relatives and fellow prisoners, who are foremost among the apostles," the text is now changed so as to be more readily translated: "Greet Andronicus and Junia, my relatives; and also greet my fellow prisoners who are foremost among the apostles." With this textual change, no longer does one need to worry about a woman being cited among the apostolic band of men!

A similar change was made by some scribes who copied the book of Acts. In chapter 17 we learn that Paul and his missionary companion Silas spent time in Thessalonica preaching the gospel of Christ to the Jews of the local synagogue. We are told in verse 4 that the pair made some important converts: "And some of them were persuaded and joined with Paul and Silas, as did a great many of the pious Greeks, along with a large number of prominent women."

The idea of women being prominent—let alone prominent converts—was too much for some scribes, and so the text came to be
changed in some manuscripts, so that now we are told: "And some of
them were persuaded and joined with Paul and Silas, as did a great
many of the pious Greeks, along with a large number of wives of
prominent men." Now it is the men who are prominent, not the wives
who converted.

Among Paul's companions in the book of Acts were a husband
and wife named Aquila and Priscilla; sometimes when they are mentioned, the author gives the wife's name *first,* as if she had some kind
of special prominence either in the relationship or in the Christian
mission (as happens in Rom. 16:3 as well, where she is called Prisca).
Not surprisingly, scribes occasionally took umbrage at this sequenc-
ing and reversed it, so that the man was given his due by having his
name mentioned first: Aquila and Priscilla rather than Priscilla and
Aquila.[6]

In short, there were debates in the early centuries of the church
over the role of women, and on occasion these debates spilled over
into the textual transmission of the New Testament itself, as scribes
sometimes changed their texts in order to make them coincide more
closely with the scribes' own sense of the (limited) role of women in
the church.

JEWS AND THE TEXTS OF SCRIPTURE

To this point we have looked at various controversies that were internal to early Christianity—disputes over christological issues and over
the role of women in the church—and have considered how they affected the scribes who reproduced their sacred texts. These were not
the only kinds of controversy with which Christians were involved,
however. Just as poignant for those involved, and significant for our
considerations here, were conflicts with those *outside* the faith, Jews
and pagans who stood in opposition to Christians and engaged in

polemical controversies with them. These controversies also played some role in the transmission of the texts of scripture. We can begin by considering the disputes that Christians of the early centuries had with non-Christian Jews.

Jews and Christians in Conflict

One of the ironies of early Christianity is that Jesus himself was a Jew who worshiped the Jewish God, kept Jewish customs, interpreted the Jewish law, and acquired Jewish disciples, who accepted him as the Jewish messiah. Yet, within just a few decades of his death, Jesus's followers had formed a religion that stood over-against Judaism. How did Christianity move so quickly from being a Jewish sect to being an anti-Jewish religion?

This is a difficult question, and to provide a satisfying answer would require a book of its own.[7] Here, I can at least provide a historical sketch of the rise of anti-Judaism within early Christianity as a way of furnishing a plausible context for Christian scribes who occasionally altered their texts in anti-Jewish ways.

The last twenty years have seen an explosion of research into the historical Jesus. As a result, there is now an enormous range of opinion about how Jesus is best understood—as a rabbi, a social revolutionary, a political insurgent, a cynic philosopher, an apocalyptic prophet: the options go on and on. The one thing that nearly all scholars agree upon, however, is that *no matter how* one understands the major thrust of Jesus's mission, he must be situated in his own context as a first-century Palestinian Jew. Whatever else he was, Jesus was thoroughly Jewish, in every way—as were his disciples. At some point—probably before his death, but certainly afterward—Jesus's followers came to think of him as the Jewish messiah. This term *messiah* was understood in different ways by different Jews in the first century, but one thing that all Jews appear to have had in common when thinking about the messiah was that he was to be a figure of grandeur and power, who in some way—for example, through raising a Jewish army or by leading the heavenly angels—would overcome Israel's enemies and establish Israel as a sovereign state that could be ruled by God himself (possibly through human agency). Christians who called Jesus the messiah obviously had a difficult time convincing others of this claim, since rather than being a powerful warrior or a heavenly judge, Jesus was widely known to have been an itinerant preacher who had gotten on the wrong side of the law and had been crucified as a low-life criminal.

To call Jesus the messiah was for most Jews completely ludicrous. Jesus was not the powerful leader of the Jews. He was a weak and powerless nobody—executed in the most humiliating and painful way devised by the Romans, the ones with the real power. Christians, however, insisted that Jesus *was* the messiah, that his death was not a miscarriage of justice or an unforeseen event, but an act of God, by which he brought salvation to the world.

What were Christians to do with the fact that they had trouble convincing most Jews of their claims about Jesus? They could not, of course, admit that they themselves were wrong. And if *they* weren't wrong, who was? It had to be the Jews. Early on in their history, Christians began to insist that Jews who rejected their message were recalcitrant and blind, that in rejecting the message about Jesus, they were rejecting the salvation provided by the Jewish God himself. Some such claims were being made already by our earliest Christian author, the apostle Paul. In his first surviving letter, written to the Christians of Thessalonica, Paul says:

> For you, our brothers, became imitators of the churches of God that are in Judea in Christ Jesus, because you suffered the same things from your own compatriots as they did from the Jews, who killed both the Lord Jesus and the prophets, and persecuted us, and are not pleasing to God, and are opposed to all people. (1 Thess. 2:14–15)

Paul came to believe that Jews rejected Jesus because they understood that their own special standing before God was related to the fact that they both had and kept the Law that God had given them

(Rom. 10:3–4). For Paul, however, salvation came to the Jews, as well as to the Gentiles, not through the Law but through faith in the death and resurrection of Jesus (Rom. 3:21–22). Thus, keeping the Law could have no role in salvation; Gentiles who became followers of Jesus were instructed, therefore, not to think they could improve their standing before God by keeping the Law. They were to remain as they were—and not convert to become Jews (Gal. 2:15–16).

Other early Christians, of course, had other opinions—as they did on nearly every issue of the day! Matthew, for example, seems to presuppose that even though it is the death and resurrection of Jesus that brings salvation, his followers will naturally keep the Law, just as Jesus himself did (see Matt. 5:17–20). Eventually, though, it became widely held that Christians were distinct from Jews, that following the Jewish law could have no bearing on salvation, and that joining the Jewish people would mean identifying with the people who had rejected their own messiah, who had, in fact, rejected their own God.

As we move into the second century we find that Christianity and Judaism had become two distinct religions, which nonetheless had a lot to say to each other. Christians, in fact, found themselves in a bit of a bind. For they acknowledged that Jesus was the messiah anticipated by the Jewish scriptures; and to gain credibility in a world that cherished what was ancient but suspected anything "recent" as a dubious novelty, Christians continued to point to the scriptures—those ancient texts of the Jews—as the foundation for their own beliefs. This meant that Christians laid claim to the Jewish Bible as their own. But was not the Jewish Bible for Jews? Christians began to insist that Jews had not only spurned their own messiah, and thereby rejected their own God, they had also misinterpreted their own scriptures. And so we find Christian writings such as the so-called *Letter of Barnabas,* a book that some early Christians considered to be part of the New Testament canon, which asserts that Judaism is and always has been a false religion, that Jews were misled by an evil angel into interpreting the laws given to Moses as literal prescriptions of how to live, when in fact they were to be interpreted allegorically.[8]

Eventually we find Christians castigating Jews in the harshest terms possible for rejecting Jesus as the messiah, with authors such as the second-century Justin Martyr claiming that the reason God commanded the Jews to be circumcised was to mark them off as a special people who deserved to be persecuted. We also find authors such as Tertullian and Origen claiming that Jerusalem was destroyed by the Roman armies in 70 C.E. as a punishment for the Jews who killed their messiah, and authors such as Melito of Sardis arguing that in killing Christ, the Jews were actually guilty of killing God.

> *Pay attention all families of the nations and observe! An extraordinary murder has taken place in the center of Jerusalem, in the city devoted to God's Law, in the city of the Hebrews, in the city of the prophets, in the city thought of as just. And who has been murdered? And who is the murderer? I am ashamed to give the answer, but give it I must. . . . The one who hung the earth in space, is himself hanged; the one who fixed the heavens in place is himself impaled; the one who firmly fixed all things is himself firmly fixed to the tree. The Lord is insulted, God has been murdered, the King of Israel has been destroyed by the right hand of Israel.* (Paschal Homily, 94–96)[9]

Clearly we have come a long way from Jesus, a Palestinian Jew who kept Jewish customs, preached to his Jewish compatriots, and taught his Jewish disciples the true meaning of the Jewish law. By the second century, though, when Christian scribes were reproducing the texts that eventually became part of the New Testament, most Christians were former pagans, non-Jews who had converted to the faith and who understood that even though this religion was based, ultimately, on faith in the Jewish God as described in the Jewish Bible, it was nonetheless completely anti-Jewish in its orientation.

Anti-Jewish Alterations of the Text

The anti-Jewishness of some second- and third-century Christian scribes played a role in how the texts of scripture were transmitted. One

of the clearest examples is found in Luke's account of the crucifixion, in
which Jesus is said to have uttered a prayer for those responsible:

> *And when they came to the place that is called "The Skull," they cru-*
> *cified him there, along with criminals, one on his right and the other*
> *on his left. And Jesus said, "Father, forgive them, for they don't know*
> *what they are doing." (Luke 23:33–34)*

As it turns out, however, this prayer of Jesus cannot be found in all
our manuscripts: it is missing from our earliest Greek witness (a papyrus called P[75], which dates to about 200 C.E.) and several other
high-quality witnesses of the fourth and later centuries; at the same
time, the prayer can be found in Codex Sinaiticus and a large range of
manuscripts, including most of those produced in the Middle Ages.
And so the question is, Did a scribe (or a number of scribes) delete the
prayer from a manuscript that originally included it? Or did a scribe
(or scribes) add it to a manuscript that originally lacked it?

Scholarly opinion has long been divided on the question. Because
the prayer is missing from several early and high-quality witnesses,
there has been no shortage of scholars to claim that it did not originally belong to the text. Sometimes they appeal to an argument based
on internal evidence. As I have pointed out, the author of the Gospel
of Luke also produced the Acts of the Apostles, and a passage similar
to this one can be found in Acts in the account of the first Christian
martyr, Stephen, the only person whose execution is described at any
length in Acts. Because Stephen was charged with blasphemy, he was
stoned to death by a crowd of angry Jews; and before he expired he
prayed, "Lord, do not hold this sin against them" (Acts 7:60).

Some scholars have argued that a scribe who did not want Jesus to
look any less forgiving than his first martyr, Stephen, added the
prayer to Luke's Gospel, so that Jesus also asks that his executioners
be forgiven. This is a clever argument, but it is not altogether convincing, for several reasons. The most compelling is this: whenever scribes
try to bring texts into harmony with each other, they tend to do so by

repeating the same words in both passages. In this case, however, we do not find identical wording, merely a similar kind of prayer. This is not the kind of "harmonization" that scribes typically make.

Also striking in conjunction with this point is that Luke, the author himself, on a number of occasions goes out of his way to show the similarities between what happened to Jesus in the Gospel and what happened to his followers in Acts: both Jesus and his followers are baptized, they both receive the Spirit at that point, they both proclaim the good news, they both come to be rejected for it, they both suffer at the hands of the Jewish leadership, and so on. What happens to Jesus in the Gospel happens to his followers in Acts. And so it would be no surprise—but rather expected—that one of Jesus's followers, who like him is executed by angry authorities, should also pray that God forgive his executioners.

There are other reasons for suspecting that Jesus's prayer of forgiveness is original to Luke 23. Throughout both Luke and Acts, for example, it is emphasized that even though Jesus was innocent (as were his followers), those who acted against him did so in ignorance. As Peter says in Acts 3: "I know that you acted in ignorance" (v. 17); or as Paul says in Acts 17: "God has overlooked the times of ignorance" (v. 27). And that is precisely the note struck in Jesus's prayer: "for they don't know what they are doing."

It appears, then, that Luke 23:34 was part of Luke's original text. Why, though, would a scribe (or a number of scribes) have wanted to delete it? Here is where understanding something about the historical context within which scribes were working becomes crucial. Readers today may wonder for *whom* Jesus is praying. Is it for the Romans who are executing him in ignorance? Or is it for the Jews who are responsible for turning him over to the Romans in the first place? However we might answer that question in trying to interpret the passage today, it is clear how it was interpreted in the early church. In almost every instance in which the prayer is discussed in the writings of the church fathers, it is clear that they interpreted the prayer as being uttered not on behalf of the Romans but on behalf of the Jews.[10] Jesus was asking God to forgive the Jewish people (or the Jewish leaders) who were responsible for his death.

Now it becomes clear why some scribes would have wanted to omit the verse. Jesus prayed for the forgiveness of *the Jews?* How could that be? For early Christians there were, in fact, two problems with the verse, taken in this way. First, they reasoned, why would Jesus pray for forgiveness for this recalcitrant people who had willfully rejected God himself? That was scarcely conceivable to many Christians. Even more telling, by the second century many Christians were convinced that God had *not* forgiven the Jews because, as mentioned earlier, they believed that he had allowed Jerusalem to be destroyed as a punishment for the Jews in killing Jesus. As the church father Origen said: "It was right that the city in which Jesus underwent such sufferings should be completely destroyed, and that the Jewish nation be overthrown" (*Against Celsus* 4, 22).[11]

The Jews knew full well what they were doing, and God obviously had not forgiven them. From this point of view, it made little sense for Jesus to ask for forgiveness for them, when no forgiveness was forthcoming. What were scribes to do with this text, then, in which Jesus prayed, "Father, forgive them, for they don't know what they are doing"? They dealt with the problem simply by excising the text, so that Jesus no longer asked that they be forgiven.

There were other passages in which the anti-Jewish sentiment of early Christian scribes made an impact on the texts they were copying. One of the most significant passages for the eventual rise of anti-Semitism is the scene of Jesus's trial in the Gospel of Matthew. According to this account, Pilate declares Jesus innocent, washing his hands to show that "I am innocent of this man's blood! You see to it!" The Jewish crowd then utters a cry that was to play such a horrendous role in the violence manifest against the Jews down through the Middle Ages, in which they appear to claim responsibility for the death of Jesus: "His blood be upon us and our children" (Matt. 27:24–25).

The textual variant we are concerned with occurs in the next verse. Pilate is said to have flogged Jesus and then "handed him over to be crucified." Anyone reading the text would naturally assume that he handed Jesus over to his own (Roman) soldiers for crucifixion. That makes it all the more striking that in some early witnesses—including one of the scribal corrections in Codex Sinaitius—the text is changed to heighten even further the Jewish culpability in Jesus's death. According to these manuscripts, Pilate "handed him over *to them* [i.e., to the Jews] in order that *they* might crucify him." Now the Jewish responsibility for Jesus's execution is absolute, a change motivated by anti-Jewish sentiment among the early Christians.

Sometimes anti-Jewish variants are rather slight and do not catch one's attention until some thought is given to the matter. For example, in the birth narrative of the Gospel of Matthew, Joseph is told to call Mary's newborn son Jesus (which means "salvation") "because he will save his people from their sins" (Matt. 1:21). It is striking that in one manuscript preserved in Syriac translation, the text instead says "because he will save *the world* from its sins." Here again it appears that a scribe was uncomfortable with the notion that the Jewish people would ever be saved.

A comparable change occurs in the Gospel of John. In chapter 4, Jesus is talking with the woman from Samaria and tells her, "You worship what you do not know; we worship what we know, because salvation comes from the Jews" (v. 22). In some Syriac and Latin manuscripts, however, the text has been changed, so that now Jesus declares that "salvation comes from Judea." In other words, it is not the Jewish people who have brought salvation to the world; it is Jesus's death in the country of Judea that has done so. Once again we might suspect that it was anti-Jewish sentiment that prompted the scribal alteration.

My final example in this brief review comes from the fifth-century Codex Bezae, a manuscript that arguably contains more interesting and intriguing variant readings than any other. In Luke 6, where the

Pharisees accuse Jesus and his disciples of breaking the Sabbath (6:1–4), we find in Codex Bezae an additional story consisting of a single verse: "On the same day he saw a man working on the Sabbath, and he said to him, 'O man, if you know what you are doing, you are blessed, but if you do not know, you are cursed, and a transgressor of the Law.'" A full interpretation of this unexpected and unusual passage would require a good deal of investigation.[12] For our purposes here it is enough to note that Jesus is quite explicit in this passage, in a way that he never is elsewhere in the Gospels. In other instances, when Jesus is accused of violating the Sabbath, he defends his activities, but never does he indicate that the Sabbath laws *are* to be violated. In this verse, on the other hand, Jesus plainly states that anyone who knows why it is legitimate to violate Sabbath is blessed for doing so; only those who don't understand why it is legitimate are doing what is wrong. Again, this is a variant that appears to relate to the rising tide of anti-Judaism in the early church.

PAGANS AND THE TEXTS OF SCRIPTURE

Thus far we have seen that internal disputes over correct doctrine or church management (the role of women) affected early Christian scribes, and so too did conflicts between church and synagogue, as the church's anti-Jewish sentiment played a role in how those scribes transmitted the texts that were eventually declared to be the New Testament. Christians in the early centuries of the church not only had to contend with heretical insiders and Jewish outsiders, they also saw themselves embattled in the world at large, a world that was for the most part made up of pagan outsiders. The word *pagan* in this context, when used by historians, does not carry negative connotations. It simply refers to anyone in the ancient world who subscribed to any of the numerous polytheistic religions of the day. Since this included anyone who was neither Jewish nor Christian, we are talking about something like 90–93 percent of the population of the empire. Christians were sometimes opposed by pagans because of their unusual form of worship and their acceptance of Jesus as the one Son of God whose death on the cross brought salvation; and occasionally this opposition came to affect the Christian scribes who were reproducing the texts of scripture.

Pagan Opposition to Christianity

Our earliest records indicate that Christians were sometimes violently opposed by pagan mobs and/or authorities.[13] The apostle Paul, for example, in a listing of his various sufferings for the sake of Christ, recounts that on three occasions he was "beaten with rods" (1 Cor. 11:25), a form of punishment used by Roman municipal authorities against criminals judged to be socially dangerous. And as we have seen, Paul writes in his first surviving letter that his Gentile-Christian congregation in Thessalonica had "suffered from your own compatriots what they [the church of Judea] did from the Jews" (1 Thess. 2:14). In the latter case, it appears that the persecution was not "official" but the result of some kind of mob violence.

In fact, most of the pagan opposition to Christians during the church's first two centuries happened on the grassroots level rather than as a result of organized, official Roman persecution. Contrary to what many people appear to think, there was nothing "illegal" about Christianity, per se, in those early years. Christianity itself was not outlawed, and Christians for the most part did not need to go into hiding. The idea that they had to stay in the Roman catacombs in order to avoid persecution, and greeted one another through secret signs such as the symbol of the fish, is nothing but the stuff of legend. It was not illegal to follow Jesus, it was not illegal to worship the Jewish God, it was not illegal to call Jesus God, it was not illegal (in most places) to hold separate meetings of fellowship and worship, it was not illegal to convince others of one's faith in Christ as the Son of God.

And yet Christians were sometimes persecuted. Why was that?

To make sense of Christian persecution, it is important to know something about pagan religions in the Roman Empire. All these religions—and there were hundreds of them—were polytheistic, worshiping many gods; all of them emphasized the need to worship these gods through acts of prayer and sacrifice. For the most part, the gods were not worshiped to secure for the worshiper a happy afterlife; by and large, people were more concerned about the *present* life, which for most people was harsh and precarious at best. The gods could provide what was impossible for people to secure for themselves—for the crops to grow, for the livestock to be fed, for enough rain to fall, for personal health and well-being, for the ability to reproduce, for victory in war, for prosperity in peace. The gods protected the state and made it great; the gods could intervene in life to make it livable, long, and happy. And they did this in exchange for simple acts of worship—worship on the state level during civic ceremonies honoring the gods, and worship on the local level, in communities and families.

When things did not go well, when there were threats of war, or drought, or famine, or disease, this could be taken as a sign that the gods were not satisfied with how they were being honored. At such times, who would be blamed for this failure to honor the gods? Obviously, those who refused to worship them. Enter the Christians.

Of course, Jews would not worship the pagan gods either, but they were widely seen as an exception to the need for all people to worship the gods, since Jews were a distinctive people with their own ancestral traditions that they faithfully followed.[14] When Christians came on the scene, however, they were not recognized as a distinctive people— they were converts from Judaism and from an entire range of pagan religions, with no blood ties to one another or any other connections except their peculiar set of religious beliefs and practices. Moreover, they were known to be antisocial, gathering together in their own communities, abandoning their own families and deserting their former friends, not participating in communal festivals of worship.

Christians were persecuted, then, because they were regarded as detrimental to the health of society, both because they refrained from worshiping the gods who protected society and because they lived together in ways that seemed antisocial. When disasters hit, or when people were afraid they might hit, who more likely as the culprits than the Christians?

Only rarely did the Roman governors of the various provinces, let alone the emperor himself, get involved in such local affairs. When they did, however, they simply treated Christians as a dangerous social group that needed to be stamped out. Christians were usually given the chance to redeem themselves by worshiping the gods in the ways demanded of them (for example, by offering some incense to a god); if they refused, they were seen as recalcitrant troublemakers and treated accordingly.

By the middle of the second century, pagan intellectuals began taking note of the Christians and attacking them in tractates written against them. These works not only portrayed the Christians themselves in negative ways. They also attacked the Christians' beliefs as ludicrous (they claimed to worship the God of the Jews, for example, and yet refused to follow the Jewish law!) and maligned their practices as scandalous. On the latter point, it was sometimes noted that Christians gathered together under the cloak of darkness, calling one another "brother" and "sister" and greeting one another with kisses; they were said to worship their god by eating the flesh and drinking the blood of the Son of God. What was one to make of such practices? If you can imagine the worst, you won't be far off. Pagan opponents claimed that Christians engaged in ritual incest (sexual acts with brothers and sisters), infanticide (killing the Son), and cannibalism (eating his flesh and drinking his blood). These charges may seem incredible today, but in a society that respected decency and openness, they were widely accepted. Christians were perceived as a nefarious lot.

In the intellectual attacks against Christians, considerable attention was paid to the founder of this newfangled and socially disreputable faith, Jesus himself.[15] Pagan writers pointed to his impoverished origins and lower-class status in order to mock Christians for thinking that he was worthy of worship as a divine being. Christians were said to worship a crucified criminal, foolishly asserting that he was some-how divine.

Some of these writers, starting near the end of the second century, actually read the Christian literature in order better to build their cases. As the pagan critic Celsus once said, concerning the basis of his attack on Christian beliefs:

> These objections come from your own writings, and we need no other witnesses: for you provide your own refutation. (Against Celsus 2, 74)

These writings were sometimes held up to ridicule, as in the words of the pagan Porphry:

> The evangelists were fiction-writers — not observers or eyewitnesses of the life of Jesus. Each of the four contradicts the other in writing his account of the events of his suffering and crucifixion. (Against the Christians 2, 12–15)[16]

In response to these kinds of attacks, claims the pagan Celsus, Christian scribes altered their texts in order to rid them of the problems so obvious to well-trained outsiders:

> Some believers, as though from a drinking bout, go so far as to oppose themselves and alter the original text of the gospel three or four or several times over, and change its character to enable them to deny difficulties in the face of criticism. (Against Celsus 2, 27)

As it turns out, we do not need to rely on pagan opponents of Christianity to find evidence of scribes occasionally changing their texts in light of pagan opposition to the faith. There are places within our surviving manuscript tradition of the New Testament that show this kind of scribal tendency at work.[17]

Before considering some of the relevant passages, I should point out that these pagan charges against Christianity and its founder did not go unanswered from the Christian side. On the contrary, as intellectuals began to be converted to the faith, starting in the mid-second century, numerous reasoned defenses, called apologies, were forth-coming from the pens of Christians. Some of these Christian authors are well known to students of early Christianity, including the likes of Justin Martyr, Tertullian, and Origen; others are lesser known but nonetheless noteworthy in their defense of the faith, including such authors as Athenagoras, Aristides, and the anonymous writer of the *Letter to Diognetus*.[18] As a group, these Christian scholars worked to show the fallacies in the arguments of their pagan opponents, arguing that, far from being socially dangerous, Christians were the glue that held society together; insisting not only that the Christian faith was reasonable but that it was the only true religion the world had ever seen; claiming that Jesus was in fact the true Son of God, whose death brought salvation; and striving to vindicate the nature of the early Christian writings as inspired and true.

How did this "apologetic" movement in early Christianity affect the second- and third-century scribes who were copying the texts of the faith?

Apologetic Alterations of the Text

Although I did not mention it at the time, we have already seen one text that appears to have been modified by scribes out of apologetic concerns. As we saw in chapter 5, Mark 1:41 originally indicated that when Jesus was approached by a leper who wanted to be healed, he became angry, reached out his hand to touch him, and said "Be cleansed." Scribes found it difficult to ascribe the emotion of anger to Jesus in this context, and so modified the text to say, instead, that Jesus felt "compassion" for the man.

It is possible that what influenced the scribes to change the text was something more than a simple desire to make a difficult passage easier to understand. One of the constant points of debate between pagan critics of Christianity and its intellectual defenders had to do with the deportment of Jesus and whether he conducted himself in a way that was worthy of one who claimed to be the Son of God. I should emphasize that this was not a dispute over whether it was conceivable that a human being could also, in some sense, be divine. That was a point on which pagans and Christians were in complete agreement, as pagans too knew of stories in which a divine being had become human and interacted with others here on earth. The question was whether Jesus behaved in such a way as to justify thinking of him as someone of that sort, or whether, instead, his attitudes and behaviors eliminated the possibility that he was actually a son of God.[19]

By this period it was widely believed among pagans that the gods were not subject to the petty emotions and whims of mere mortals, that they were, in fact, above such things.[20] How was one to determine, then, whether or not an individual was a divine being? Obviously, he would have to display powers (intellectual or physical) that were superhuman; but he would also need to comport himself in a way that was compatible with the claim that he originated in the divine realm.

We have a number of authors from this period who insist that the gods do not get "angry," as this is a human emotion induced by frustration with others, or by a sense of being wronged, or by some other petty cause. Christians, of course, could claim that God became "angry" with his people for their misbehavior. But the Christian God, too, was above any kind of peevishness. In this story about Jesus and the leper, however, there is no very obvious reason for Jesus to get angry. Given the circumstance that the text was changed during the period in which pagans and Christians were arguing over whether Jesus comported himself in a way that was appropriate to divinity, it is altogether possible that a scribe changed the text in light of that controversy. This, in other words, may have been an apologetically driven variation.

Another such alteration comes several chapters later in Mark's Gospel, in a well-known account in which Jesus's own townsfolk wonder how he could deliver such spectacular teachings and perform such spectacular deeds. As they put it, in their astonishment, "Isn't this the carpenter, the son of Mary and brother of James and Joseph and

Judas and Simon, and aren't his sisters here with us?" (Mark 6:3). How, they wondered, could someone who grew up as one of them, whose family they all knew, be able to do such things?

This is the one and only passage in the New Testament in which Jesus is called a carpenter. The word used, TEKTŌN, is typically applied in other Greek texts to anyone who makes things with his hands; in later Christian writings, for example, Jesus is said to have made "yokes and gates."[21] We should not think of him as someone who made fine cabinetry. Probably the best way to get a "feel" for this term is to liken it to something more in our experience; it would be like calling Jesus a construction worker. How could someone with *that* background be the Son of God?

This was a question that the pagan opponents of Christianity took quite seriously; in fact, they understood the question to be rhetorical: Jesus obviously could not be a son of God if he was a mere TEKTŌN. The pagan critic Celsus particularly mocked Christians on this point, tying the claim that Jesus was a "woodworker" into the fact that he was crucified (on a stake of wood) and the Christian belief in the "tree" of life.

> And everywhere they speak in their writings of the tree of life . . . I
> imagine because their master was nailed to a cross and was a carpenter
> by trade. So that if he happened to be thrown off a cliff or pushed into
> a pit or suffocated by strangling, or if he had been a cobbler or stone-
> mason or blacksmith, there would have been a cliff of life above the
> heavens, or a pit of resurrection, or a rope of immortality, or a blessed
> stone, or an iron of love, or a holy hide of leather. Would not an old
> woman who sings a story to lull a little child to sleep have been
> ashamed to whisper tales such as these? (Against Celsus 6, 34)

Celsus's Christian opponent, Origen, had to take seriously this charge that Jesus was a mere "carpenter," but oddly enough he dealt with it not by explaining it away (his normal procedure), but by denying it altogether: "[Celsus is] blind also to this, that in none of the

Gospels current in the Churches is Jesus himself ever described as being a carpenter" (*Against Celsus* 6, 36).

What are we to make of this denial? Either Origen had forgotten about Mark 6:3 or else he had a version of the text that did *not* indicate that Jesus was a carpenter. And as it turns out, we have manuscripts with just such an alternative version. In our earliest manuscript of Mark's Gospel, called P^{45}, which dates to the early third century (the time of Origen), and in several later witnesses, the verse reads differently. Here Jesus's townsfolk ask, "Is this not the *son of* the carpenter?" Now rather than being a carpenter himself, Jesus is merely the carpenter's son.[22]

Just as Origen had apologetically motivated reasons for denying that Jesus is anywhere called a carpenter, it is conceivable that a scribe modified the text—making it conform more closely with the parallel in Matthew 13:55—in order to counteract the pagan charge that Jesus could not be the Son of God because he was, after all, a mere lower-class TEKTŌN.

Another verse that appears to have been changed for apologetic reasons is Luke 23:32, which discusses Jesus's crucifixion. The translation of the verse in the New Revised Standard Version of the New Testament reads: "Two others also, who were criminals, were led away to be put to death with him." But the way the verse is worded in the Greek, it could also be translated "Two others, who were also criminals, were led away to be put to death with him." Given the ambiguity of the Greek, it is not surprising that some scribes found it necessary, for apologetic reasons, to rearrange the word order, so that it unambiguously reports that it was the two others, not Jesus as well, who were criminals.

There are other changes in the textual tradition that appear to be driven by the desire to show that Jesus, as a true son of God, could not have been "mistaken" in one of his statements, especially with regard to the future (since the Son of God, after all, would know what was to happen). It may have been this that led to the change we have already discussed in Matthew 24:36, where Jesus explicitly states that no one knows the day or the hour in which the end will come, "not even the angels of heaven nor even the Son, but the Father alone." A significant number of our manuscripts omit "nor even the Son." The reason is not hard to postulate; if Jesus does not know the future, the Christian claim that he is a divine being is more than a little compromised.

A less obvious example comes three chapters later in Matthew's crucifixion scene. We are told in Matt. 27:34 that while on the cross Jesus was given wine to drink, mixed with gall. A large number of manuscripts, however, indicate that it was not wine that he was given, but vinegar. The change may have been made to conform the text more closely with the Old Testament passage that is quoted to explain the action, Psalm 69:22. But one might wonder if something else was motivating the scribes as well. It is interesting to note that at the Last Supper, in Matt. 26:29, after distributing the cup of wine to his disciples, Jesus explicitly states that he will not drink wine again until he does so in the kingdom of the Father. Was the change of 27:34 from wine to vinegar meant to safeguard that prediction, so that he in fact did not taste wine after claiming that he would not?

Or we might consider the alteration to Jesus's prediction to the Jewish high priest at his trial in Mark 14:62. When asked whether he is the Christ, the Son of the Blessed, Jesus replies, "I am, and you will see the Son of Man seated at the right hand of power and coming with the clouds of heaven." Widely considered by modern scholars to embody or approximate an authentic saying of Jesus, these words have proved discomforting for many Christians since near the end of the first century. For the Son of Man never did arrive on the clouds of heaven. Why then did Jesus predict that the high priest would himself see him come? The historical answer may well be that Jesus actually thought that the high priest would see it, that is, that it would happen within his lifetime. But, obviously, in the context of second-century apologetics, this could be taken as a false prediction. It is no wonder that one of our earliest witnesses to Mark modifies the verse by eliminating the offending words, so that now Jesus simply says that the high priest will see the Son of Man seated at the right hand of power with the clouds of heaven. No mention remains of an imminent appearance by One who, in fact, never came.

In sum, a number of passages in our surviving manuscripts appear to embody the apologetic concerns of the early Christians, especially as these relate to the founder of their faith, Jesus himself. Just as with theological conflicts in the early church, the question of the role of women, and the controversies with Jews, so too with the disputes raging between Christians and their cultured despisers among the pagans: all of these controversies came to affect the texts that were eventually to become part of the book that we now call the New Testament, as this book—or rather this set of books—was copied by nonprofessional scribes in the second and third centuries, and occasionally came to be altered in light of the contexts of their day.

One of the most famous and ornate manuscript pages in existence, the frontispiece of the Gospel of John in the Latin Lindisfarne Gospels (off the northeast coast of Northumberland, England).

Conclusion

CHANGING SCRIPTURE

Scribes, Authors, and Readers

I began this book on a personal note by describing how I became interested in the question of the New Testament text and why it took on so much importance for me. I think what has held my interest over the years has been the mystery of it all. In many ways, being a textual critic is like doing detective work. There is a puzzle to be solved and evidence to be uncovered. The evidence is often ambiguous, capable of being interpreted in various ways, and a case has to be made for one solution of the problem over another.

The more I studied the manuscript tradition of the New Testament, the more I realized just how radically the text had been altered over the years at the hands of scribes, who were not only conserving scripture but also changing it. To be sure, of all the hundreds of thousands of textual changes found among our manuscripts, most of them are completely insignificant, immaterial, of no real importance for anything other than showing that scribes could not spell or keep focused any better than the rest of us. It would be wrong, however, to say—as people sometimes do—that the changes in our text have no real bearing on what the texts mean or on the theological conclusions that one draws from them. We have seen, in fact, that just the opposite is the case. In some instances, the very meaning of the text is at stake, depending on how one resolves a textual problem: Was Jesus an angry man? Was he completely distraught in the face of death? Did he tell his disciples that they could drink poison without being harmed? Did he let an adulteress off the hook with nothing but a mild warning? Is the doctrine of the Trinity explicitly taught in the New Testament? Is Jesus actually called the "unique God" there? Does the New Testament indicate that even the Son of God himself does not know when the end will come? The questions go on and on, and all of them are related to how one resolves difficulties in the manuscript tradition as it has come down to us.

It bears repeating that the decisions that have to be made are by no means obvious, and that competent, well-meaning, highly intelligent scholars often come to opposite conclusions when looking at the same evidence. These scholars are not just a group of odd, elderly, basically irrelevant academics holed up in a few libraries around the world; some of them are, and always have been, highly influential on society and culture. The Bible is, by all counts, the most significant book in the history of Western civilization. And how do you think we have *access* to the Bible? Hardly any of us actually read it in the original language, and even among those of us who do, there are very few who ever look at a manuscript—let alone a group of manuscripts. How then do we know what was originally in the Bible? A few people have gone to the trouble of learning the ancient languages (Greek, Hebrew, Latin, Syriac, Coptic, etc.) and have spent their professional lives examining our manuscripts, deciding what the authors of the New Testament actually wrote. In other words, someone has gone to the trouble of doing textual criticism, reconstructing the "original" text based on the wide array of manuscripts that differ from one another in thousands of places. Then someone else has taken that reconstructed Greek text, in which textual decisions have been made (what was the original form of Mark 1:2? of Matt. 24:36? of John 1:18? of Luke 22:43–44? and so on), and translated it into English. What you read is that English translation—and not just you, but millions of people like you. How do these millions of people know what is in the New Testament? They "know" because scholars with unknown names, identities, backgrounds, qualifications, predilections, theologies, and personal opinions have *told* them what is in the New Testament. But what if the translators have translated the wrong text? It has happened before. The King James Version is filled with places in which the translators rendered a Greek text derived ultimately from Erasmus's edition, which was based on a single twelfth-century manuscript that is one of the worst of the manuscripts that we now have available to us! It's no wonder that modern translations often differ from the King James, and no wonder that some Bible-believing Christians prefer to pretend there's never been a problem, since God inspired the King James Bible instead of the original Greek! (As the old saw goes, If the King James was good enough for Saint Paul, it's good enough for me.)

Reality is never that neat, however, and in this case we need to face up to the facts. The King James was not given by God but was a translation by a group of scholars in the early seventeenth century who based their rendition on a faulty Greek text.[1] Later translators based their translations on Greek texts that were better, but not perfect. Even the translation you hold in your hands is affected by these textual problems we have been discussing, whether you are a reader of the New International Version, the Revised Standard Version, the New Revised Standard Version, the New American Standard Version, the New King James, the Jerusalem Bible, the Good News Bible, or something else. They are *all* based on texts that have been changed in places. And there are some places in which modern translations continue to transmit what is probably not the original text (so I've argued for Mark 1:41; Luke 22:43–44; and Heb. 2:9, for example; there are other instances as well). There are some places where we don't even know what the original text was, places, for example, about which highly intelligent and impressively trained textual critics continue to dispute. A number of scholars—for reasons we saw in chapter 2—have even given up thinking that it makes *sense* to talk about the "original" text.

I personally think that opinion may be going too far. I do not mean to deny that there are difficulties that may be insurmountable in reconstructing the originals: for example, if Paul dictated his letter to the Galatians and the secretarial scribe writing down what he said misheard a word because someone in the room coughed, then the "original" copy would already have a mistake in it! Stranger things have happened. Even so—despite the imponderable difficulties—we do have manuscripts of every book of the New Testament; all of these manuscripts were copied from other, earlier manuscripts, which were themselves copied from earlier manuscripts; and the chain of transmission has to end *somewhere,* ultimately at a manuscript produced either by an author or by a secretarial scribe who was producing the "autograph"—the first in the long line of manuscripts that were copied for nearly fifteen centuries until the invention of printing. So at least it is not "non"-sense to talk about an original text.

When I was a student just beginning to think about those fifteen centuries of copying and the vicissitudes of the text, I kept reverting to the fact that whatever else we may say about the Christian scribes— whether of the early centuries or of the Middle Ages—we have to admit that in addition to copying scripture, they were changing scripture. Sometimes they didn't mean to—they were simply tired, or inattentive, or, on occasion, inept. At other times, though, they did mean to make changes, as when they wanted the text to emphasize precisely what they themselves believed, for example about the nature of Christ, or about the role of women in the church, or about the wicked character of their Jewish opponents.

This conviction that scribes had changed scripture became an increasing certitude for me as I studied the text more and more. And this certitude changed the way I understood the text, in more ways than one.

In particular, as I said at the outset, I began seeing the New Testament as a very human book. The New Testament as we actually have it, I knew, was the product of human hands, the hands of the scribes who transmitted it. Then I began to see that not just the scribal text but the original text itself was a very human book. This stood very much at odds with how I had regarded the text in my late teens as a newly minted "born-again" Christian, convinced that the Bible was the inerrant Word of God and that the biblical words themselves had come to us by the inspiration of the Holy Spirit. As I realized already in graduate school, even if God had inspired the original words, we don't have the original words. So the doctrine of inspiration was in a sense irrelevant to the Bible as we have it, since the words God reputedly inspired had been changed and, in some cases, lost. Moreover, I came to think that my earlier views of inspiration were not only irrelevant, they were probably wrong. For the only reason (I came to think) for God to inspire the Bible would be so that his people would have his actual words; but if he really wanted people to have his actual words, surely he would have miraculously preserved those words, just as he had miraculously inspired them in the first place. Given the circumstance that he didn't preserve the words, the conclusion seemed inescapable to me that he hadn't gone to the trouble of inspiring them.

The more I reflected on these matters, the more I began to see that the authors of the New Testament were very much like the scribes who would later transmit those authors' writings. The authors too were human beings with needs, beliefs, worldviews, opinions, loves, hates, longings, desires, situations, problems—and surely all these things affected what they wrote. Moreover, in an even more tangible way these authors were like the later scribes. They too were Christians who had inherited traditions about Jesus and his teachings, who had learned about the Christian message of salvation, who had come to believe in the truth of the gospel—and they too passed along the traditions in their writings. What is striking, once one sees them for the human beings they were, with their own beliefs, worldviews, situations, and so on, is that all these authors passed along the traditions they inherited in *different* words. Matthew, in fact, is not exactly like Mark; Mark is not the same as Luke; or Luke as John; or John as Paul; or Paul as James. Just as scribes modified the words of the tradition, by sometimes putting these words "in other words," so too had the authors of the New Testament itself, telling their stories, giving their instructions, and recording their recollections by using their *own* words (not just the words they had heard), words that they came up with to pass along their message in ways that seemed most appropriate for the audience and the time and place for which they were writing.

And so I began to see that since each of these authors is different, it was not appropriate to think that any one of them meant the same thing as some other author meant—any more than it is fair to say that what I mean in this book must be the same as what some other author writing about textual criticism means in his or her book. We might mean different things. How can you tell? Only by reading each of us carefully and seeing what each of us has to say—not by pretending that we are both saying the same thing. We're often saying very different things.

The same is true of the authors of the New Testament. This can be seen in a very tangible way. As I pointed out earlier in this book, it has been clear to most scholars since the nineteenth century that Mark was the first Gospel written, and that Matthew and Luke both used Mark as one of the sources for their stories about Jesus. On the one hand, there's nothing particularly radical about this claim. Authors have to get their stories somewhere, and Luke himself indicates that he had read and used earlier accounts in coming up with his own (1:1–4). On the other hand, this means that it is possible to compare what Mark says with what Matthew and/or Luke say, in any story shared between them; and by doing so, one can see how Mark was *changed* by these later authors.

Engaging in this different kind of detective work can also be interesting and enlightening. For these later authors sometimes borrowed Mark's sentences wholesale, but on other occasions they changed what he had to say, sometimes radically. In that sense, they, like the scribes, were changing scripture. We have seen some examples in the course of our study. Mark, for example, portrays Jesus as in deep agony in the face of death, telling his disciples that his soul was "sorrowful unto death," falling on his face in prayer, and beseeching God three times to take away the cup of his suffering; on his way to be crucified he is silent the entire time, and he says nothing on the cross when mocked by everyone, including both robbers, until the very end when he calls out in anguish, "My God, my God, why have you forsaken me?" He then utters a loud cry and dies.

Luke had this version of the story available to him, but he modified it significantly. He removed Mark's comment that Jesus was highly distraught, as well as Jesus's own comment that he was sorrowful unto death. Rather than falling on his face, Jesus simply kneels, and instead of pleading three times to have the cup removed, he asks only once, prefacing his prayer with "if it be your will." He is not at all silent on the way to his crucifixion but speaks to a group of weeping women, telling them to grieve not for him but for the fate to befall themselves. While being crucified he is not silent but asks God to forgive those responsible, "for they don't know what they're doing." While on the cross he is not silent: when one of the robbers mocks him (not both, as in Mark), the other asks for his help, and Jesus replies in full assurance of what was happening, "Truly I tell you, today you will be with me in paradise." And at the end, rather than asking God why he had been forsaken—there is no cry of dereliction here—he instead prays in full confidence of God's support and care: "Father, into your hands I commend my Spirit."

Luke has changed the account, and if we wish to understand what Luke wanted to emphasize, we need to take his changes seriously. People don't take his changes seriously, I came to see, when they pretend that Luke is saying the same thing as Mark. Mark wanted to emphasize the utter forsakenness and near-despair of Jesus in the face of death. Interpreters differ in their explanations of *why* this is what Mark wanted to emphasize; one interpretation is that Mark wanted to stress that God works in highly mysterious ways, and that seemingly inexplicable suffering (Jesus at the end seems to be in the throes of doubt: "Why have you forsaken me?") can in fact be the way of redemption. Luke wanted to teach a different lesson. For him, Jesus was not in despair. He was calm and in control, knowing what was happening to him, why it was happening, and what would occur later ("today you will be with me in paradise"). Again interpreters are divided on why Luke portrayed Jesus this way in the face of death, but it may be that Luke wanted to give an example to persecuted Christians about how they themselves should face death, in full assurance that God is on their side despite their torments ("into your hands I commend my spirit").

The point is that Luke changed the tradition he inherited. Readers completely misinterpret Luke if they fail to realize this—as happens, for example, when they assume that Mark and Luke are in fact saying the same thing about Jesus. If they are not saying the same thing, it is not legitimate to assume they are—for example, by taking what Mark says, and taking what Luke says, then taking what Matthew and John say and melding them all together, so that Jesus says and does *all* the things that each of the Gospel writers indicates. Anyone who interprets the Gospels this way is not letting each author have his own say; anyone who does this is not reading what the author wrote in order to understand his message; anyone who does this is not reading the Gospels themselves—he or she is making up a *new* Gospel consisting of the four in the New Testament, a new Gospel that is not like any of the ones that have come down to us.

The idea that Luke changed the text before him—in this case the Gospel of Mark—does not put him in a unique situation among the early Christian authors. This, in fact, is what all the writers of the New Testament did—along with all the writers of all the Christian literature outside the New Testament, indeed writers of every kind everywhere. They modified their tradition and put the words of the tradition in their own words. John's Gospel is quite different from each of the other three (he never has Jesus tell a parable, for example, or cast out a demon; and in his account, unlike theirs, Jesus gives long discourses about his identity and does "signs" in order to prove that what he says about himself is true). The message of Paul is both like and unlike what we find in the Gospels (he doesn't say much about Jesus's words or deeds, for example, but focuses on what for Paul were the critical issues, that Christ died on the cross and was raised from the dead). The message of James differs from the message of Paul; the message of Paul differs from the message of Acts; the message of the Revelation of John differs from the message of the Gospel of John; and so forth. Each of these authors was human, each of them had a different message, each of them was putting the tradition he inherited into his own words. Each of them, in a sense, was changing the "texts" he inherited.

This, of course, is also what the scribes were doing. On one level, ironically perhaps, the scribes were changing scripture much *less* radically than the authors of the New Testament themselves were. When Luke prepared his Gospel and used Mark as his source, it was not his intention simply to *copy* Mark for posterity. He planned to alter Mark in light of other traditions that he had read and heard about Jesus. Later scribes who were producing our manuscripts, on the other hand, were principally interested in copying the texts before them. They, for the most part, did not see themselves as authors who were writing new books; they were scribes reproducing the old books. The changes they made—at least the intentional ones—were no doubt seen as improvements of the text, possibly made because the scribes were convinced that the copyists before them had themselves mistakenly altered the words of the text. For the most part, their intention was to conserve the tradition, not to change it.

But change it they did, sometimes accidentally, sometimes intentionally. In numerous places, the scribes altered the tradition they inherited; and on occasion they did this in order to make the text say what it was already supposed to mean.

As the years went by and I continued to study the text of the New Testament, I gradually became less judgmental toward the scribes who changed the scriptures they copied. Early on, I suppose I was a bit surprised, maybe even scandalized, by the number of changes these anonymous copyists of the text had made in the process of transcription, as they altered the words of the texts, putting the text in their own words rather than the words of the original authors. But I softened my view of these transcribers of the text as I (slowly) came to realize that what they were doing with the text was not all that different from what each of us does every time we read a text.

For the more I studied, the more I saw that reading a text necessarily involves interpreting a text. I suppose when I started my studies I had a rather unsophisticated view of reading: that the point of reading a text is simply to let the text "speak for itself," to uncover the meaning inherent in its words. The reality, I came to see, is that meaning is not inherent and texts do not speak for themselves. If texts could speak for themselves, then everyone honestly and openly reading a text would agree on what the text says. But interpretations of texts abound, and people in fact do *not* agree on what the texts mean. This is obviously true of the texts of scripture: simply look at the hundreds, or even thousands, of ways people interpret the book of Revelation, or consider all the different Christian denominations, filled with intelligent and well-meaning people who base their views of how the church should be organized and function on the Bible, yet all of them coming to radically different conclusions (Baptists, Pentecostals, Presbyterians, Roman Catholics, Appalachian snake-handlers, Greek Orthodox, and on and on).

Or think back on the last time you were involved in a heated debate in which the Bible was invoked, and someone volunteered an interpretation of a scripture verse that left you wondering, How did he (or she) come up with *that?* We hear this all around us in discussions of homosexuality, women in the church, abortion, divorce, and even American foreign policy, with both sides quoting the same Bible—and sometimes even the same verses—to make their case. Is this because some people are simply more willful or less intelligent than others and can't understand what the text plainly says? Surely not—surely the texts of the New Testament are not simply collections of words whose meaning is obvious to any reader. Surely the texts have to be interpreted to make sense, rather than simply read as if they can divulge their meanings without the process of interpretation. And this, of course, applies not just to the New Testament documents, but to texts of every kind. Why else would there be such radically different understandings of the U.S. Constitution, or *Das Kapital,* or *Middlemarch?* Texts do not simply reveal their own meanings to honest inquirers. Texts are interpreted, and they are interpreted (just as they were written) by living, breathing human beings, who can make sense of the texts only by explaining them in light of their other knowledge, explicating their meaning, putting the words of the texts "in other words."

Once readers put a text in other words, however, they have changed the words. This is not optional when reading; it is not something you can choose *not* to do when you peruse a text. The only way to make sense of a text is to read it, and the only way to read it is by putting it in other words, and the only way to put it in other words is by having other words to put it into, and the only way you have other words to put it into is that you have a life, and the only way to have a life is by being filled with desires, longings, needs, wants, beliefs, perspectives, worldviews, opinions, likes, dislikes—and all the other things that make human beings human. And so to read a text is, necessarily, to change a text.

That's what the scribes of the New Testament did. They read the texts available to them and they put them in *other* words. Sometimes, however, they *literally* put them in other words. On the one hand, when they did this, they did what all of us do every time we read a text, but on the other, they did something very different from the rest of us. For when we put a text in other words in our minds, we don't actually change the physical words on the page, whereas the scribes sometimes did precisely that, changing the words so that the words later readers would have before them were different words, which then had to be put into yet other words to be understood.

In that respect, the scribes changed scripture in ways that we do not. In a more basic sense, though, they changed scripture the way we all change scripture, every time we read it. For they, like we, were trying to understand what the authors wrote while also trying to see how the words of the authors' texts might have significance for them, and how they might help them make sense of their own situations and their own lives.

Notes

Introduction

1. My friend Jeff Siker says that reading the New Testament in Greek is like seeing it in color, whereas reading it in translation is like seeing it in black and white: one gets the point but misses a lot of the nuances.

2. The book that comes closest is David C. Parker's *The Living Text of the Gospels* (Cambridge: The Univ. Press, 1997).

Chapter 1

1. Scholars today use the "common era" (abbreviated C.E.) for the older designation *anno Domini* (= A.D., or "in the year of the Lord"), since the former is more inclusive of all faiths.

2. For a sketch that deals with the formation of the Jewish canon of scripture, see James Sanders's "Canon, Hebrew Bible" in the *Anchor Bible Dictionary*, ed. David Noel Freedman (New York: Doubleday, 1992), 1:838–52.

3. By calling Jesus a rabbi I do not mean to say that he had some kind of official standing within Judaism but simply that he was a Jewish teacher. He was, of course, not only a teacher; he can perhaps best be understood as a "prophet." For further discussion, see Bart D. Ehrman, *Jesus: Apocalyptic Prophet of the New Millennium* (New York: Oxford Univ. Press, 1999).

4. For this abbreviation, see n. 1 above.

5. These would include the three "Deutero-Pauline" letters of Colossians, Ephesians, and 2 Thessalonians and, especially, the three "pastoral" letters of 1 and 2

Timothy and Titus. For scholars' reasons for doubting that these letters were from Paul himself, see Bart D. Ehrman, *The New Testament: A Historical Introduction to the Early Christian Writings*, 3d ed. (New York: Oxford Univ. Press, 2004), chap. 23.

6. At a later time, there were several forged letters claiming to be the letter to the Laodiceans. We still have one of them, which is usually included in the so-called New Testament Apocrypha. It is little more than a pastiche of Pauline phrases and clauses, patched together to look like one of Paul's letters. Another letter called *To the Laodiceans* was evidently forged by the second-century "heretic" Marcion; this one no longer survives.

7. Although Q obviously no longer exists, there are good reasons for thinking that it was a real document—even if we cannot know for sure its complete contents. See Ehrman, *The New Testament*, chap. 6. The name *Q* is short for the German word *Quelle*, which means "source" (that is, the source for much of Matthew's and Luke's sayings material).

8. For example, in the tractates known as the *Apocalypse of Peter* and the *Second Treatise of the Great Seth*, both discovered in 1945 in a cache of "Gnostic" documents near the village of Nag Hammadi in Egypt. For translations, see James M. Robinson, ed., *The Nag Hammadi Library in English*, 3d ed. (San Francisco: HarperSanFrancisco, 1988), 362–78.

9. The name Gnostic comes from the Greek word *gnosis*, which means "knowledge." Gnosticism refers to a group of religions from the second century onward that emphasized the importance of receiving secret knowledge for salvation from this evil, material world.

10. For a fuller discussion, see Bart D. Ehrman, *Lost Christianities: The Battles for Scripture and the Faiths We Never Knew* (New York: Oxford Univ. Press, 2003), esp. chap. 11. More information about the entire process can be found in Harry Gamble, *The New Testament Canon: Its Making and Meaning* (Philadelphia: Fortress Press, 1985). For the standard authoritative scholarly account, see Bruce M. Metzger, *The Canon of the New Testament: Its Origin, Development and Significance* (Oxford: Clarendon Press, 1987).

11. For a recent translation of the letter of Polycarp, see Bart D. Ehrman, *The Apostolic Fathers* (Loeb Classical Library; Cambridge: Harvard Univ. Press, 2003), vol. 1.

12. For further information on Marcion and his teachings, see Ehrman, *Lost Christianities*, 103–8.

13. See especially William V. Harris, *Ancient Literacy* (Cambridge: Harvard Univ. Press, 1989).

14. For literacy rates among Jews in antiquity, see Catherine Hezser, *Jewish Literacy in Roman Palestine* (Tübingen: Mohr/Siebeck, 2001).

15. See the discussion of Kim Haines-Eitzen, *Guardians of Letters: Literacy, Power, and the Transmitters of Early Christian Literature* (New York: Oxford Univ. Press, 2000), 27–28, and the articles by H. C. Youtie that she cites there.

16. The standard English translation is by Henry Chadwick, *Origen's "Contra Celsum"* (Cambridge: The Univ. Press, 1953), which I follow here.

Chapter 2

1. For further discussion, see Harry Y. Gamble, *Books and Readers in the Early Church: A History of Early Christian Texts* (New Haven: Yale Univ. Press, 1995), chap. 3.

2. *Seneca: Moral Essays,* ed. and trans. John W. Basore (Loeb Classical Library; London: Heinemann, 1925), 221.

3. *Martial: Epigrams,* ed. and trans. Walter C. A. Ker (Loeb Classical Library; Cambridge: Harvard Univ. Press, 1968), 1:115.

4. The fullest discussion is in Haines-Eitzen's *Guardians of Letters.*

5. I borrow this example from Bruce M. Metzger. See Bruce M. Metzger and Bart D. Ehrman, *The Text of the New Testament: Its Transmission, Corruption, and Restoration,* 4th ed. (New York: Oxford Univ. Press, 2005), 22–23.

6. This is stated in the famous Muratorian Canon, the earliest list of the books accepted as "canonical" by its anonymous author. See Ehrman, *Lost Christianities,* 240–43.

7. This is one of the key conclusions of Kim Haines-Eitzen, *Guardians of Letters.*

8. By professional I mean scribes who were specially trained and/or paid to copy texts as part of their vocation. At a later period, monks in monasteries were typically trained, but not paid; I would include them among the ranks of professional scribes.

9. *Commentary on Matthew* 15.14, as quoted in Bruce M. Metzger, "Explicit References in the Works of Origen to Variant Readings in New Testament Manuscripts," in *Biblical and Patristic Studies in Memory of Robert Pierce Casey,* ed. J. Neville Birdsall and Robert W. Thomson (Freiburg: Herder, 1968), 78–79.

10. *Against Celsus* 2.27.

11. See Bart D. Ehrman, *The Orthodox Corruption of Scripture: The Effects of Early Christological Controversies on the Text of the New Testament* (New York: Oxford Univ. Press, 1993).

12. Origen, *On First Principles,* Preface by Rufinus; as quoted in Gamble, *Books and Readers,* 124.

13. See n. 8 above.

14. For other notes added to manuscripts by tired or bored scribes, see the examples cited in Metzger and Ehrman, *Text of the New Testament,* chap. 1, sect. iii.

15. On only one occasion does one of Paul's secretarial scribes identify himself; this is a man named Tertius, to whom Paul dictated his letter to the Romans. See Rom. 16:22.

16. See, especially, E. Randolph Richards, *The Secretary in the Letters of Paul* (Tübingen: Mohr/Siebeck, 1991).

17. Even the New Testament indicates that the Gospel writers had "sources" for their accounts. In Luke 1:1–4, for example, the author states that "many" predecessors had written an account of the things Jesus said and did, and that after reading them and consulting with "eyewitnesses and ministers of the word," he decided to produce his own account, one which he says is, in contrast to the others, "accurate." In other words, Luke had both written and oral sources for the events he narrates—he was not himself an observer of Jesus's earthly life. The same was probably true of the other Gospel writers as well. On John's sources, see Ehrman, *The New Testament,* 164–67.

18. Later we will see how some manuscripts can be established as "better" than others.

19. In fact, there were different endings added by different scribes—not just the final twelve verses familiar to readers of the English Bible. For an account of all the endings, see Bruce M. Metzger, *A Textual Commentary on the Greek New Testament,* 2d ed. (New York: United Bible Society, 1994), 102–6.

20. See Ehrman, *The New Testament,* chap. 5, esp. 79–80.

Chapter 3

1. For my understanding of the term *professional scribe,* see n. 8 in chapter 2.

2. For an argument that there is no evidence of scriptoria in the earlier centuries, see Haines-Eitzen, *Guardians of Letters,* 83–91.

3. Eusebius is widely known today as the father of church history, based on his ten-volume account of the church's first three hundred years.

4. For an account of these early "versions" (i.e., translations) of the New Testament, see Metzger and Ehrman, *Text of the New Testament,* chap. 2, sect. ii.

5. On the Latin versions of the New Testament, including the work of Jerome, see Metzger and Ehrman, *Text of the New Testament,* chap. 2, ii.2.

6. For fuller information on this, and on the other printed editions discussed in the following pages, see Metzger and Ehrman, *Text of the New Testament,* chap. 3.

7. See, especially, the informative account in Samuel P. Tregelles, *An Account of the Printed Text of the Greek New Testament* (London: Samuel Bagster & Sons, 1854), 3–11.

8. The Latin reads: "textum ergo habes, nunc ab omnibus receptum: in quo nihil immutatum aut corruptum damus."

9. See Metzger and Ehrman, *Text of the New Testament,* chap. 3, sect. ii.

10. Whitby's emphasis. Quoted in Adam Fox, *John Mill and Richard Bentley: A Study of Textual Criticism of the New Testament, 1675–1729* (Oxford: Blackwell, 1954), 106.

11. Fox, *Mill and Bentley,* 106.

12. Phileleutherus Lipsiensis, *Remarks upon a Late Discourse of Free Thinking,* 7th ed. (London: W. Thurbourn, 1737), 93–94.

13. My friend Michael Holmes points out to me that of the seven thousand copies of the Greek Bible (both Greek New Testament and Greek Old Testament),

fewer than ten, to our knowledge, ever contained the *entire* Bible, both Old and New Testaments. All ten of these are now defective (missing pages here and there); and only four of them predate the tenth century.

14. Manuscripts—handwritten copies—continued to be made after the invention of printing, just as some people continue to use typewriters today, even though word processors are available.

15. It will be seen that the four categories of manuscripts are not grouped on the same principles. The papyri are written in majuscule script, as are the majuscules, but on a different writing surface; the minuscules are written on the same kind of writing surface as the majuscules (parchment) but in a different kind of script.

16. For additional examples of accidental changes, see Metzger and Ehrman, *Text of the New Testament,* chap. 7, sect. I.

17. Those interested in seeing how scholars debate back and forth concerning the virtues of one reading over another should consult Metzger, *Textual Commentary.*

18. I owe this example, along with several of the preceding ones, to Bruce M. Metzger. See Metzger and Ehrman, *Text of the New Testament,* p. 259.

19. For a further discussion of this variant, see pp. 203–04.

20. For a fuller discussion of the variants in the traditions of the Lord's Prayer, see Parker, *Living Text of the Gospels,* 49–74.

21. There are a number of textual variants among the witnesses that attest this longer form of the passage.

Chapter 4

1. For a classic study of how the Bible was understood and treated in the Middle Ages, see Beryl Smalley, *The Study of the Bible in the Middle Ages* (Oxford: Clarendon Press, 1941).

2. Richard Simon, *A Critical History of the Text of the New Testament* (London: R. Taylor, 1689), Preface.

3. Simon, *Critical History,* pt. 1, p. 65.

4. Simon, *Critical History,* pt. 1, pp. 30–31.

5. Simon, *Critical History,* pt. 1, p. 31.

6. Quoted in Georg Werner Kümmel, *The New Testament: The History of the Investigation of Its Problems* (Nashville: Abingdon Press, 1972), 41.

7. The fullest biography is still that by James Henry Monk, *The Life of Richard Bentley, D.D.,* 2 vols. (London: Rivington, 1833).

8. Quoted in Monk, *Life of Bentley,* 1:398.

9. Monk, *Life of Bentley,* 399.

10. *Proposals for Printing a New Edition of the Greek New Testament and St. Hieroms Latin Version* (London, 1721), 3.

11. See Monk, *Life of Bentley,* 2:130–33.

12. Monk, *Life of Bentley,* 136.

13. Monk, *Life of Bentley,* 135–37.

14. For a full biography, see John C. F. Burk, *A Memoir of the Life and Writings of John Albert Bengel* (London: R. Gladding, 1842).

15. Burk, *A Memoir,* 316.

16. We have seen this principle at work already; see the examples of Mark 1:2 and Matt. 24:36 discussed in chapter 3.

17. C. L. Hulbert-Powell, *John James Wettstein, 1693–1754: An Account of His Life, Work, and Some of His Contemporaries* (London: SPCK, 1938), 15, 17.

18. Hulbert-Powell, *John James Wettstein,* 43.

19. Lachmann is famous in the annals of scholarship as one who, more than any other, devised a method for establishing the genealogical relationship among manuscripts in the textual tradition of the classical authors. His primary professional interest was not, in fact, the writings of the New Testament, but he did see these writings as posing a unique and interesting challenge to textual scholars.

20. Cited in Metzger and Ehrman, *Text of the New Testament,* 172.

21. Constantine von Tischendorf, *When Were Our Gospels Written?* (London: The Religious Tract Society, 1866), 23.

22. Tischendorf, *When Were Our Gospels Written?,* 29.

23. To this day the monks of Saint Catherine's monastery maintain that Tischendorf was not "given" the manuscript but absconded with it.

24. Since Tischendorf's day, even more significant manuscripts have been discovered. In particular, throughout the twentieth century archaeologists unearthed numerous papyrus manuscripts, which predate Codex Sinaiticus by up to 150 years. Most of these papyri are fragmentary, but some are extensive. To date, some 116 papyri are known and catalogued; they contain portions of most of the books of the New Testament.

25. Caspar R. Gregory, "Tischendorf," *Bibliotheca Sacra* 33 (1876): 153–93.

26. Arthur Fenton Hort, ed., *Life and Letters of Fenton John Anthony Hort* (London: Macmillan, 1896), 211.

27. Hort, *Life and Letters,* 250.

28. Hort, *Life and Letters,* 264.

29. Hort, *Life and Letters,* 455.

30. For a summary of the text-critical principles that Westcott and Hort used in establishing their text, see Metzger and Ehrman, *Text of the New Testament,* 174–81.

31. See n. 24., above.

Chapter 5

1. For further explanation of these methods, see Metzger and Ehrman, *Text of the New Testament,* 300–15.

2. Among other things, this means that the readings in the "Byzantine" majority text are not necessarily the *best* readings. They simply have the most manuscript

support in terms of sheer numbers. As an old text-critical adage says, however: Manuscripts are to be weighed, not counted.

3. Some scholars take this to be the most basic and reliable text-critical principle of all.

4. Much of what follows is taken from my article "Text and Tradition: The Role of New Testament Manuscripts in Early Christian Studies," found in *TC: A Journal of Textual Criticism* [http://rosetta.reltech.org/TC/TC.html] 5 (2000).

5. For a fuller discussion of this variant, and its significance for interpretation, see my article "A Sinner in the Hands of an Angry Jesus," in *New Testament Greek and Exegesis: Essays in Honor of Gerald F. Hawthorne,* ed. Amy M. Donaldson and Timothy B. Sailors (Grand Rapids: Eerdmans, 2003). I have relied on this article for much of the following discussion.

6. See Ehrman, *The New Testament,* chap. 6.

7. On only two other occasions in Mark's Gospel is Jesus explicitly described as compassionate: in Mark 6:34, at the feeding of the five thousand, and in Mark 8:2, at the feeding of the four thousand. Luke tells the first story completely differently, and he does not include the second. Matthew, however, has both stories and retains Mark's description of Jesus's being compassionate on both occasions (Matt. 14:14 [and 9:30]; 15:32). On three additional occasions in Matthew, and yet one other occasion in Luke, Jesus is explicitly described as compassionate, with this term (SPLANGNIZŌ) used. It is difficult to imagine, then, why they both, independently of each other, would have omitted the term from the account we are discussing if they had found it in Mark.

8. For these various interpretations, see Ehrman, "A Sinner in the Hands of an Angry Jesus."

9. For a more detailed discussion of why scribes changed the original account, see pp. 200–01, below.

10. For a fuller discussion of this variant, see Ehrman, *Orthodox Corruption of Scripture,* 187–94. My first treatment of this passage was co-written with Mark Plunkett.

11. For a discussion of why scribes added the verses to Luke's account, see pp. 164–65, below.

12. For a fuller discussion of this variant reading, see Ehrman, *Orthodox Corruption of Scripture,* 146–50.

Chapter 6

1. For primary texts from this period, see Bart D. Ehrman, *After the New Testament: A Reader in Early Christianity* (New York: Oxford Univ. Press, 1999). A nice introduction to the period can be found in Henry Chadwick, *The Early Church* (New York: Penguin, 1967).

2. For a fuller discussion of the material covered in the following paragraphs, see especially Ehrman, *Lost Christianities,* chapter 1.

3. For a full discussion, see Ehrman, *Orthodox Corruption of Scripture.*

4. For a fuller discussion of adoptionistic views, and of those who held them, see Ehrman, *Orthodox Corruption of Scripture,* 47–54.

5. For a fuller discussion of docetism and docetic Christologies, see Ehrman, *Orthodox Corruption of Scripture,* 181–87.

6. See pp. 33–34, above.

7. He also accepted ten letters of Paul as scripture (all those in the New Testament except 1 and 2 Timothy and Titus); he rejected the entire Old Testament, since it was the book of the Creator God, not of the God of Jesus.

8. The quotations come from Justin's *Dialogue with Trypho,* 103.

9. For further demonstration that these verses were not original to Luke but were added as an antidocetic polemic, see Ehrman, *Orthodox Corruption of Scripture,* 198–209.

10. For another textual addition, and a fuller discussion of this one, see Ehrman, *Orthodox Corruption of Scripture,* 227–32.

11. For further information on separationist Christologies, and the Gnostic groups that held them, see Ehrman, *Orthodox Corruption of Scripture,* 119–24.

12. For additional discussion of Gnosticism, see Ehrman, *Lost Christianities,* chap. 6.

13. *Against Heresies* 3, 11, 7.

Chapter 7

1. See Ehrman, *The New Testament,* chap. 24. I have depended on this chapter for much of the following discussion. For fuller discussion and documentation, see Ross Kraemer and Mary Rose D'Angelo, *Women and Christian Origins* (New York: Oxford Univ. Press, 1999). See also R. Kraemer, *Her Share of the Blessings: Women's Religions Among Jews, Pagans, and Christians in the Graeco-Roman World* (New York: Oxford Univ. Press, 1992), and Karen J. Torjesen, *When Women Were Priests: Women's Leadership in the Early Church and the Scandal of Their Subordination in the Rise of Christianity* (San Francisco: HarperSanFrancisco, 1993).

2. For further elaboration, see Ehrman, *Jesus,* 188–91.

3. See Ehrman, *The New Testament,* chap. 23.

4. For a fuller discussion that shows that Paul did not write verses 34–35, see especially the commentary by Gordon D. Fee, *The First Epistle to the Corinthians* (Grand Rapids: Eerdmans, 1987).

5. The fullest recent discussion is by Eldon Jay Epp, "Text-critical, Exegetical, and Sociocultural Factors Affecting the Junia/Junias Variation in Rom 16:7," in A. Denaux, *New Testament Textual Criticism and Exegesis* (Leuven: Univ. Press, 2002), 227–92.

6. For other changes of this sort in Acts, see Ben Witherington, "The Anti-Feminist Tendencies of the 'Western' Text of Acts," *Journal of Biblical Literature* 103 (1984): 82–84.

7. For two standard treatments in the field, see Rosemary Ruether, *Faith and Fratricide: The Theological Roots of Anti-Semitism* (New York: Seabury, 1974), and John Gager, *The Origins of Anti-Semitism: Attitudes Toward Judaism in Pagan and Christian Antiquity* (New York: Oxford Univ. Press, 1983). A more recent study is Miriam Taylor's *Anti-Judaism and Early Christian Identity: A Critique of the Scholarly Consensus* (Leiden: Brill, 1995).

8. See Ehrman, *Apostolic Fathers,* 2:3–83.

9. Translation of Gerald Hawthorne; the entire translation of the homily may be found in Bart D. Ehrman, *After the New Testament,* 115–28.

10. See especially David Daube, "For They Know Not What They Do," in *Studia Patristica,* vol. 4, ed. by F. L. Cross (Berlin: Akademie-Verlag, 1961), 58–70, and Haines-Eitzen, *Guardians of Letters,* 119–23.

11. Translations of *Against Celsus* are taken from Henry Chadwick's edition; *Origin: Contra Celsum* (Oxford: Clarendon, 1953).

12. See Ernst Bammel, "The Cambridge Pericope: The Addition to Luke 6.4 in Codex Bezae," *New Testament Studies* 32 (1986): 404–26.

13. The classic study of early Christian persecution is W.H.C. Frend's *Martyrdom and Persecution in the Early Church* (Oxford: Blackwell, 1965). See also Robert Wilken, *The Christians as the Romans Saw Them* (New Haven: Yale Univ. Press, 1984).

14. Moreover, before 70 C.E. (when the Temple was destroyed), Jews were known to perform sacrifices on behalf of the emperor, a sign of their loyalty to the state.

15. For a fuller discussion, see the recent book by Wayne Kannaday, *Apologetic Discourse of the Scribal Tradition* (Atlanta: Society of Biblical Literature Press, 2004), esp. chap. 2.

16. Translation of R. Joseph Hoffman (Amherst, NY: Prometheus, 1994).

17. The fullest study is that of Wayne Kannaday, cited in n. 15 above.

18. See Robert M. Grant, *Greek Apologists of the Second Century* (Philadelphia: Westminster Press, 1988).

19. See, especially, Eugene Gallagher, *Divine Man or Magician: Celsus and Origen on Jesus* (Chico, CA: Scholars Press, 1982).

20. See Dale B. Martin, *Inventing Superstition* (Cambridge: Harvard Univ. Press, 2005).

21. Justin Martyr, *Dialogue with Trypho,* 88.

22. There is a hole in the manuscript P[45] at this point, but it is clear by counting the number of letters that could fill this gap that this was its original reading.

Conclusion

1. For a recent discussion, see Adam Nicolson, *God's Secretaries: The Making of the King James Bible* (New York: HarperCollins, 2003).

Index

Citations of Biblical and ancient texts appear in bold print.